Dyslexia and Learning Style
A Practitioner's Handbook

Dyslexia and Learning Style

A Practitioner's Handbook

by

TILLY MORTIMORE

Mark College, Somerset
and the University of Cardiff

Consultant in Dyslexia

MARGARET SNOWLING
University of York

W
WHURR PUBLISHERS
LONDON AND PHILADELPHIA

© 2003 Whurr Publishers Ltd
First published 2003
by Whurr Publishers Ltd
19b Compton Terrace
London N1 2UN England and
325 Chestnut Street, Philadelphia PA 19106 USA

Reprinted 2003 (twice)

British Library Cataloguing in Publication Data

A catalogue record for this book
is available from the British Library.

ISBN 1 86156 313 2

Printed and bound in the UK by Athenaeum Press Ltd,
Gateshead, Tyne & Wear.

Contents

Preface

This book aims to share with others a range of proven teaching techniques that have been successful with dyslexic students in schools and colleges.

In my work, I have always been fortunate to have the support of talented colleagues who will, no doubt, recognise their contribution, as will those dyslexic students themselves who have taught me so much about the different ways in which learning can be accomplished. The range of ingenious and creative ways in which these students approached their learning was the inspiration for the contents of this book. It made me want to investigate the relationship between dyslexia and learning style and also to discover if research existed to explain why certain approaches seemed to be more successful than others.

This book includes teaching strategies, which I hope will be of instant use to practitioners, and also it places these within the context of some of the most recent research into memory, learning and dyslexia in an attempt to suggest why some of these techniques work. In this way I hope that it can provide a real bridge between theory and practice. It is also the first practical book to apply learning style research to dyslexia.

Historically I feel that there has been an overemphasis upon the medicalised deficit models of dyslexia and that more attention must be paid to removing the academic and social barriers confronting those individuals with dyslexia who attempt to realise their potential. I hope this book will contribute in some way to their emancipation.

I am indebted to the inspiration. I have received from students and colleagues at Mark College, my research supervisor Dr Ray Crozier and the support of Phil, Lekki, Elly and Max Wdowski and Mary Mortimore.

Advanced organiser

Some learners find an advanced organiser or preview of the contents of a book extremely helpful. Here is one for this book.

PART ONE: LEARNING STYLE

Chapter 1
Provides and discusses definitions for cognitive or learning style. Cognitive style is a person's relatively consistent way of dealing with incoming information from the environment. Learning style is this cognitive style applied in a learning situation. Controversial aspects are discussed, and the Riding model for diagnosis of cognitive style is introduced.

Chapter 2
Examines why certain ways of presenting information can cause difficulties to some learners. Looks at the evidence in favour of matching learning and presentational style. Weighs up two major approaches to diagnosis and presents a range of tools for diagnosing style.

PART TWO: DYSLEXIA

Chapter 3
Discusses definitions of specific learning difficulties or dyslexia, the underlying causes and ways of identifying the condition.

Chapter 4
Looks at the patterns of difficulties associated with dyslexia throughout an individual's lifespan and some other learning difficulties, which can sometimes co-exist with dyslexia.

Chapter 5
Examines the evidence for the possession of superior visuo-spatial talents by some dyslexic people.

PART THREE: APPLYING LEARNING STYLE THEORY TO LEARNING

Chapter 6
Provides more detail about the importance of cognitive or learning style to the development of learning strategies in education for students who might or might not have dyslexia. Emphasises the importance of encouraging students to become more flexible in their approaches. Introduces the research background to the strategies described in this book – schema theory and memory function.

PART FOUR: STRATEGIES FOR WHOLISTIC AND ANALYTIC LEARNERS

Chapter 7
Provides a description of the likely learning preferences of wholistic learners and a range of strategies for absorbing, processing, revising and producing information.

Chapter 8
Provides a description of the likely learning preferences of analytic strategies absorbing, processing, revising and producing information.

PART FIVE: WORDS OR PICTURES?

Chapter 9
Provides a range of strategies to utilise and develop visualising skills.

Chapter 10
Provides a range of strategies to help students develop and utilise the verbal mode.

PART SIX: WHAT WERE THOSE LAST TEN CHAPTERS ABOUT?

Chapter 11
Provides strategies for dyslexic and non-dyslexic students to reduce memory overload, interact with material to be learnt, use the creative power of the imagination and use structures to organise material.

PART ONE
Learning Style

CHAPTER 1

Different ways of seeing

Introduction

Jack is 12 years old, and he is angry. Despite regular attendance at a good village school and all the attention paid to him by concerned teachers, his reading and writing skills have simply failed to develop. While classmates are in the process of becoming good readers, Jack still struggles with the most basic sight words. For all the years spent trying, Jack has barely progressed beyond being able to write his own name. The humiliation of having his younger sister quickly outpace him is already a bitter memory.

Jack's anger is born of frustration. No one can explain to him why he should be so hopeless in this all-important area, especially when he is very good at other things. This is a lively, articulate boy, full of ideas, both practical and imaginative. He has helped to build car engines at home. He adores drawing up plans for fantasy machines and futuristic houses. These plans are scrupulously detailed and competently executed. And Jack can explain his ideas to a listener in a most engaging way. Not only this but also the quick understanding he shows in discussion – the ready ability to draw links and infer-ences – coupled with good general knowledge and an associated fund of references with which to back his opinions are skills one immediately associates with an able twelve-year-old, not with a boy of Jack's reading age.

For Jack, at 12, this is a dangerous time. He has watched teachers trying to do their best for him. He has listened to his parents' constant words of encouragement. He has tried, and tried again: tried to improve, tried to learn how to read those troublesome words, to trap those ideas on paper. If only he could! All these efforts appear to have been entirely in vain, There is a limit, after all. At the same time that Jack is beginning to question the point of continuing to try to improve, he is facing the upheaval of the tricky transition from junior to secondary school – a transition fraught with extra difficulties for him. Rapidly growing in size and strength, his energy levels are increasing. His parents are increasingly concerned. Will Jack gravitate towards the more disruptive element among the students at the new school? Will he seek to bolster his self-esteem in unproductive ways, venting his frustrations upon the system that has evidently failed him? He is already angry and confused. What will he be like at sixteen?

Jack's case is not that uncommon. What is going wrong for him and how does 'learning style' come into it? Fortunately, his story has a happy ending, but this is not always the case. Jack's difficulties, in fact, stem from his severe dyslexia, which has now been diagnosed, and he is doing well at a specialist school. He is well on the way to becoming a fully independent reader, uses IT to communicate his ideas and has plans to go on to higher education as the first step to becoming an engineer.

His success is the product of three things:

- his own grit and determination
- appropriate teaching methods
- his discovery of his preferred learning style, which allows him to use his strengths and compensate for his weaknesses

It is swiftly evident to anybody who has attempted to teach a class of students, co-operate on a project with a group of colleagues or simply negotiate a survivable holiday route through a foreign city with partner or family without coming to blows that we do not all solve problems in the same way. We do not process incoming information in the same way, neither do we store it, organise it or retrieve it in the same way. Some people can always remember a face but cannot put a name to it. Others can memorise telephone numbers or birthdays simply by reciting them. Some teachers cannot recall the names of their students until they have seen them written on exercise books; others only need one rehearsal before they can identify any student anywhere in the room. Some travellers can follow oral directions unerringly; others can find their way swiftly to any previously visited destination by retracing their steps but are unable to give reliable directions. These all illustrate the diversity of the survival techniques people use spontaneously in everyday life.

Take a household example. It is eight a.m. Everyone is getting ready for work and school. The cry goes up, 'Where are my football boots?' How do you locate them? Do you picture a nightmare bedroom in your mind's eye with the boots peeping out from under a pile of *Beano* comics and last night's pyjamas or do you logically think through the steps they and their owner might have taken between football practice and this morning? Either of these approaches can locate the boots, and the approach you take spontaneously can give you some idea as to your particular *learning style*.

What is Jack's preferred learning style? Is he a 'pictures' or 'words' man?

His strengths are his active practical mind, his inventiveness, his ability to visualise and to create visual representations, his ability to remember detail when really engaged and his willingness to experiment with ways of working in order to take responsibility for himself. However, he finds it hard to remember anything other than the basic outlines of information if it is only presented verbally, and, at 14, although writing clear accounts and simple stories, he remains reluctant to expand his writing beyond what is strictly necessary. He resists any form of playing with written words and states that he is hopeless at poetry. This may, of course, be due to a lack of confidence and to the difficulty he still experiences with spelling. However, many equally dyslexic members of his group are poets, attempt to write at length and experiment with words. This does not seem to come naturally to Jack, despite the fact that his received-vocabulary score is well above average, and he is a persuasive talker. He also responds far more strongly to material presented through film or diagrams and has spontaneously adopted visual ways of mapping out ideas.

This pattern would suggest that his style of learning is far more visual than verbal and that he prefers to use mental pictures rather than words. This was, in fact, borne out by his scores on a test for learning style preferences. He will flounder in an environment where words are the only tools of communication. However, he is not extreme, as he is fortunate in that he both understands a wide range of vocabulary and expresses himself well orally. Many able visual learners are far less able to deal with words than Jack and are therefore even more disadvantaged in learning situations that do not take this into account.

Being verbal or visual is not, however, the whole story of learning style. Jack is also one of those students who always wants to know in advance what the group will be doing and likes to plan in advance rather than taking things step by step as they come. He always prefers reading or listening to action stories or practical information. When really involved in a story, and able to visualise events, he not only gets the gist of events and makes interesting links and inferences but remembers details really well. However, he consistently finds the retention of step-by-step information harder than the overall concept, particularly if the texts are longer and more theoretical and therefore less easy to visualise.

This tendency to respond more to the overall scope of a topic than its step-by-step structure is another aspect of learning style and one that is as crucial to successful learning as the pictures or words.

Current research into patterns of learning behaviour is now providing a wealth of information about the influence learning style can have on the success people make of their lives – particularly in the world of education with its specific demands and restrictions. No one approach or style is in itself more or less effective than any other. The crucial factor is whether it is suited to a particular everyday task or situation. It is when individuals are placed within an educational context and the pressure is on to retain and utilise information that some students may begin to find that their particular approaches are less well catered for by the ways in which information is structured and presented to them. This is when research into learning style may offer insights into ways of making academic information more accessible to the diverse groups of learners in our schools and universities.

Before introducing the more practical aspects of using learning style to help students learn, it is perhaps necessary to present some of the theoretical and research background to the whole area of cognitive or learning styles.

What are cognitive or learning styles?

Learning style is one aspect of cognitive style. The term *cognitive* may be unfamiliar. *Cognitive* is to do with cognition. Cognition refers to knowing, and the study of cognition examines the ways in which people structure and organise knowledge, including the higher-order mental processes, such as reasoning and problem-solving, through which humans attempt to understand the world. A range of research has been carried out into both cognitive and learning style. Current research into patterns of learning behaviour tends to agree that cognitive style is an individual's characteristic and relatively consistent way of processing incoming information of all types from the environment. A distinction is made between *cognitive* style, which is seen as a fairly fixed way in which people *process* all incoming information and *learning* style, which is seen more in terms of the *strategies* people use to cope when learning. One accepted definition of cognitive style states that cognitive styles are characteristic modes of thinking, remembering and problem-solving that vary between individuals and develop around personality differences (Messick 1982 cited by Schmeck 1988). These fixed styles underlie the more flexible strategies that are used in everyday activity. *Learning style* is simply the type of strategy used when an individual's cognitive style is applied to a learning situation.

Two different approaches to cognitive style have emerged. One (Riding 1997) tends to focus upon the way in which people process incoming information from the environment. This approach takes cognitive style as being 'an individual's characteristic and consistent approach to organising and processing information'. (Tennant 1988, quoted by Riding et al 1993, p. 268). It attempts to measure cognitive style objectively by comparing the approaches of different individuals to simple cognitive tasks.

The other approach is slightly different, more broadly based and incorporates emotional, sociological, environmental and physiological aspects of the individual's styles into what is termed a cognitive style 'map' or 'profile'. Gregorc (1982) and Keefe (1987) suggest that the pattern of behaviour and performance that an individual brings to educational experience can be termed his or her learning style. They suggest that this pattern arises from the interplay between the developing structure of neural pathways in the learner's brain and the learning experiences gained from home, school and society in general. Once established, however, these learning styles will persist regardless of experience of teaching methods or content. Given and Reid (1999) provide a more extensive account of this way of compiling a profile, which will be discussed in chapter 2.

Any area of research inevitably throws up as many controversial questions as it answers. The definitions of *cognitive style* above agree broadly over two points.

1. *Cognitive style* is an individual's characteristic and relatively consistent way of processing incoming information from the environment.
2. A student's *learning style* describes the strategies used in a learning situation.

However, although there is broad agreement over these two points, other issues over learning style are more controversial.

Five controversial aspects of cognitive and learning style

Issue One

Is cognitive style genetically determined and fixed or environmentally developed and changeable?

 This is the old nature-nurture debate, which was applied to all areas of behavioural psychology and occupied researchers throughout much of the twentieth century. Are tendencies towards particular personality traits and behaviour patterns laid down in the genes a newborn baby inherits from its parents or is a baby born as a blank slate later to develop consistent patterns of learned behaviour through interaction with the environment?

 When applied to cognitive style theory, evidence from studies in behaviour genetics and personality research suggests that individuals have a certain range of potential that can be shaped and developed through their interaction with the opportunities the environment presents. Geisler-Brenstein and Schmeck (1995) review a range of research including evidence from brain researchers and state that 'traits are not repetitive habits, but inherently dynamic dispositions that interact with the opportunities and challenges of the moment' (p. 15).

 In other words genes predispose people to a particular style of processing, but this is shaped by experience. Yes, the newborn baby already has inherited tendencies towards particular types of behaviour, but the infant brain is so plastic and malleable that neural

pathways are shaped by experience to create a person's own characteristic ways of dealing with life. Nature is moulded by nurture to
create each individual.

Issue Two

Is cognitive or learning style specific to a particular situation or task
or consistent across a range of tasks and areas of life?

Do styles, as Gregorc (1982) suggests above, persist regardless of
the content or delivery of lessons? If students tend towards particular ways of storing information, will they stick to these methods
across the curriculum regardless of the content and demands of the
tasks?

A range of researchers would answer 'yes' to this question (Witkin
1969, Entwistle 1981, Schmeck 1988). They suggest that personal
characteristics influence response to a learning situation and that
these characteristics are stable enough to lead to consistency in
behaviour across a range of both academic and social situations.
This is, however, still the subject of some debate.

Issue Three

Does learning style develop and change with age?

There are two ways in which style could be said to change with
age. One is as part of a *staged developmental process*. The other is in
response to learning experiences.

What is a *staged process*? Generally, stage theorists, of whom Piaget
can be said to be the most well-known educational figure, contend
that all humans go through common stages of development in a set
order in a journey towards maturity. Thus a teenager should, for
example, be capable of some abstract reasoning where a five-year-
old is probably not. There are no value judgements implicit in this.
There is no suggestion that five-year-olds are somehow lacking
because they have trouble with philosophy. It is just the stage they
are at and everyone has to go through it. Thus expectations of
behaviour change according to age. It is a physiologically determined developmental process and, for example, very young children should not be expected to be able to work out the implications
of their actions in the same way as their older teenage brothers and
sisters.

Figure 1.1 gives an example of how stage theory can be applied to learning style.

Level 1   associative thinking (rote or memorising)

Level 2a   analytic reasoning

Level 2b   imaginative thought   seen as two distinct learning styles

Level 3   synthesis of 2a and 2b into a versatile (Pask and Scott 1972 cited in
            Schmeck 1988) or synthetic (Kirby 1988) style

Figure 1.1 A stage theorist's perspective showing the development of a versatile or synthetic learning style from levels 1–3.

This is an illustration of the approach of a number of the stage theorists (Entwistle 1981). It shows how they might explain the development of academic learning style as going through distinct stages starting, in this case, with rote memorising and progressing to the higher-order skills of level 3, where true understanding necessitates either a 'versatile' or 'flexible' style (Pask and Scott 1972) or a 'synthetic' style (Kirby 1988), which merges both analytic and imaginative reasoning. These theorists imply that students will ideally move towards a flexible integrated approach which will allow versatility in the use of learning style. Most older students do see reality from new points of view as they mature; however, one study of university students found such versatility to be rare (Entwistle 1988). Few students seemed able to carry through all the component processes demanded by a full and deep level of understanding!

Such stage theorists would strongly suggest that learning style changes with age even if many people never achieve full maturity. This is the first way in which learning style can be said to change, although it is still unclear whether this development involves a complete change in style or more an increased flexibility and adaptability.

The second way in which cognitive or learning style may change with age is in response to learning experiences.

What role does experience play in the determination of cognitive style? Cognitive style influences a person's approach to learning and that approach to learning determines the nature of the learning outcome. Some research has even suggested that these learning outcomes may change the nervous system. How can this happen?

Contemporary research into the biochemical basis for learning (see Hulme and Snowling 1997) suggests that learning outcomes may result both in chemical changes within the brain and the formation of neural traces and pathways, which, in effect, may actually alter the learner's cognitive style and hence learning strategies or style. There is some argument in favour of the suggestion that experience of the environment directly influences our style of learning. Schmeck (1988) cites Shapiro's (1965) suggestion that the style we practise most leaves traces that will predispose us to use the same style in the future. He says:

> What we perceive is a result of what we attend to, and what we attend to is a result of the actual stimulus situation plus what we remember about that type of situation from our last experience of it. If we form global impressions, we will remember global impressions and notice global features in the future. (1965, cited by Schmeck 1988)

The suggestion is that this process is gradually crystallised through regular reinforcement. So, for example, school situations are approached with a mind-set developed through past experiences of school. This mind-set become less and less flexible. This would suggest that this crystallisation is a subconscious process beyond the control of the individual learner.

The environment is thus seen to be playing a very strong role in the setting down of the particular neural pathways that determine a person's cognitive style. The approach does change with maturity, but, if cognitive style is rigid, fundamental changes in the direction of flexibility are not easily accomplished in adulthood since styles of functioning and personality become deeply engrained (Geisler-Brenstein and Schmeck 1995). A person's operating system tends automatically to force him or her to process information suited to existing thought structures more efficiently. It may even not only be a waste of time but be psychologically damaging to attempt to change styles in the interests of versatility (Miller 1991).

It seems rather pessimistic to consider that, if cognitive style changes with maturity, it is only to become more entrenched and less flexible! Some researchers and educators argue that it is here that the development of conscious self-knowledge about our style can enhance learning so that particular skills and approaches are used intentionally rather than automatically (Das, Kirby and Weinstein, cited in Schmeck 1988).

These researchers emphasise how important it is for students to know their own style tendencies and to take personal responsibility for making use of their learning strengths. This should give students greater self-awareness and a positive academic self-concept or image of themselves as learners. Metacognition, or knowledge about one's own way of thinking, plays an important role in this process. It is argued strongly that this knowledge should be extended and self-esteem enhanced as a key to success with any learning task.

Issue Four

How do different teaching styles affect learners?

Just as there are specific and differing *learning* styles, so are there also different *teaching* styles. What might be the effect of a match or mismatch of the teacher's and learners' styles on the acquisition of skills and knowledge? Riding and Rayner (1998) and Keefe (1982) have carried out a range of classroom studies that show that people do tend to learn more effectively and remember more when the style of presentation matches their own predominant learning style.

It is important for any teacher to be aware of the fact that different students of seemingly similar ability may well absorb information in very different ways. However, this obviously throws up problems of classroom management to cater for this range of students with differing styles. For the individual student, monitoring his or her own progress, it is important to know what his or her predominant style is so that the most effective way of studying can be established. Ultimately the buck must stop with the student, and the aim of this book is to help both teachers and students to develop useful self-knowledge and ways in which to make use of it.

Issue Five

How flexible is learning style?

How far do people tend to stick rigidly to certain types of approach, regardless of the nature of the task?

Nisbet and Shucksmith suggest (1986) that successful learners have three traits:

1. they will be acutely aware of their learning style
2. they will be aware of the requirements of each learning situation
3. they will have developed a range of strategies that they can then apply according to their own style

The emphasis here is upon the importance of metacognition or knowledge of one's own patterns of behaviour in a learning situation. However, knowledge is of little use if one is too inflexible to adapt. The importance of this will be discussed in more detail in a later chapter.

Recap

So far in this chapter the following points have been established:

Cognitive style describes the way in which an individual processes information from the environment; *learning* style is *cognitive* style applied to a learning task.

A body of research supports the existence of learning style and its importance in both day-to-day life and education.

It has also introduced a range of controversies to which, as yet, there are no conclusive answers:

- Is cognitive style a stable, long-lasting trait?
- What role does the environment play in the development of cognitive style?
- Does the learning style of a student change in a develop mental way?
- How do different teaching styles affect learners?
- How flexible is learning style?

For practical use, most of the essential background knowledge to cognitive or learning style theory has been presented. The only other aspect that might need some explanation is the fact that different researchers subscribe to different models of cognitive or learning style. How does a student or teacher pick the most practical way to identify and use learning style? Which 'model' or 'construct' should they go for? This book chooses to use Riding's two-dimensional model. The next section gives a brief description of some of the main models and explains why Riding's has been selected.

Models of cognitive or learning style

What exactly do researchers mean when they talk about a *model* or *construct* of learning style? It is clear that each researcher will tend to see cognitive style in a different way. Is cognitive style a question of whether people prefer to use visual or verbal channels? Is cognitive style to do with motivation and its effect upon approaches to learning? Is it to do with what strategies are used, consciously or unconsciously, to memorise? Is it to do with how deeply or superficially people think? To put it another way, each researcher will have a different *model* or *construct* of cognitive style.

When a researcher sets up a project to measure an aspect of behaviour, certain research methodology questions must be settled before any investigation begins.

In particular, anyone looking at the results of an experiment needs to be absolutely clear as to what was being measured. A research team will agree on a particular model or construct of what they think the behaviour involves. For example, if they wished to measure levels of anger, would they measure levels of adrenalin or blood pressure across a range of stressful situations? In that case they would be creating a *medical* model or construct of 'anger' in terms of reflex bodily responses. They could, alternatively, use a questionnaire asking people to rate their anger levels from 1 to 5 in intensity in a range of situations. This would be creating a different model or construct of anger as an *emotional* state, measured by self-report. These are just two of a whole possible range of different models or constructs of anger, each of which would involve measuring or describing the behaviour in different ways. In the same way, before a researcher is able to measure someone's learning style, the model of learning style being used must be clear.

The first impression one has of cognitive or learning style research projects is of a bewildering range of varying models or constructs for learning style, each of which gives a picture of a different type. Closer inspection can divide all these varying approaches into six major different models. Each one focuses upon the specific aspect of behaviour that the particular researchers felt was the central factor in the way people respond to a learning situation. These aspects of behaviour usually relate to one of the following six factors:

1. personality
2. intellectual development
3. motivation
4. self-concept
5. types of processing
6. hemispheric specialisation

Personality

Some approaches to identifying learning style examine the impact personality type has upon cognitive and learning style. For example, is a student introverted or extroverted (Eysenck 1967, 1976), impulsive or reflective? Any tests used by researchers favouring this approach for measuring learning style will be based upon a specific type of personality theory that may not necessarily be universally accepted as valid.

Intellectual development

Another approach is that of the stage theorists who link cognitive or learning style with stages of intellectual development leading towards a particular mature style that is seen as desirable.

Motivation

Some researchers have defined learning style by the type of motivation that spurs a student on. Biggs (1987) sees style of learning as heavily influenced by types of motivation, such as personal, vocational or competitive. He suggests that there are three approaches to learning, all linked with motivation – surface, deep and achieving. *Surface* learners are pragmatically motivated by, for example, a desire for a qualification. Tasks are seen as demands to be met, therefore the strategies involve focusing upon essentials, usually facts rather than deeper meanings authors may wish to convey. *Deep* learners are motivated by an intrinsic interest in the task; consequently, they adopt strategies that will satisfy their curiosity and focus upon the study material as a whole with the aim of digging out the meanings the author intended to convey and linking these with their own experience and interest. *Achieving* learners are motivated by the competitive instinct and characterised by attempts at highly efficient task management. Biggs states that the achieving approach is usually found in conjunction with either the deep or surface approaches, and frequently the mixture of deep and achieving strategies is the characteristic of high-achievement students.

Self-concept

Many researchers focus upon the academic self-concept or how individuals see themselves as learners. Are they frightened of failure, and does this influence the way they take information in? Do they feel inadequate as learners and therefore copy the strategies of others? Are they able to take responsibility for their own successes and failures as learners or do they blame the environment?

Types of processing

Another group of theories are built upon a *processing* model, where the mind is compared with a computer that processes information in a range of different ways. These theories frequently tend to deny the existence of any centralised consciousness or personality in the brain and define an individual in terms of the processing systems involved in the input of information and the carrying out of actions. Cognitive styles are seen as the patterns of processing favoured by an individual. They might be simultaneous or sequential; they may favour input from ears or eyes or even differ as to the level or depth of processing involved. For example, Ausubel (1981) defines four levels or styles of thinking:

1. *associative*, involving rote and memorising
2. *analytic*, which combines use of long-term memory and narrowly focused search strategies
3. *imaginative*, which combines long-term memory and wide-ranging leisurely strategies
4. *intelligent*, *creative*, which combines the imaginative and the analytic

Style 1 is seen as more superficial involving less-extensive processing while the others bring deeper levels of processing into play.

Hemispheric specialisation

The brain is not perfectly symmetrical. The left hemisphere or side of the brain is usually more specialised for language performance and the right side for spatial and mathematical tasks – hence the term *hemispheric specialisation*. The development of brain-imaging techniques, such as positron emission tomography (PET), has confirmed, through pictures, that the left side of the brain is more active during language tasks and the right side more active during mathematical tasks. However, this is an oversimplification, and these pictures also show that most tasks like reading and listening involve many areas of the brain (Posner et al 1998, cited Vasta et al. 1992). A number of researchers, such as West (1991) or Torrance and Rockenstein (1988), suggest that there are links between a particular learning style and an individual's tendency to favour a particular hemisphere when processing incoming information. The right hemisphere is linked with the non-verbal, wholistic, concrete, spatial, creative and intuitive style. The left hemisphere favours the verbal, analytical, abstract, temporal and digital style.

Each of these six types of approach to learning style involves a different interpretation of what learning style is and therefore how it can be measured in any individual or how it might be used to help that person in the world of education. The range of these models makes it clear that there is no universally accepted single model of learning style.

How can this picture be simplified?

Simplifying the picture – two inclusive approaches

Attempts have been made to correlate a range of models into a few non-contradictory, all-inclusive models, which can then form the basis for research projects, style diagnosis and educational strategies. However, when researchers or educationalists select a particular model or construct, they take the risk either of oversimplifying the picture or of overextending the construct in a way that might invalidate findings (Moran 1991, Dunn and Dunn 1991). In some cases both risks may co-exist. Is there any way around this that can make the research findings of this fascinating field practically relevant to those in the business of teaching and learning?

It seems that there are, in fact, two major ways of looking at learning style, which can gather all these seemingly disparate models under two umbrellas.

The broad approach

Keefe (1982) reviews the range of styles described in American research. He divides them into *cognitive, affective* (or emotional) and *physiological* styles reflecting, as mentioned earlier, the broader perspective of American learning style research. Given and Reid (1999) provide a detailed and useful discussion of the impact upon learning of emotional styles. Within the cognitive style category, Keefe divides the range of styles into two types:

1. *reception styles*, or ways in which people absorb information
2. *concept formation and retention styles*, or ways in which people store information

He also provides a comprehensive list of research and diagnostic tests where they were available.

The cognitive approach

Much recent work has been carried out by Riding and his associates. They concentrate upon cognitive style rather than emotional or physiological styles and, like Keefe, have been concerned to come up with a broadly based model that not only is of practical use for research and diagnosis but also is of benefit in education and the workplace. This present book deals with the use of *cognitive* or *learning* style to enhance study and therefore focuses on the effect upon learning of cognitive rather than emotional or physiological styles.

Riding (1997) argues that research has established correlations or links between many of these labels and that a number of the seemingly different cognitive styles which other researchers have labelled are actually describing the same thing. Riding and Cheema (1991) conclude that all the different styles described can be boiled down into two principal cognitive style groups. They called these the Wholistic-Analytic and Verbaliser–Imager style continua and summed them up as follows:

The Wholistic-Analytic continuum is whether an individual tends to process information in wholes or parts. The extreme wholistic learner is at one end of the continuum, the extreme analytic at the other.

The Verbaliser–Imager continuum is concerned with whether an individual is inclined to represent information during thinking in words or in mental images. Extreme verbalisers form one end of this continuum, extreme imagers the other.

Each is a very broadly based, clearly distinct style continuum linking two extreme styles. Each individual learner's style falls somewhere along the continuum. On the first continuum, the Wholistic-Analytic, individuals can be assessed as to how far they take a broadly based inclusive approach or one that is sharply focused. On the second continuum, the Verbaliser–Imager, can be determined their tendency to use verbal or visual pathways to process and store information.

Each individual will be placed at some point along the continuum from extreme wholistic to extreme analytic and at another point along the continuum from extreme verbaliser to extreme imager (Riding and Mathias 1991). These two dimensions are independent – where an individual falls upon the Wholistic-Analytic style continuum will have no bearing on his or her position of the Verbaliser–Imager continuum. There is no suggestion that any type of cognitive style is more or less effective than any other.

Figure 1.2 is taken from Riding and Rayner (1998, p. 99) and shows the two cognitive style continua or dimensions.

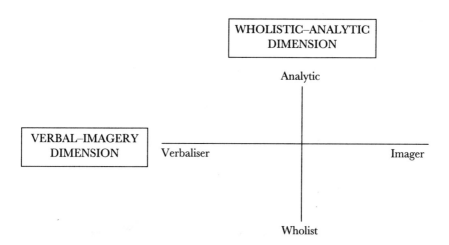

Figure 1.2 The cognitive style dimensions.

Riding and his associates do not deny the existence of other models for cognitive style. Having established the validity for these two broadly based constructs, Riding and Mathias (1991) find research to back the grouping of other constructs, including many of the American ones, within these two dimensions. In this they are independently supported by Schmeck (1988), who collected and reviewed a large number of these cognitive style constructs and states that he considers all cognitive styles to be reflections of a single dimension that he labels 'global versus analytic' (p. 327).

This clear, broadly based, two-dimensional mode both encompasses a wide range of approaches and offers a simple and accessible way of analysing style. Bearing the two dimensions of the model in mind, it is useful to refer back to Jack, the student described earlier. Judging from his most successful ways of learning, he is likely to fall towards the imager end of the Verbaliser–Imager continuum and the Wholistic end of the Wholistic-Analytic continuum. When he was formally assessed using Riding's instrument, this was confirmed. When helped to use his particular style to compensate for his difficulties, his school life began to be more successful. For all these reasons, Riding's model of cognitive style analysis is the one that will be used as a basis for diagnosis and practical action for students, parents and teachers.

Chapter summary

Definitions for cognitive and learning style are provided and discussed.

Cognitive style is an individual's characteristic and relatively consistent way of processing incoming information of all types from the environment.

Learning style is the application of this cognitive style to a learning situation.

The major controversies around cognitive and learning style have been presented:

Is cognitive style a stable, long-lasting trait?

What role does the environment play in the development of cognitive style?

Does the learning style of student change in a developmental way?

How do different teaching styles affect learners? How flexible is learning style?

Slightly differing research backgrounds to the variety of contemporary approaches to cognitive and learning style (termed cognitive and broad to distinguish them) have been described.

The Riding model of the two cognitive style dimensions, which both encompasses a wide range of approaches and offers a simple way of analysing style, is presented as a reliable and practical approach to the definition and diagnosis of cognitive or learning style.

Based upon the two style dimensions, Wholistic-Analytic and Verbaliser–Imager, it is the model that will be used as a basis for diagnosis and practical action for students, parents and teachers.

Chapter 2 explores the different methods of learning employed by students with dyslexia.

CHAPTER 2

Different ways of learning

Introduction

The previous chapter introduces a body of fairly academic information much of which may have been new, particularly to readers whose primary interest may well be dyslexia rather than learning style. How would you go about remembering the bulk of this information? Anyone familiar with the work of Tony Buzan (1982) might create a mind map (see opposite).

How do you respond to this? Does it resonate with and reinforce the impressions of chapter one that you have carried with you or does it irritate you? What are the implications of your response for your knowledge of your own learning methods?

Concept maps – a visuo-spatial tool

Students are frequently encouraged to use this form of noting information when 'brainstorming' or collecting ideas for writing, and the later chapters on visual and wholistic methods will look into creating and using these for dyslexic students. They are, however, also invaluable as a tool for storing or revising information and, once students feel confident with them, many frequently find themselves using them for virtually everything, whether it be revising for secondary-school examinations or planning the layout of a book. However, does this approach work for everyone?

It is likely that in any group of students there will be one or more who complain that concept maps 'do their heads in'. The previous chapter should have given some indication as to why this might be. A mind map is primarily a visual tool. Frequently, words are kept to a minimum, and some students will use symbols where appropriate.

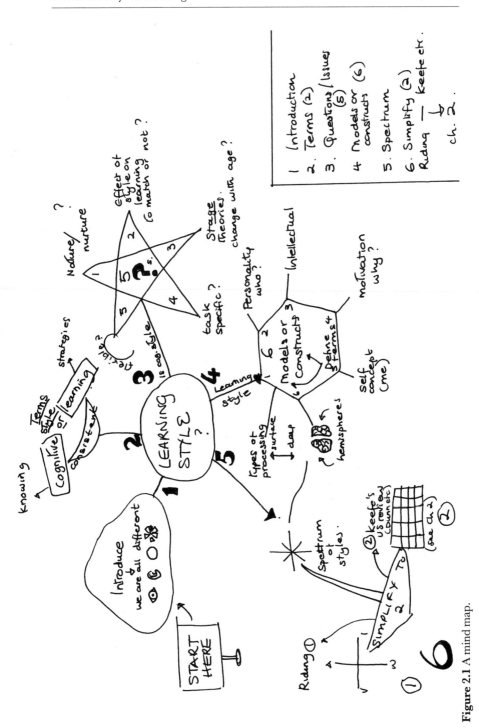

Figure 2.1 A mind map.

Ideas are not spelled out verbally and emphasis is placed upon the brain's ability to make connections in order to retrieve associated items or details from memory. Another characteristic of a concept map is that it is a map of the whole of a topic, and it is not, at first glance, orderly or sequential. Where does it start? Where does it finish? Can the reader follow it step by step? For some students it is simply a bewildering spidery maze that gets between the student and the information, increasing tension and reducing their ability to retrieve the facts they need.

Which students might find themselves in this predicament? Arguably, it will be those whose style strengths are not predominantly visual or wholistic – the student whose first tool is language, whose approach to learning is linear, detail orientated and focused upon a logical approach to learning where aspects of any topic are learned separately and stored in a logical, orderly sequence. These students will probably find other methods more congenial, unless they are shown ways in which to adapt the concept map approach to their own style. (Chapters 7 and 8, which look at analytic and wholistic learners, should provide some help here.)

Helping students cope with the teaching methods of secondary school

Recently, many teachers in secondary schools have been introducing some of these more visuo-spatial methods into their classrooms, and this is greatly to be welcomed for the following reasons.

Several research projects, including Galton and Willcocks (1983) and Lunzer and Gardner (1979), highlight the key differences in teaching and presentation styles between primary and secondary classrooms. These include:

- a move away from practical work and the presentation of concrete ideas supported by 'context-embedded referents' – an environment that contains objects and activities to clarify and make 'concrete' the spoken message (Cummins 1978)
- a move towards the verbal introduction of more abstract ideas despite the fact that many young adolescents do not consistently show competence in working with abstract ideas at this stage (Coleman and Hendry 1989)

- the tendency to spend substantially more time sitting listening to oral material presented by a teacher (Lunzer and Gardner 1979)
- the change from group work, where students interact with the teacher on an individual or small-group basis, to the whole-class work situation, where information is delivered from the front of the class by the teacher, frequently verbally, with little opportunity for visual cues or concrete experience
- an increase in the cognitive and linguistic demands of the language used, for example, in a study about weather, the use of cognitively undemanding terms such as *hot/cold*, *sunny/cloudy*, in the primary school changes in the secondary school to abstract meteorological terminology, such as *pressure, fronts* and *humidity*, where words may either be previously unknown, such as *humidity*, or given a distinct context-specific technical meaning, such as *front*, which the students probably last came across in relation to doors or dinner queues!

Overall, these changes, particularly the move from concrete to abstract reasoning, can do considerable damage to the progress of a significant minority of pupils (Galton and Willcocks 1983). This is exacerbated by the fact that many of these transferring children have not yet reached the stage of development where they are ready for this more abstract and verbal mode of presentation. In the previous chapter reference was made to Piaget's concept that children move through distinct stages in their cognitive development, as described here. (For further detail and discussion, see Silva and Lunt 1982, Donaldson 1978 or Wood 1988.)

Summary of Piaget's Four Stages

Approximate ages

1.	Sensory motor	Birth–2 years
2.	Pre-operations	2 years–7 years
3.	Concrete operations	7 years–11 years
4.	Formal operations	11 years

Only at stage 3, the concrete operational stage, do children begin either to be able to see the world from any standpoint but their own or to be able to provide logical or sensible answers to practical problems closely related to the immediate concrete environment. Abstract reasoning does not begin until the child reaches the fourth stage of formal operations, where they begin to be able to go beyond defining problems in terms of physical actions and their outcomes and to be able to apply logical thought to abstract problems and concepts, for example issues of morality, religion or politics.

It is only at this stage that students begin to be able to hold and test a range of hypotheses in their heads, and it is debatable as to whether many students are capable of doing this effectively even by the age of 15, let alone 11.

Some learning style theorists also suggest the possibility of stages of development. Carbo (1995, cited in Dunn 1995) suggests the following progression:

[up points] tactual/kinesthetic → psychomotor → visual → auditory

However, this is much less extensively researched and not necessarily accepted. It would, however, show that a verbal style, based upon listening, is the most mature style and that many students might not have developed this.

Both these stage theories would suggest that those students particularly at risk at transfer time would be those whose learning style is less verbal or auditory, who have survived the practically orientated, context-rich curriculum of the primary school and now find themselves floundering in a sea of abstract academic language. Carbo does actually suggest that a significant proportion of students entering the secondary school are still predominantly kinesthetic learners. Appendix 2 contains a few suggestions as to how to help them learn.

For these students, the introduction of visuo-spatial techniques and some of the accelerated learning ideas developed by the Accelerated Learning Centre (Smythe 2001) are beginning to provide some counterbalance to the predominantly verbal, abstract and theoretical delivery of the curriculum in the secondary school. However, it would be unwise to expect all learners to respond positively to this approach. It thus seems vital to be able to develop awareness of style, in both teachers and learners, as cognitive style will inevitably affect both the teacher's preferred modes of presentation and the student's receptiveness.

Matching the mode to the style

It seems clear that different modes of presentation suit different students. However, is it simply a matter of matching the presentation mode to the student's preferred style for optimum results? As always, nothing is quite that simple.

Common sense might suggest that the most effective learning would take place when instruction and style are matched. As Chasty suggests (1985), if a student cannot learn in the way a teacher teaches, the teacher must teach in the way the student learns. Using a preferred processing style is likely to be more spontaneous, to use up less energy and neural space and therefore to leave more potential for other simultaneous processing activity, such as reflection or analysis (Dunn and Dunn 1991). Strong research evidence does exist to support this claim (Given and Reid 1999), but some research has been criticised on the grounds that it is difficult to attribute learning success to a match between style preference and presentation rather than to any of a range of other influences in the classroom, including teacher skill, group dynamic, student motivation or interest.

Dunn's 1995 meta-analysis of 36 studies from American colleges (described by Given and Reid 1999) came to these conclusions:

- Students with strong style preferences made greater gains than those with weak preferences when instructed in matching style.
- Small-group studies showed more pronounced gains than medium- or large-sized samples.
- College and adult learners made greater gains than younger students.
- Middle-class students made greater gains than any other socioeconomic class.
- Average students were more responsive than high- or low-ability students.

From these conclusions it might be inferred that greater gains occurred in a situation where the small size of the group, or the level of student maturity, allowed greater focusing on metacognitive processes.

In its turn, this meta-analysis was strongly criticised on a range of grounds related to the way the studies were carried out. Given and Reid (1999) describe the course of the controversy. However, despite the criticism, they finally decide that there is considerable evidence of success being achieved through matching instruction to learning style. They therefore suggest that educators continue to explore methodology that seems to work and leave the researchers to continue the debate!

Riding and Rayner (1998) present a range of studies that investigate the links between mode of presentation and student success. There are some predictable findings. For example, Riding and Staley (1998) find that, even though university students are not very consciously aware of their style strengths, their performance is still improved by a match between presentation and verbaliser–imagery styles. Secondary-school students, when given a choice of versions of a sheet giving information, also instinctively choose the materials that suit their own styles (Riding and Watts 1997). Most of the research cited echoes Keefe's and Dunn's views, that matching style and presentation leads to success, particularly for the initial presentation of any task. However, there are some interesting exceptions, particularly to do with gender differences.

There is much ongoing research in the area of gender differences in learning and academic achievement from the much-publicised concern over the comparative underachievement of boys in secondary schools to suggested differences in underlying cognitive processing in boys and girls. Interpretation is always difficult as it is hard to distinguish between cultural and biological influences upon behaviour. It is therefore useful to look at the most basic levels of information processing and how this is expressed in cognitive style. There do not appear to be overall gender differences with respect to cognitive style (Riding and Rayner 1998).

However, there was a suggestion that there is a difference in the processing of information with males processing information faster but more as a superficial scan while females were slower and more thorough. This may be linked with a gender difference in the location of activity within the brain. There is also a suggestion that, in some situations, females, unlike males, do better when their cognitive style does not theoretically suit the task. These issues of gender and brain activity are examined more thoroughly later in relation to dyslexia and its impact upon each particular learning style.

The overall conclusions Riding and his associates come to is, however, that any student's learning performance will be affected by the interaction between cognitive style and three aspects of any study material:

- the structure of the material
- the mode of presentation
- the type of content

It would therefore seem crucial to give both students and teachers a chance to explore their own underlying preferences and to take responsibility for using the approaches that work best for them and for the full range of their students.

The next question, of course, is *how?*

Diagnosing cognitive or learning style

An individual's learning style needs to be diagnosed. Chapter one introduces the range of models of cognitive and learning style that can be used as a basis for diagnosing an individual's preferred style. It also outlines the basic differences in focus and scope between two major approaches:

- the learning style profile
- the cognitive style analysis

The Learning Style profile

A style mapping or profiling approach is the more widely based of the two approaches and takes into account a range of domains of experience. Given and Reid (1999) describe in detail the Dunn and Dunn Learning Styles Model, a representative and well-used example of this approach (Figure 2.1). This has been extensively researched in classroom settings and covers five domains of experience: the reflective, emotional, sociological, physical and psychological. Stylistic preferences within these five domains influence learning outcomes.

- the *reflective* covers environmental factors, such as sound, light and temperature, and internal factors, such as tendencies to reflect, explore, record and analyse performance
- the *emotional* covers motivation, responsibility, persistence and personal goals
- the *sociological* covers the kind of social groupings or relationships a student prefers for maximum success
- the *physical* involves the need for mobility or tactile experiences and the physical influence of surroundings
- the *psychological* covers cognitive needs, such as a preference for a particular mode of presentation or for a wholistic or analytic approach

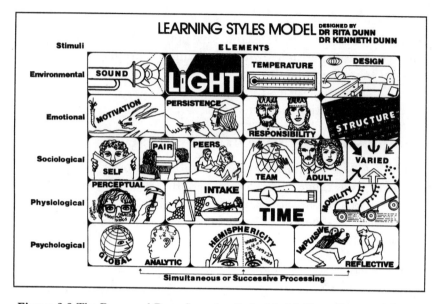

Figure 2.2 The Dunn and Dunn Learning Styles Model. From Dunn and Dunn: Teaching Secondary School Students Through Their Individual Learning Styles. Published by Allyn and Bacon MA. Copyright 1993 by Pearson Education. Reprinted by permission of the publishers.

To tailor a learning situation so that it suits a student it is necessary to have a clear picture of the student's learning style profile. This can be compiled in a number of ways:

Using a *formal standardised inventory* The Learning Styles Inventory is one example that has been studied extensively. This does, however, have various drawbacks, not the least being the practical fact that it has 104 items and therefore takes considerable time to administer. It has also been criticised on statistical grounds. It could be argued too that this type of learning styles profile is, in fact, trying to cover too wide a range of learning situations and is therefore unreliable as students' preferences could vary from situation to situation. It is, however, widely in use in the United States with much reported success.

Another example of an inventory is Levine's (1993) PEEX and PEERAMID assessment batteries, which support his model of Neurodevelopmental Diversity. Levine divides learning into a number of areas: attention, language, temporal-sequential ordering, spatial ordering, memory, neuromotor function, higher-order cognition and social cognition. His inventory assesses each area's own set of subskills and compiles a profile of strengths and weaknesses.

Using informal questionnaires

These can be very useful, both as diagnostic measures and as ways of raising a student's or teacher's awareness as to his or her own preferred styles. They can be designed for the students themselves to answer, as in Ostler and Ward (2001) or for teachers to record observations about children or to monitor their own style. One example is Given and Reid's (1999) questionnaire, (Figure 2.3) designed to raise

Understanding preferred learning styles
In order to maximise learning, it is useful to understand preferred learning styles. Preferred learning styles refer here to the auditory, visual and physical/motor skill strengths and weaknesses. Through this understanding you can maximise your learning potential.

Learning Style Inventory

Name: _____

Date: _____

Score 3 for mostly, 2 for sometimes and 1 for rarely.

Tick what applies to you	Mostly	Sometimes	Rarely
1. I am physically demonstrative and find clapping, hugging, patting friends on the back quite natural.			
2. I find it easier to learn by listening rather than by reading.			
3. I follow verbal directions more easily than written ones.			
4. I prefer to 'talk my way' through illustrations, charts and diagrams.			
5. I prefer to transfer written text into illustrations, charts and diagrams to understand them.			
6. I prefer written instructions to verbal instructions.			
7. I need to highlight keywords in order to understand the question.			
8. I tape notes to help me revise.			
9. I prefer text that is written on pastel rather than white paper.			
10. My hand aches if I write for more than ten minutes.			
11. I learn best through physically undertaking a task when possible.			
12. I remember best by creating a mental picture of information.			
13. I close my eyes to 'see' a word that I cannot spell easily.			
14. I have two or three tries at some spellings to 'see' which one looks correct.			
15. I find it easier to listen if I can 'fiddle' with something like plasticene or a ball of paper.			
16. I need to read information or an instruction aloud in order to understand it.			
17. When reading silently I mentally 'hear' the words and add emphasis in my mind where necessary.			
18. I recognise friends' voices on the telephone with ease even if I haven't seen them for ages.			
19. I chew the ends of pens and pencils when thinking.			
20. I enjoy research-type activities where I can search out information on the Internet or in the library.			
21. I enjoy walking round when revising where possible.			

Figure 2.3 Given and Reid's questionnaire. Reproduced by permission of the authors.

the readers' awareness of preference for style from the following range: global, wholistic, visual, auditory, tactual and kinesthetic.

Holloway (2000) has also devised two questionnaires; the first is for determining whether a student is 'left-brained' or 'right-brained'. She describes 'right-brained' students as those who learn best by: 'doing, touching, being creative, thinking visually and by bringing colour, rhythm, creativity and movement' (p. 28) into learning and 'left-brained' as those who learn well from text and like facts and precise detail. A selection of items from the second is shown here (Figure 2.4) and is designed to pinpoint preferences for auditory, visual or physical/ motor approaches to learning. Each question is linked to a particular modality.

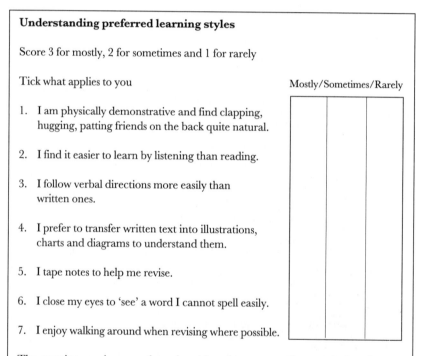

Figure 2.4 Selection from the 20 question Learning Style Inventory (Holloway 2000). Reproduced by permission of the author.

Another example (Figure 2.5) comes from Bridgwater College, Somerset, where it is issued to students on induction to encourage them to think more about their preferred learning styles.

FINDING OUT YOUR PREFERRED LEARNING STYLES

Look at each question and then decide which method you would choose to help you learn- there are no right or wrong answers. Put a tick in the box to make your choice.

1 **Timestable/Multiplication**
   (a) Cover over and picture it ☐
   (b) Saying out aloud ☐
   (c) Adding on fingers ☐

2 **Spelling A Word**
   (a) Write it down ☐
   (b) Imagine what it looks like ☐
   (c) Say each letter out ☐

3 **Learning A Foreign Word**
   (a) Repeating it out loud to yourself ☐
   (b) Writing it out over and over again ☐
   (c) Looking at a picture next to the word ☐

4 **Learning A History Fact**
   (a) Watch a video ☐
   (b) Listen to a person on a radio explaining what happened ☐
   (c) Role play – act out what happened ☐

5 **Learning How Something Works**
   (a) Take the object apart and try to put it back together ☐
   (b) Look at a diagram or a picture on the board ☐
   (c) Listen to a speaker telling you about it ☐

6 **Learning A Story**
   (a) Tell someone else the story ☐
   (b) Draw pictures/cartoons to tell the story ☐
   (c) Imagine the story ☐

7 **Learning A New Sport**
   (a) Watch a demonstration ☐
   (b) Repeat back instructions to the coach ☐
   (c) Do it ☐

8 **Learning A New Move On a Trampoline**
   (a) Let the coach support you through the movements so you feel how to do it ☐
   (b) Look at diagrams of the move on cards (flash cards) ☐
   (c) Talk through the movements with a friend ☐

Figure 2.5 Finding out your preferred learning styles. Devised by Sue Thatcher, based on materials from FEDA College Based Research Networks (1997–8)   (contd)

9 **Learning How To Use A New Tool In The Workshop**
   (a) Listen to your friend explain how to use it ☐
   (b) Teach someone else how to use it ☐
   (c) Watch someone else use it ☐

10 **Learning How To Make A Curry**
   (a) Look at the instructions on the packet ☐
   (b) Listen to a tape about what to do ☐
   (c) Try to make it ☐

11 **Learning To Count In A Foreign Language**
   (a) Sing the words ☐
   (b) Look at cards/posters ☐
   (c) Play French bingo ☐

12 **Learning How The Eye Works**
   (a) Listen to a Doctor telling you ☐
   (b) Make a model ☐
   (c) Look at a diagram of the eye ☐

Figure 2.5 (contd).

This questionnaire focuses upon auditory/listening, practical and visual/seeing styles. It takes as its basis a range of academic and everyday tasks and makes the student think about what kind of approach he or she would take to each one. Each answer is allegedly linked to a particular mode and as such throws up questions, such as whether saying letters out load when learning spellings really represents an auditory method. It is simplistic, fairly representative of its kind and useful as a way of getting students to focus upon the way they learn, possibly for the first time in their academic lives.

All self-report-style questionnaires have inherent weaknesses, including individuals' conscious or unconscious distortion of the truth, unwillingness to make the necessary effort to respond accurately and their bias due to social pressures or a desire to please or irritate. These 'blunt instruments' have a real role to play in increasing awareness but, for greater accuracy and consistency, need to be combined with more in-depth measures.

Using observation

The advantages of observing behaviour are that it occurs in real or natural settings across alternative situations, it is direct rather than relying on reported strategies, it is diagnostic and it can go on informally within ordinary class work. The focus can be upon the student's behaviour or use of strategies. It does need to be systematic, and ideally a teacher or classroom assistant should use an observational record sheet they have devised to suit the requirements of the situation. For example, when trying to determine which modality – visual, auditory or tactual – a student favours, Given and Reid (1999) suggest that some of the following aspects of behaviour can be significant:

1. Use of language – visual learners will often tend to use 'visual' vocabulary: 'I *see* what you mean. Do you get the *picture*? I don't like the *look* of this!'
2. Auditory learners may use expressions like 'That *sounds* like a good plan. *Talk* me through that.'
3. Spontaneous choice of ways of showing knowledge – would it be writing, drawing, talking or demonstrating?
4. What type of learning generates signs of tension?
5. What types of instructions does the student find easiest to follow-written, oral, visual or demonstrated?
6. What does the student choose to do with spare time – listen to music, draw, construct, play sports or other physical exercise?
7. Does the student spontaneously use maps, diagrams, notes or oral rehearsal when trying to remember something?

Checklists

It might be convenient and time saving to devise a checklist that can be used by a number of observers to build up a comprehensive picture of a student's approach to learning over a variety of tasks and a period of time. It would be possible to do this across all or some of the five domains – reflective, emotional, sociological, physical and psychological – according to the teacher's focus. Figure 2.6 shows an example overleaf.

Further observational methods

The Neurolinguistic Programming approach (O'Connor and Seymour 1990) suggests that a student is either visual, audile or kinesthetic in their approach to information. They claim that this can be estimated by observing a student's eye movement when asked

Example of an Observational Checklist

Choose a range of lessons or activities and observe the incidence of the following types of behaviour. Tick appropriate column each time behaviour is observed.

Date _____   Lesson _____   Observer _____

Verbal	Yes	No
• Follows oral instructions successfully		
• Shows ability to follow verbal events		
• Asks questions		
• Follows answers		
• Listens attentively		
• Contributes to discussions		
• Fluent communicator – good vocabulary		
• Willing to work in groups		
• Works successfully in groups		
• Chooses to learn from books, tapes and text		
• Good at explaining things		
• Likes to take notes		
• *General comments*		
Visual		
• Chooses to learn from film, illustration, diagrams etc.		
• Good with maps and graphs		
• Chooses to use symbols, pictures to store information		
• Observant		
• Visualises, sees things in mind's eye		
• Good navigator		
• Uses visual terminology		
• Chooses to spend time drawing etc.		
• *General comments*		
Wholist		
• Asks for advance organisers		
• Sees links between ideas		
• Looks for patterns and relations		
• Finds retention of detail difficult		
• Finds lists and sequences difficult		
• *General comments*		
Analytic		
• Able to follow logical sequences		
• Likes to follow step-by-step instructions		
• Enjoys sequential problem solving activities		
• Uses lists spontaneously		
• Doesn't automatically see links and patterns		
• Good recollection of detail		
• *General comments*		

Ticks in the No column of the verbal section may be an indication of a visual learning style.
Ticks in the No column of the wholist section may be an indication of an analytic learning style.

Figure 2.6 Example of an observational checklist.

to tackle a mental problem – even something as simple as calculating the number of windows on the front of their house. Figure 2.7 shows the NLP diagnostic eye-movement diagram. Briefly, if the eye movement is upwards, the student is visual. If it is to the side, the student is audile or auditory. A downward movement indicates a kinesthetic learner who depends upon feelings and emotions.

Another simple observational trick for distinguishing between auditory and visual processors is to tell the student to pinch his or her cheek while, at the same time, pinching your nose. Observe what the student does. An auditory learner will pinch their cheek, a visual learner their nose.

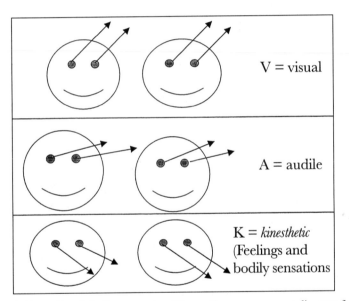

Figure 2.7 Neuro-linguistic Programming Diagnostic eye-movement diagram (based on O'Connor & Seymour 1990).

Using a combination of techniques

Within the area of mathematics, where two specific categories (quantitative and qualitative learners or 'inchworms and grasshoppers') have been identified (Bath et al 1986), Chinn and Ashcroft (1998) use a combination of techniques to create a maths profile, which includes a measurement of cognitive style in mathematics. Chinn has developed the IANS, (Chinn 2000) an Informal Assessment of

Numeracy Skills, which is a diagnostic battery of tests, including a cognitive style test. Along with this they support Sharma's suggestion(1989) of using the order in which the Rey Osterrieth Complex Figure (see Figure 2.8) is copied as an informal method of diagnosis. Sharma predicts that a qualitative learner will start with the outline, whereas a quantitative learner will start with the detail.

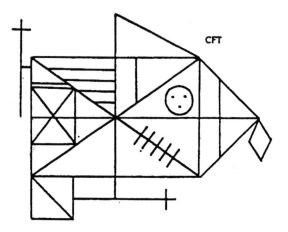

Figure 2.8 The Rey Osterrieth Complex Design Test.

Chinn and Ashcroft also suggest that observation of the mathematical strategies a child uses, such as whether fingers are counted to add the numbers 8 and 7 or (2 x 8) minus 1 used, or how a subtraction sum such as 1000 minus 699 is done, will give a good idea as to whether the child is a quantitative or qualitative learner. This is a good example of combining a range of assessment measures.

RECAP

This broad-based approach to learning style has its supporters and its detractors.

Supporters claim:

- the diagnostic methods enable an individual's unique learning style profile to be mapped
- the range of domains covered takes into account the variety of factors that influence successful learning

- lessons can be planned and executed to address students' basic psychological needs
- students can be encouraged to learn about their learning and take responsibility for it
- its efficacy has been shown in a range of classroom studies

Critics suggest:

- the diagnostic tools have technical flaws and are too time-consuming
- there is too much reliance either upon questionnaires or observation both of which are subjective and can give unreliable information
- the range of domains covered is too wide for precision
- it is too easy to attribute behaviours wrongly to underlying learning styles
- behaviour may be more random and inconsistent than can be shown by a limited amount of observation in the time available
- it is not practically possible to set up the kind of differentiated classrooms that the learning style approach demands
- the classroom studies showing the success of this kind of teaching are empirically flawed

It is obviously up to educators to come to their own conclusions about this method and its implementation. There is, however, another approach that may avoid some of the pitfalls.

The Cognitive Styles Analysis

(See Figure 1.2, page 19)
This model concentrates upon the **processing** of incoming information and gives a picture of a learner's preferred mode of presentation. It focuses on the cognitive basis for organising incoming information and establishes a style profile based upon this. There is, however, also a body of research that links particular styles with social behaviours, which is described later in this book. So it is possible to ascertain the social settings that will be most congenial to learners. This simple two-dimensional continuum does actually

contain a whole range of other models of cognitive style within itself; so, although it is simple, it is not simplistic.

Riding has developed the Cognitive Styles Analysis (1991a) to assess an individual's cognitive style. It has the following advantages:

- It is a computer-presented assessment, which is quick and simple to administer. It takes about 20 minutes and does not need teacher input.
- It is self-explanatory and consists of a series of very simple tasks, which most adults and children are able to perform with ease.
- It avoids using self-report or questionnaires, because of their inherent weaknesses.
- It assesses more directly the underlying sources of an individual's behaviour patterns by assessing performance on simple tasks, which might then be representative of an individual's general characteristics of processing. Although simple in themselves, they reflect very fundamental underlying tendencies within the individual's information processing system and so allow the cognitive styles to be detected.
- It is not threatening or intrusive, because it does not ask for personal details or attitudes and only requires simple neutral judgments. It is, therefore, relatively stress-free and is unlikely to raise anxiety levels that might change an individual's approach.
- It is free from culture and context.
- It prints out an individual score for both the Wholistic-Analytic and Verbaliser–Imager dimensions showing at what point on each continuum it falls. An accompanying handbook (Riding 1991b) gives information as to the learning and behavioural implications for this style.

How does it measure each dimension?

- For the Verbaliser–Imager dimension, the Cognitive Styles Analysis (CSA) assesses the balance between verbal and imagery representation by comparing the ease and speed with which an individual responds to a statement that requires a verbal judgement with the ease and speed for one that is based on a mental image. It does this by comparing a person with themselves; so it is not a test of overall speed but of a person's performance in the verbal mode relative to their performance in the imagery mode. The computer records the response time to each statement and calculates the Verbaliser–Imager ratio. A low ratio indicates a Verbaliser and a high ratio an Imager with the intermediate position being described as Bimodal. In this approach individuals have to read both the verbal and the imagery items so that reading ability and reading speed have no effect on the outcome (Riding 1997).

- With respect to the Wholistic-Analytic dimension, the CSA assesses the balance between the ability to see a figure as a whole and the ability to *dis-embed* or see it divided into its parts. This reflects the way an individual organises information – either in parts or as a whole.

Each individual will be placed at some point along each dimension; the higher or lower the score, the more extreme the cognitive style and the more difficulty the individual may have in absorbing information presented in the less-favoured mode. It is likely that a person will be further from the central position on one style than on the other, and this will mean that the effect of one style will probably be more noticeable and will be dominant.

Is the CSA considered empirically sound?

Riding (1997) and Riding and Rayner (1998) provide considerable evidence, through a range of studies, that it is valid or, in other words, that it does measure what it sets out to do. An index of reliability is, to some extent, built into the CSA by the speed index and percentage correct scores which indicate (a) how carefully an individual did the CSA and (b) whether they were able to do it. The ongoing development of a further parallel form for re-testing will also help to confirm reliability.

The simplest and most accurate way of determining an individual's cognitive style is obviously to use the instrument designed for the purpose. However, the same methods of questionnaires and observation referred to earlier can be used. It can also be instructive to try delivering teaching material in different structures and modes of presentation, to compare results and to discuss students' feelings about the methods. This will not have the same precision or objective validity as using the assessment instrument.

Once a cognitive style profile has been assessed, students or teachers can choose to investigate social and behavioural implications of style as indicated by the Riding research or to get involved in some of the other domains discussed earlier. At this point, observation techniques to gather information about preferences in other domains can be used if required, but this is not essential.

Are there any serious disadvantages?

The main disadvantage is that, to be confident about any diagnosis, it is necessary to use the CSA that is sold under licence and would therefore be expensive for individual use. For schools and institutions, however, the annual cost is no more than one standard piece of CD software.

A caution

Everything is open to interpretation, including this chapter. It is easy to oversimplify the results and implications of any research.

Here are three examples:

1. 'Once a student's learning style has been diagnosed, he or she will **always** respond better to material presented in the way that matches the style.' Well, if he or she is an able student with dyslexia who scores fairly highly on the verbalising continuum, this may be true ... until he or she has enough trouble reading more complex language to prevent him or her understanding the arguments.
2. 'Observing a student's behaviour in a range of situations will give you a **clear** picture of their preferred mode of learning.' Well, yes. Until you notice that on Tuesday, when given the choice of a range of sources to research his project, Toby, a 13-year-old able student with dyslexia, chose to take notes from a fairly complex library book. On Wednesday he rejected this and insisted on using a video to make a mind map. On Thursday he used written material cut and pasted from a CD Rom and on Friday he announced he would like to present his findings as a mixture of posters and oral explanation. What is going on here?
3. 'A student who scores highly on the imaging side of the CSA continuum is **bound** to like mind maps.' Well, it depends how they are presented...

Joe, a 16-year-old student with dyslexia and mild receptive language difficulties, strongly visual and artistic, had sat through a couple of superb and dynamic sessions on the use of mind maps or brain-imaging techniques complete with diagrams and maps. When asked to produce his own mind map of the events of the play *Romeo and Juliet,* he looked completely bewildered. 'What's drains got to do with Shakespeare?' he said.

What went wrong there? Discuss.

Arguably the most valuable conclusion is that nothing can be taken for granted. However, there is enough evidence to suggest that the following are important:

- diagnosis of a student's learning style or a teacher's presentational style
- enabling students to try out a range of presentational and study styles to develop self-awareness of what works for them
- use of a range of styles to accommodate the range of students in any group

This resonates strongly with one of the most established techniques of teachers working with students with dyslexia – the **multi-sensory approach**.

Chapter summary

This chapter examines visuo-spatial modes of presentation, such as mind maps and why not all students relate to them.

It investigates the changes in presentational style confronted by children on transfer from primary to secondary schools and the difficulties for those whose verbal or abstract skills are less fully developed.

It discusses evidence for and against the efficacy of matching learner and presentational style with the conclusion that giving the individual student the chance to identify preferences is crucial.

It presents and weighs up two major approaches to diagnosis:

- the learning style profile
- the cognitive style analysis

It looks at the advantages and disadvantages of a range of diagnostic tools:

- formal inventories
- informal questionnaires

- classroom observation techniques
- Riding's computer presented Cognitive Styles Analysis (CSA, 1991a)

It also cautions against oversimplifying the role played in learning by style.

Chapter 3 starts to apply learning style theory to working with students with dyslexia or specific learning difficulties.

PART TWO
Dyslexia

CHAPTER 3

The 3 'D's: Dyslexia, Definitions and Diagnosis

Introduction: What is dyslexia?

There is a student at the front of the class. The students are talking about the environment, the threats posed by pollution and global warming. Her hand goes up again and again. Each time her comment is both original and to the point. Not only that but she can talk at some length and discusses eagerly with her friends when they go into groups to collect ideas for written homework. Next day she hands in her work. It is half a side, untidy, simplistic. The teacher challenges her. 'Didn't have time, Miss,' she says. Another lunchtime spent in detention.

There is another student at the back of the class. His legs are stuck out across the gangway. His file seems to have exploded onto his desk. His shirt is hanging out; his tie is nowhere. When the teacher turns his back there always seems to be a ripple of counter-culture from that corner of the room. He always seems to be doodling when he should be following the text the teacher is reading, but from time to time produces a comment that shows he's taken in the content. Homework? Forget it.

There is a little boy at the side of the class. Other students seem to pick on him a bit. Written work is dragged out of him. He doesn't say a lot, but occasionally, if students have been asked to read aloud around the class, his pen will suddenly cover him with ink or he will stick a compass into the girl next to him just before he is due to read. He doesn't seem to mind being sent out of the room.

Which of these students has dyslexia or specific learning difficulties (sometimes termed Sp.LD)? The answer is that all or none of them could. The first girl could either be stroppy, have problems at home or be severely dyslexic and unable to express herself on paper despite obvious ability. The back-row boy could be Jack the Lad or concealing his dyslexic difficulties by opting out, acting the class clown, causing trouble – the range of displacement behaviours is limited only by ingenuity. The little boy at the front could have all-round mild learning difficulties, language difficulties or could exhibit intermittent inappropriate behaviours or he could be a dyslexic virtual non-reader concealing his difficulty. It is not particularly easy to identify dyslexic students by their behaviour.

Defining dyslexia

The difficulty is increased by the fact that the establishing of definitions and boundaries for dyslexia or specific learning difficulties continues to be a problematic and sometimes contentious task.

First, the terminology. Should the discussion be about 'dyslexia' or 'specific learning difficulties'? Originally, the term 'dyslexia' referred strictly to an impairment in the processing of written language. However, it has been recognised (Pumfrey and Reason 1991) that the two terms now seem to be used interchangeably to cover the particular pattern of difficulties experienced. Consequently, the term 'dyslexia' is used throughout this book with no suggestion that the characteristics are confined solely to difficulties with written language.

Secondly, what is dyslexia? The definition has changed subtly over the last thirty years. In 1968 the World Federation of Neurologists defined it as follows:

> Dyslexia is a disorder manifested by difficulty in learning to read despite conventional instruction and sociocultural opportunity. It is dependent upon fundamental cognitive disabilities which are frequently of constitutional origin. (World Federation of Neurologists 1968, cited by Reid 1994, p. 2)

Here the focus is upon literacy difficulties. However, Miles' research (1993) concluded that difficulties with spelling and reading form part of a wider disability involving distinguishing between, and naming, forms of symbolic material, such as graphemes or number systems. By 1989 the International Dyslexia Association provided an expanded and clearer definition that highlights the range of difficulties dyslexic students may experience:

> Specific Learning Difficulties can be defined as organising or learning deficiencies which restrict the students' competencies in information processing, in motor skills and working memory, so causing limitations in some or all of the skills of speech, reading, spelling, writing, essay writing, numeracy and behaviour. (*Dyslexia* 1989)

This definition is far less vague than that of the World Federation of Neurologists (1968) quoted above and now refers to a wider range of behaviour. However, it is still a 'deficit' definition, and the majority of researchers have focused upon analysis of deficits and mostly confine themselves to difficulties with symbolic material or phonological processing. More detailed reviews of research are presented by Snowling (2000), Snowling and Stackhouse (1996) or Grigorenko (2001).

Deficit definitions

A 'deficit' definition characterises a condition by what it *lacks* rather than by *positive* characteristics. In fact, for some time dyslexia seemed to be viewed as simply a difficulty with the processing and retention of symbolic material with no real analysis of any other possible strengths or weaknesses. Much of the research literature in the area of dyslexia focuses upon a deficit model of weaknesses in one or more of the following areas:

- phonological processing
- short-term memory
- visual deficits
- automaticity

Phonological processing is the way people process *phonemes*, or sounds within words at the cognitive level rather than the hearing level. People with adequate hearing can still find it hard to identify, sequence and reproduce sounds within a word. (See Snowling 2000, Bradley and Bryant 1978 and 1983, Frith 1995, 1997 or Stanovich 1988 for further details.)

Short-term memory represents the phase in processing where information, sounds or symbols are stored temporarily before being discarded or transferred into long-term memory. Chasty (1985), along with other researchers in the area of memory processing, reaches the conclusion that inefficient short-term memory forms one of the basic causal factors. (See Chasty 1985, Gathercole and Baddeley 1993.)

Visual deficits: Stein and Walsh (1997) suggest that dyslexia is caused by a sensory defect in the large nerve cells in the eye, known as 'magnocells'. These cells, which form part of the pathway between the retina and the visual cortex of the brain, carry information about rapid movement or changes in the environment. Defects in these result in the brain receiving slightly unstable images – obviously causing enormous problems with the processing of print or symbols.

Automaticity: Many tasks, such as reading or driving, consist of a number of simultaneous subskills. For example, to be able to drive a car, one must be able to focus upon appropriate objects within the visual field, judge distance and speed, analyse events seen in at least two rear-view mirrors, co-ordinate feet on three separate pedals, judge appropriate pressure on the clutch and brake, manipulate a gear stick – and that's way before one might whip out a mobile phone or a sandwich! This hierarchy of subskills must be performed simultaneously; therefore most of them must become automatic rather than conscious, and use up very little processing capacity, to allow effortless performance. Hence *automaticity* refers to the ability to perform an action automatically without focusing upon it. Nicolson and Fawcett's (1994) research indicates that dyslexic students need to devote more energy to the conscious control of mental activities and even physical activities, such as balance, that would usually quickly become automatic for non-dyslexic people. Students with dyslexia therefore have greater problems than others in coping with simultaneous mental processes. This is a far more deep-seated processing problem, which affects far wider areas of life than simply identifying and distinguishing between symbols. Nicolson and Fawcett suggest that the root of the problem lies in the part of the brain known as the 'cerebellum'. This 'deficit' definition does, however, suggest a certain 'otherness' in the way people with dyslexia perceive and order their lives.

These are all deficit definitions; is there more to dyslexia than deficits? It was another development that began to offer some support to those people whose day-to-day contact with dyslexic people in a range of social and educational contexts led them to feel that the deficit approach did not seem adequately to address the range of behaviours exhibited by dyslexic school students in the classroom rather than the research laboratory or to take into consideration the considerable strengths exhibited by many dyslexic students despite their difficulties.

This second development was the research of Galaburda (1993), among others, into laterality and hemispheric asymmetry with its implications for 'right- and left-brained' learning styles. This will be defined and discussed further in chapter 4. These findings support the contention that dyslexia is not simply a difficulty with symbolic material but a much wider approach to the processing of experience involving a range of basic executive-function or organisational difficulties, including organisation in time and space (Vail 1997), which do not simply disappear once a student masters the written word. They also lend credence to the contention that the effect of dyslexia goes way beyond working with symbols or phonological processing and that many dyslexic people possess considerable strengths.

The opportunity for a move beyond the definitions that do not simply concentrate upon deficits was also provided by the increasing sophistication and sensitivity of techniques allowing researchers to observe brain functions.

Diagnosing dyslexia

Establishing a definition begins to provide a foundation for diagnosis. It is worrying to find that by 1994 Reid was still able to observe that around 15% of the children who were identified as having specific learning difficulties were not identified until they reach secondary education (Riddell, Duffield, Brown and Ogilvy 1992, cited by Reid 1994). The existence of many individuals who are not identified until, as adults, they wish to return to the education system they dropped out of earlier must support the contention that many others will remain unidentified. Recent research carried out at Pentonville Prison and Feltham Young Offenders Unit (cited by Williams 1999) suggests the existence of a significant group of unidentified dyslexics within the prison population. This all suggests that the process of identification is anything but infallible.

There are various approaches to diagnosis. The range of options includes:

- behavioural observation
- interpretation of psychometric tests – the ACID profile
- diagnostic interviews
- formal screening tests
- informal self-report questionnaires
- brain scanning
- genetic indicators

Behavioural observation

Pollock and Waller (1994) provide a helpful guide to this kind of diagnosistic approach. In general, if the answer to three or more of the following questions is 'yes', further investigation is definitely warranted.

Does a seemingly able and frequently articulate student

1. have difficulties with expressing himself or herself on paper – poor and sometimes bizarre spelling, slow or poorly formed handwriting, untidy presentation?
2. seem resistant to or need extra time for written work?
3. have unexpected difficulties with reading or maths?
4. have difficulties with organisation within time and space?
5. have difficulties with situations that involve memory (bringing the right equipment on the right day, remembering spoken instructions, remembering phone numbers, learning multiplication tables)?
6. use inappropriate behaviour to avoid classroom situations in which dyslexic-type learning difficulties might be revealed in public?
7. frequently seem worried, switched off or lagging behind?

Interpretation of psychometric testing – the ACID profile

A range of psychometric tests can be used to produce a pattern of subtest scores and provide details of discrepancies between different areas of ability. Some of these can only be administered by qualified psychologists (e.g. The WISC or Wechsler Intelligence Scale for

Children). Until comparatively recently, the emphasis upon the study of observable behaviours and not the unobservable mind as the legitimate object of scientific study meant that discussions about dyslexia were frequently restricted to an area totally defined by surface behaviours that could be observed, such as performance on reading, spelling and IQ tests and the differences or discrepancies between them (Frith 1997).

This 'discrepancy' definition involved identifying dyslexia through the observation of unexpectedly low scores on specific areas within such psychometric instruments as the Wechsler Intelligence Scale for Children (WISC-III, or third edition 1991) or the adult version, the Wechsler Adult Intelligence Scale Revised, the WAIS-R 1981). This is one of a number of instruments commonly used by psychologists to measure both verbal and performance intelligence and combine the scores to produce a full-scale intelligence quotient, or IQ. A child or adult undertakes a number of activities based on verbal or practical ability such as repeating sequences of digits, answering general knowledge questions, solving maths problems or arranging blocks to replicate the shape of a two-dimensional pattern. Each subtest provides a score and the amalgamation provides the full-scale IQ.

This enables a psychologist to look more closely at the pattern of scores for different skills, including visual memory, auditory memory and ability to sequence, and to emerge with a clearer profile for each individual. It also enables the observation of discrepancies, for example between verbal and performance skills, which can be masked by combining all scores into one averaged-out total. For example, a student scoring 120 (superior) on performance skills and 80 (well-below average) on verbal skills would still emerge with a full-scale average IQ of 100 despite the fact that verbal skills are well below average.

Throughout the 1980s a profile called the ACID profile was seen as a strong indication of specific learning difficulties. (Thomson 1984). This profile is evident when a student scores unexpectedly low – for example, below 5 or 6 where scores elsewhere are 10 or above – on Arithmetic, Coding (a measure of visual memory), Information and Digit Span (a measure of auditory sequential memory) hence the term 'ACID'. These areas of weakness tie in with the major research findings – that dyslexia involves a core phonological processing problem and difficulties with memory. This 'discrepancy' definition was seen as the only scientifically objective way of defining dyslexia and explanations for this discrepancy, through analysis of underlying differences in cognitive function, were yet to be investigated.

Drawbacks of the ACID profile

The ACID profile is now felt to be less reliable as an indicator. As Frith (1997) points out the concept of a 'discrepancy' definition is that an individual's difficulty must be *specific* to particular areas of ability to qualify as dyslexia. How specific is the deficit supposedly underlying dyslexia? Do qualitative differences in the underlying problems result in different subtypes? Are there degrees of severity? These questions have yet to be answered.

One further problem of definition emerges from this discrepancy model. Research into brain processes (Hulme and Snowling 1997, Grigorenko 2001) takes us beyond the discrepancy definition and any suggestion that, once reading problems have been overcome, the individual ceases to be dyslexic. A range of studies are collected in Frith (1997). These include longitudinal studies by Bruck (1992), Elbro et al. (1994), Pennington et al (1990) and Gallagher et al (1996), which show the persistence into adulthood of underlying problems linked mainly with phonological processing but also subtle impairments in visual ability (Slaghuis et al. 1993) and a wide range of abilities involving motor control (Nicolson and Fawcett 1995). Paulesu et al's 1996 (cited in Frith 1997) brain-imaging study of five dyslexic adults, who had seemingly compensated well for their dyslexia, showed also that, although the dyslexic adults were capable of performing a set of simple phonological tasks, the brain activity involved in performing these tasks was abnormal.

In many case of adult dyslexics, a discrepancy might have been present at a particular point in time but not at later stages, when, according to test results, reading has improved. This can cause difficulties when attempting to diagnose adults with dyslexia. Most dyslexic children who stick with education eventually learn to read at least to around a level that allows them to 'get by' in schools, if not at anything like their full potential. They also frequently manage to get around the writing problem in a number of ways, although spelling nearly always remains depressed. However, as

Frith states:

> no one with experience of dyslexia would doubt that dyslexic children become
> dyslexic adults, regardless of the improvements they show in reading and the
> improvement they can show on certain phoneme awareness tests. Probably no
> one would doubt that dyslexia also exists in languages where orthography is so
> consistent that learning to read is relatively easy, even for dyslexic children ...
> dyslexia is not a disease which comes with school and goes away with adult-
> hood. (Frith 1997, p. 8)

This provides a reminder that, if the conservative estimate of incidence of dyslexia in the general population is one in twenty-five
(Osmond 1994), there must be considerable numbers of dyslexic
adults about. For some of these, particularly adults entering higher
education needing support or concessions, credible diagnosis of their
condition is essential. Use of discrepancy definitions may well mask
their problems. This is one of the reasons why professionals working
with adults with Sp.LD frequently prefer to use another approach,
that of the structured diagnostic interview.

Diagnostic interviews

Klein (1995) provides both a justification and clear methodology for
structuring an in-depth diagnostic interview that includes measures
of specific skills, such as reading, writing, spelling, difficulties with
memory, visual-motor or spatial and temporal skills. She also justifies
the use of this qualitative approach rather than the quantitative or
measurement-based approach of psychometric tools, such as the
WAIS. This approach also gives more opportunity for contact with
the student and the devising of an individualised support package
including scope for feedback. It is, of course, very time consuming so
is only really practical for use with students who have already been
diagnosed as 'at risk' by other screening methods, such as reading or
spelling assessments or checklists for dyslexia. There are a range of
formal screening tests and checklists, varying in complexity.

Formal screening tests

There are a number of screening procedures available, specifically
designed to identify students with dyslexia, which can all be administered by teaching professionals. They all examine performance in a
range of activities not dependent on taught skills, such as reading,

which give an indication of performance across areas that will include visual and auditory memory, phonological discrimination, sequencing, automaticity, laterality and others. These include tests such as:

- Fawcett and Nicolson's Dyslexia Early Screening Test (DEST 1996)
- Singleton, Thomas and Leedale's computer administered CoPs (1996)
- Miles's Bangor Dyslexia Test (1983)
- The Aston Index (Newton and Thompson 1982)

Reid (1994) gives a helpful résumé of the range of alternative methods of assessment and screening.

Informal screening self-report questionnaires

There are a number of these, frequently used with adults. Figure 3.1, which was devised by Matty, Chasty and Vinegrad (1994) and taken with permission from the *Dyslexia Handbook* 2000 (ed. Smythe) is an example.

It is clear that all these methods contain advantages and disadvantages. The diagnosis of specific learning difficulties is not clear cut. Assessment needs to be seen as a process in which different

---

Checklist for dyslexic adults

Below is a checklist designed to help the dyslexic adult identify areas of weakness, not just in language skills, but also other areas such as organisational skills. Only when the difficulties have been identified can appropriate assistance be offered.

1. Do you find difficulty telling left from right?

2. Is map reading or finding your way to a strange place confusing?

3. Do you dislike reading aloud?

4. Do you take longer than you should to read a page of a book?

5. Do you find it difficult to remember the sense of what you have read?

Figure 3.1 Checklist for dyslexic adults.

6. Do you dislike reading long books?

7. Is your spelling poor?

8. Is your writing difficult to read?

9. Do you get confused if you have to speak in public?

10. Do you find it difficult to take messages on the telephone and pass them on correctly?

11. When you have to say a long word, do you sometimes find it difficult to get all the sounds in the right order?

12. Do you find it difficult to do sums in your head without using your fingers or paper?

13. When using the telephone, do you tend to get the numbers mixed up when you dial?

14. Do you find it difficult to say the months of the year forwards in a fluent manner?

15. Do you find it difficult to say the months of the year backwards?

16. Do you mix up dates and times and miss appointments?

17. When writing cheques do you frequently find yourself making mistakes?

18. Do you find forms difficult and confusing?

19. Do you mix up bus numbers like 95 and 59?

20. Did you find it hard to learn your multiplication tables at school?

If you have any further problems please telephone the BDA Helpline 0118 966 8271.

Reference
This list is based on the work of Jo Matty, Harry Chasty and Michael Vinegrad. For a full report of the Michael Vinegrad research see – A revised Dyslexia Checklist. Educare, No 48, March 1994

Figure 3.1 (contd).

forms can be used to complement each other. Frequently, diagnosis may well arise from observation of classroom behaviours that lead the teacher to suspect that something isn't right and needs investigation. An approach that is practical and matches the situation should then be followed.

Brain scans

As stated earlier, the increasing sophistication and sensitivity of techniques allowing researchers to observe brain functions offer scope for both the provision of explanations as to why certain processing skills cause difficulty for dyslexics and also possible diagnostic tools.

A range of studies discussed at the 1997 British Dyslexia Association International Conference on Dyslexia, Biological Causes and Consequences suggest that it is beginning to be possible, through post-mortem or neuro-imaging studies, to identify the relationship between variability in brain morphology (or architecture) and the deficits observed in dyslexia. There are cognitive abilities underlying visible behaviours, and these are based on neural systems in the brain. These systems can be monitored using a range of brain-scanning techniques. These include brain-imaging techniques where pictures of the activity occurring within the brain during particular activities can be generated through such processes as MRI (magnetic resonance imaging) or PET (positron-emission tomography). In PET scanning, blood flow to areas of the brain is made visible by means of a radioactive tracer and therefore enables the measurement of increasing and decreasing neural activity showing which areas of the brain are involved in particular types of processing. Establishing models for normal performance should enable those whose brains are functioning differently to be identified with the possibility of distinguishing in this way between dyslexic and non-dyslexic individuals. (Cornelissen et al 1995, cited by Frith 1997)

Genetic indicators

Another diagnostic approach may emerge from research into genetics. Studies with dyslexic families or twins have identified chromosomes possibly involved in dyslexic behaviours (De Fries et al 1997), which might very well provide indicators for the diagnosis of dyslexia in the future.

Chapter summary

This chapter discussed three questions:

- What are Specific Learning Difficulties or dyslexia?
- What are the underlying causes of dyslexia?
- How can dyslexia be identified?

What are Specific Learning Difficulties or dyslexia?

> Specific Learning Difficulties can be defined as organising or learning deficiencies which restrict the students' competencies in information processing, in motor skills and working memory, so causing limitations in some or all of the skills of speech, reading, spelling, writing, essay writing, numeracy and behaviour. (*Dyslexia* 1989)

The 1989 *Dyslexia* definition still provides a clear picture of the range of difficulties experienced. It goes beyond the earlier concentration upon dyslexia as being simply a difficulty with phonological processing or mastering symbolic material.

Research has moved on from the limited definition of dyslexia as an unexpected difficulty with literacy. The definition has broadened from focusing upon dyslexia as purely a phonological processing difficulty to an awareness that dyslexia can cause a wide range of difficulties in information processing. At the same time, there has been a shift from the 'discrepancy'-based definitions, which were closely linked with the need to rely upon observable behaviours for a diagnosis of dyslexia, to the suggestion that the dyslexic cognitive profile involves strengths as well as limitations.

What are the underlying causes of dyslexia?

Despite the scope and range of research interest in dyslexia over the last thirty years, it is still evident that, with the exception of the phonological processing deficit, which is widely accepted as a factor, there is currently no one biological or neuropsychological condition to which the pattern of difficulties termed 'dyslexia' can safely be attributed (Frith 1997).

However, recent developments in techniques for the investigation of the underlying neural systems within the brain suggest that, even though many people with dyslexia master literacy, the brain activity involved remains different from that of people who do not have dyslexia and that it may eventually be possible both to establish the patterns of brain function and to identify genetic patterns typical of the dyslexic student for the purposes both of diagnosis and educational support. Dyslexia, with its accompanying strengths and difficulties, is for life.

How can dyslexic students be identified?

Individual situations will require different approaches. Choose from a combination of:

- behavioural observation
- psychometric assessment, which can identify skill discrepancies
- diagnostic interviews
- use of test batteries designed for the purpose
- use of brain-imaging techniques or genetic indicators

Chapter 4 investigates some of the difficulties experienced by people with dyslexia.

Dyslexia – curse or blessing?

Introduction: What impact does dyslexia have on daily life?

The dyslexic profile can include both strengths and difficulties. However, this chapter focuses on the difficulties.

Traditionally, the classic 'dyslexic' individual has been seen as a bright student with difficulties focused upon reading, spelling and handwriting. It is, however, absolutely clear to anyone who lives or works with a dyslexic person that the condition frequently affects more than the ability to read and write. In 1993, the Moray House Centre for Specific Learning Difficulties consulted a wide range of professionals and concluded that dyslexia can be identified in terms of patterns of information-processing difficulty, ranging from the very mild to the extremely severe, which can result in not only literacy restrictions but also discrepancies in performance throughout the curriculum (Reid 1994).

This makes two important points very clear:

- Within the distinctive pattern of difficulties that constitutes dyslexia, each dyslexic student is an individual with his or her own relative areas of strength and difficulty and own learning style. Thus a dyslexic individual can be relatively good at reading but poor at maths, or good at reading yet unable to spell or very poor at reading and writing but an inspired mathematician or designer.
- Different people show widely differing degrees of difficulty.

The pattern of difficulties

Difficulties associated with dyslexia can be broadly divided into two
types:

1. Day-to-day organisational problems linked with unreliable
   memory or organisational skills. Parents of these children have
   already found that life is less simple than they had hoped. Their
   children have already discovered the day-to-day hurdles dyslexia
   can present.
2. Difficulties associated with the processing of symbols, whether
   they be letters or numbers. Difficulty with the processing and
   manipulation of symbols must mainly be associated with formal
   education. Not all individuals with dyslexia seem to suffer from
   organisational problems, therefore for some parents there is no
   clue, pre-school, that their child may have any kind of learning
   difficulty.

Dyslexia at home

> Life is just so confusing. (Alan, 15, dyslexic student)

Organisational problems are all-pervasive, they colour home and
school. Everyone is capable of suffering from embarrassing 'dyslexic-
type' moments when words get mixed up or equipment forgotten
because of tiredness or loss of concentration. The essential thing to
remember is that, for the individual with dyslexia, this is normal. It
doesn't go away after a good night's sleep. Even at home, getting
though an ordinary multi-tasked day, which frequently involves skir-
mishes with the written word in shopping lists or TV guides, can
demand that bit of extra concentration and build up levels of frustration when things that other people seem to do without thinking go
embarrassingly wrong.

Many dyslexic people will have difficulties with any types of situation that involve:

- memory
- sequencing
- concepts of time

- orientation
- left-right confusion
- managing simultaneous activities

Memory difficulties

Research indicates (Gathercole and Baddeley 1993) that it is an over-simplification to see memory processing as being a simple transposition of information, by way of a range of information-processing strategies, from a short-term processing 'box' into a long-term memory store. However, the storage-box metaphor is easily understood, and, initially, it is perhaps convenient to describe people with dyslexia as frequently having difficulties both with the processing and storage of information within the short-term working-memory box and with the subsequent retrieval of information from the long-term store. Memory processing, or working memory, involves four major components: the audio memory, the visual memory, movement or procedural memory and the semantic memory (storage of the meanings of words). An individual with dyslexia can suffer from a weakness in any of these channels, and this will put pressure upon the others.

Any task involving short- or long-term memory can cause unexpected difficulty to a person with dyslexia. This can include remembering phone numbers, remembering what you have been asked to get from the shop or remembering what you need to put into your school bag for the day. Performing simultaneous activities or automaticity (Nicolson and Ayres 1997) can cause problems, and these difficulties will be exacerbated if the individual is asked to follow several instructions in sequence or is expected to rely purely upon listening. If, in addition, the instructions are given while attention is elsewhere or there is particular pressure to get things right, failure is frequently guaranteed. Unfortunately, many everyday tasks do indeed involve sequences of instructions or simultaneous activities. 'While you're in the kitchen making a cup of tea, please could you turn the oven off and put the cat out?' Obviously, failing in these seemingly simple tasks both causes inconvenience to others and makes the people feel stupid. In future they may think twice about offering to help or even co-operating when asked, preferring to be seen as bolshy rather than as an idiot.

Sequencing

People with dyslexia frequently suffer from difficulties with sequencing. This does not simply involve problems with times-tables or the order of the alphabet. Children may well have little concept of the days of the week and live in a world where days are determined by the different activities that take place rather than any concept of Monday to Sunday. Their memory difficulties may erase the less-interesting activities in their lives and remove even more points of reference. How can you possibly remember your cooking ingredients on Thursday if you aren't aware it's Wednesday today? Days of the week are hard. The months of the year are doubly difficult as there are twice as many and they recur less often. Some months contain nothing memorable, like Christmas or a birthday, to help children remember them. It is not unusual to find teenagers who will tell you that summer comes before spring and after autumn (Pollock and Waller 1994).

In the face of such fundamental difficulties, it is not surprising that people with dyslexia have trouble with sequences of instructions or remembering phone numbers, let alone with following a more complex set of mathematical steps. To their embarrassment, sequences such as days of the week, months or seasons of the year and letters of the alphabet are considered easy by the majority of their classmates who are frequently quick to point this out.

Concepts of time

By the age of 12 or 13, the average child can usually cope with telling the time and with planning the week to include the wide range of activities, from football training to sleep-overs, that have to be fitted in. Concepts of time, however, are an area where the dyslexic child has difficulties. Telling the time involves sequencing, spatial and directional skills, memory and mastery of the linguistic expression of numbers (Pollock and Waller 1994). With dyslexia, these may all be problem areas, but this is not the only difficulty. Some teenagers can struggle with temporal concepts such as 'yesterday', 'today' and 'tomorrow', be confused by the fact that 'fifteen minutes' is also 'quarter of an hour' and have little sense of how much time has passed or how long half an hour 'feels like'.

This is particularly the case when he or she is absorbed in an activity and totally unable to keep any other considerations in mind.

This obviously causes friction at home when dinner is spoiled or with friends when people are let down, but it can cause real distress in the world of school where so much is organised by timetables, so much specific equipment has to be brought on the right day and where teachers may be unable to understand how a seemingly able student can be so forgetful.

Orientation and left-right confusion

Handedness seems to develop late in people with specific learning difficulties. In 1925 Samuel Taylor Orton, one of the earliest researchers into dyslexia, commented upon the fact that significant numbers of dyslexic individuals seemed to be left-handers. This may be linked with the difficulties in orientation experienced by those dyslexic people who find following maps and plans hard. Again, this is a difficulty that does not cause inordinate problems at home but can be thrown into relief on the first day in a large secondary school where the dyslexic student spends the whole day trying to find out where his or her group is supposed to be.

Dyslexia at school

As suggested earlier, there is one group of parents of dyslexic children for whom the onset of their children's problems coincides with the start of formal schooling. Until then the child has been a happy, normal, bright pre-schooler, full of chat and busy fun, interested in the new world about him or her and all it has to offer – the sort of child, in short, who would be expected to take to school like the proverbial duck to water. For these parents, the first year in the reception class may be fine. Reading books brought home may well be likely to contain more pictures than print, with stories that are talked about rather than read. If writing seems to begin and end with the child's name, there are lots of others in the class at the same stage, and life tends to revolve around active learning through play, construction, paint and playdough.

It is only when this stage seems to be going on rather longer than would be expected for an able and articulate child or when other people's children seem to be bringing home books containing three times as much writing that parents may begin to question. Quite frequently, they will then be told that children all develop at different rates, that their child is happy, sociable and obviously absorbing lots of information and that they shouldn't worry. So they don't, with mixed results!

From the information discussed so far, it should be clear what is happening. The dyslexic child is now having to do a number of things that he or she finds hard. In reading and writing he or she is struggling with the sequence of the order of the letters of the alphabet, is having problems with distinguishing between the different letter sounds and remembering the letter patterns that can represent them, cannot retain the visual images of words in his or her long-term memory and at best is guessing from the first letter. In maths he or she is encountering difficulties with sequencing and remembering numbers, with dealing with the language of mathematics and with working out which way the numbers are facing.

For some children this may be the first time they have encountered failure and disapproval from peers or adults. Many of these children will have genuine difficulty following instructions and will be trying their hardest to remember what they have been asked to do. They will be bewildered by their failures and distressed by the fact that everyone else seems to be able to do everything so easily. Other children may well be beginning to taunt them or avoid them. Their teachers may be equally puzzled and frustrated and not always convinced that the difficulties this seemingly bright child is experiencing are caused by anything other than naughtiness or carelessness.

This may well be the moment when the teacher complains that the child is lazy or is beginning to behave inappropriately or is having trouble making friends. For the parents this may well be the very first indicator that their child has a learning difficulty and that this is beginning to affect the way that child feels about himself or herself and other children or adults. It can be really unexpected and distressing after such a trouble-free start.

There are a number of books that deal very effectively with the problems dyslexic children and their parents encounter at primary school. These include Pollock and Waller (1994) and Raymond (2001). Others are listed in the further reading list at the end of this book. These discuss some of the behaviour problems that can begin to emerge as children develop avoidance strategies, which can include anything from hitting the child in the next desk to playing the class clown. They also provide a range of suggestions as to how the parents, child and the teacher can minimise and cope with these difficulties.

Learning difficulties sometimes related to dyslexia

For another group of parents, however, the news of difficulties does not come as such a surprise. All parents tend to dread the 'terrible twos' and often, however battle scarred they may be by the toddler stage, they hope that any difficulties they may have encountered are simply a manifestation of this phase. Earlier in this chapter, it is discussed how the typical difficulties with short-term memory and organisation experienced by many dyslexic children can complicate life at home. Increasingly, however, research is finding dyslexia co-existing with some other difficulties. These can include:

- problems in the development of language – either receptive, expressive or the social use of language (Stackhouse and Wells 1997)
- developmental dyspraxia (so-called 'clumsy' children) or developmental verbal dyspraxia
- attentional deficit hyperactivity disorder (ADHD) – the inability to concentrate

Children suffering from any of these three difficulties may have caused parents some anxiety well before entering school.

Any or all of these conditions can exist alongside dyslexia, greatly increasing the difficulty a child has in coping with life both at home and at school. However, care must be taken with both diagnosis and the type of provision offered. Some seeming weaknesses in language, social skills or behaviours that might indicate ADHD may well be the result of the accumulation of negative experiences.

Dyslexia and speech and language difficulties

The popular conception of a dyslexic child is of an articulate talkative child whose difficulties with literacy, mathematics or organisation appear inconsistent with performance in other verbal and non-verbal areas. As mentioned in chapter 3, one aspect of the deficit method of identifying dyslexia was to look for an uneven profile in standardised tests of intelligence, such as the Wechsler Intelligence Scale for Children (WISC-R) where, in contrast to low scores on subtests that were linked with types of memory processing, dyslexic children were expected to score average or above average on a range of verbal subtests.

Although much emphasis has been placed on the key role played by phonological-processing weaknesses in reading disabilities (Fey 1999, Stanovich 1988, Snowling and Stackhouse 1996), it was not immediately apparent that some students with dyslexia suffer from a range of speech and language difficulties. However, Stackhouse and Wells (1997) state that, although not all children with literacy problems have underlying speech and language difficulties, it is likely that the incidence of 'hidden' speech and language difficulties among individuals with dyslexia has been underestimated.

The investigative work of Stackhouse and Wells (1997) and Tallal and her associates (1988, 1997) has thrown much light upon the links between persistent speech difficulties and later literacy problems. In many cases a child's underlying language-processing problem only belatedly comes to light when subsequent failure with literacy leads to in-depth investigation of the causes. This growing awareness of language difficulty is matched by an increasing number of Statements of Special Educational Needs for students with dyslexia referring to speech and language difficulties and a need for specialist support in this field over and above the usual appropriate support given to students with dyslexia. There is growing co-operation between organisations, such as the British Dyslexia Association and Speech and Language Therapists, and an increase in collaborative work across professions such as teaching, speech and language therapy and psychology. Snowling and Stackhouse's *Dyslexia, Speech and Language* (1996) contains an excellent review of the literature with reference to case studies.

There is sometimes some confusion over exactly what a 'language' problem is. It is often imagined that the only children with language problems are either those who struggle with English as a second language or those whose articulation of spoken language is obviously hampered by some difficulty, such as a stutter, which makes them hard to understand. In fact, teaching English as a foreign language is not part of the speech and language therapist's brief, nor will the majority of cases consist purely of working with articulation. It has been estimated that one in a thousand children may suffer from severe and specific language impairments (Webster and McConnell 1987).

The field of study linked with the development of speech and language is huge. Readers with a specific interest in this area will find Martin and Miller (1996) both useful and practical. It is hard to underestimate the extent and range of communication difficulties that can be experienced by these children and adults especially when combined with dyslexia. An understanding of the following aspects of speech and language theory may help to explain some of the misunderstandings and distress experienced by children and adults with these difficulties.

- the nature of human communication
- the three main tools of communication

<u>Human communication</u> involves three main overlapping components, which are clearly presented by Bloom and Lahey's Venn diagram (see Figure 4.1) (1978, cited by Martin and Miller 1996).

The three overlapping circles represent the *content, form* and *use* of language. Content refers to semantics: topics, ideas, memory and meaning. Form refers to the method of communicating – spoken,

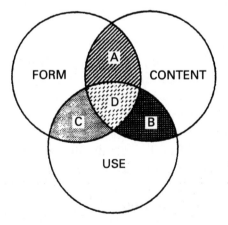

Figure 4.1 The intersection of content, form and use in language (based on Bloom and Lahey 1978).

written or signed (phonology, morphology and syntax in spoken language). Use refers to pragmatics or the goals and social use of language. The diagram shows how these three aspects of language interconnect, yet can be identified and examined separately to show how an individual's difficulties can, and often do, arise in any or all of these areas.

These are the **three main tools of successful communication**:

- *receptive* language or the processing of incoming verbal information
- *expressive* language, including retrieval of the required vocabulary speech, voice and fluency
- *non-verbal communication*, including production and interpretation of facial expressions, body posture, gestures, turn-taking and other frequently subtle social conventions that make communication meaningful. Disorders or delays can occur in any of these tools.

Difficulty with *receptive* language means that a child finds it hard to pick up on word meanings, particularly when words start to have technical implications as well as the previously understood day-to-day ones – 'I thought currants came in buns!' (Tom, 12, after a science lesson.) It makes following instructions and processes hard. Understanding and remembering, using the spoken word alone, becomes a problem.

Difficulty with *expressive* language or word retrieval means that, even if you know the answer, you're frequently too slow to select the words you need to express it before somebody else jumps in. It makes writing up experiments a challenge and giving an oral account in front of a group an ordeal.

Problems with the *social* or *pragmatic* forms of language can cause much distress as children frequently alienate their peers through their inability to know when they are boring them, how close they should stand or that the last remark was a joke. This is particularly true of students suffering from Asperger's Disorder, which is a disorder within the autistic spectrum where normal cognitive skills and verbal intelligence co-exist with impaired social or pragmatic skills that can make the individual a challenging companion.

It only takes a little imagination to begin to understand the difficulties, misunderstandings and frustrations, both with adults and peers, that can arise. Even in technical subjects or maths, information is communicated through written and spoken language, particularly in the secondary school.

Like dyslexia, specific language difficulties are frequently a 'hidden handicap'. People suffering from them can be misjudged as selfish, taciturn or difficult. Martin and Miller (1996) suggest that many students seen as having behavioural problems may well be suffering from an undiagnosed language difficulty.

Dyslexia and dyspraxia

Dyspraxia is in some ways a controversial term. Williams (in Smythe, 2001) defines it as 'difficulties in achieving purposeful, sequential movement in the absence of muscular paresis (weakness)' (p. 285), and the Dyspraxia Foundation states that: 'Dyspraxia is an impairment or immaturity of the organisation of movement. Associated with this, there may be problems of language, perception and thought.'

If a child seems exceptionally accident prone, seems to lack awareness of where peripheral parts of their body are in relation to the environment, is consistently clumsy and experiences difficulty with physical activities, such as dressing, ball games and balancing, or with the fine motor control needed to draw or write, he or she may be showing some of the signs of dyspraxia. These pupils may have difficulties with practical tasks across the curriculum, including in the science and DT areas and on the sports field. Some of these symptoms are considered to be typical of some dyslexic people and some individuals certainly appear to have some of the symptoms of both these conditions. Goedkoop (2001) considers that there is as much of an overlap as 40% between dyslexia and dyspraxia, but she presents a useful contrasting list of dyslexic and dyspraxic symptoms.

Verbal dyspraxia is a speech-production disorder, possibly related to damage to Brocas's area of the brain, characterised by difficulty processing sound sequences and an inability to organise and produce longer words or utterances. It is neurologically based and is presumed to be due to defective programming of verbal motor output, of the translation of verbal 'images' into the motor commands for their execution by the muscles of the mouth and face (Rapin 1996). Some individuals with dyslexia can also be dyspraxic and, as with speech and language difficulties, an increasing number of Statements of Special Educational Needs refer to the co-existence of the two conditions and the need for additional special support for those children with the co-ordination and motor-programming problems associated with dyspraxia. Some dyslexic teenagers who no longer suffer from articulatory difficulties continue to have to cope with slower processing speeds and response times.

Dyspraxia	Dyslexia
Late motor development	Early or normal development
Weak posture and muscle tone	Normal
Verbal IQ greater than performance IQ (often)	Performance IQ greater than Verbal (often)
Poor gross motor skills and PE	Often good at sports
Poor fine motor skills, craft and art	Strengths in art and craft (often)
Difficulty with social skills	Often strong social skills
Usually no reading difficulty	Usually reading problems
	Problems with word finding, rhymes, phonological awareness
More writing than spelling difficulty	Always spelling problems

A child who is dyspraxic may well have caused concern well before school due to his or her excessive clumsiness in play and everyday life often combined with a delay in producing intelligible speech.

Dyslexia and ADHD

ADHD (attentional deficit hyperactivity disorder) is a psychiatric diagnosis that has recently begun to be applied to children who are experiencing significant difficulty, both at home and at school and in their personal relationships, due to problems of impulse control, hyperactivity and attentional deficits. There is some controversy surrounding the question of whether this collection of difficulties is part of a specific syndrome. There is also controversy over the use of drugs, such as Ritalin in the treatment of the disorder (Volkow 2001).

ADHD often occurs alongside both behavioural and emotional disorders and low academic achievement in relation to intellectual ability (Barkley 1990). Interestingly, there is some suggestion of a link between high levels of creativity and ADHD (Cramond 1994). There is clearly an overlap between the profiles of some children with ADHD and some with dyslexia in that both may have trouble with working memory and maintaining concentration and may be behaving inappropriately, but the reasons for this may be different, and many children with ADHD do not exhibit the same literacy difficulties as those with dyslexia. Thus, despite the fact again that some Statements of Special Educational Needs do mention ADHD as well as dyslexia, great care must be taken with diagnosis and provision of the right kind of support.

Self-esteem and dyslexia – the effects of early negative experiences

Many dyslexic teenagers may have endured a lifetime of being told – or simply telling themselves – that they are hopeless. Teachers at school have been driven mad by exploding briefcases and lost assignments. At home the best intentioned of families can lose patience with misplaced belongings and forgotten arrangements. Frequently, the child will find himself or herself the odd one out in a high-achieving family where neither the student nor the parents can understand why little sister is reading far more difficult books than he or she can cope with. Sadly, parents can sometimes be the worst people to help their child with reading or homework. Instead of the home being a refuge from the pressures of school, Mum becomes 'teacher' and all the school-related problems and tensions reappear at home, exacerbated by the parent's own anxieties and insecurities.

Alternatively, other members of the family may also be struggling with dyslexia-related problems; so home may be chaotic. Some dyslexic children have younger or older brothers and sisters who tease them when they make mistakes. Accumulations of small failures and humiliations both at home and at school can damage self-esteem almost beyond repair. It's easy to laugh at oneself for the odd lapse if it happens within the context of a normally efficient and successful lifestyle. If it becomes the rule rather than the exception, one's sense of humour begins to vanish, particularly if friends and family start to lose patience or, worse, ridicule one's best efforts. Good humour is replaced by outbursts of frustration. What's the point of trying? I'll only make a mess of it!

Edwards (1994, p. 142) describes the sense of alienation, lack of confidence and self-doubt experienced by many dyslexic adolescents. She gives a vivid picture of eight 'outwardly secure, confident young men' who had 'all except one been pushed to extremes of misery during primary school ... had been teased, humiliated and insulted, by staff, children or both ... with evidence of truancy, total demoralisation, psychosomatic pain and isolation'. She also cites a range of quantitative and qualitative studies that examine the emotional reactions to dyslexia. These include lack of confidence, self-doubt, sensitivity to criticism, behavioural problems, truancy, competitiveness disorders, withdrawal, isolation and psychosomatic pain.

Psychologists frequently refer to low self-esteem when writing up statements of special educational needs for dyslexic students. 'Self-esteem' has been defined as 'the extent to which we like or approve of ourselves or how worthwhile we think we are' (Gross and McIlveen 1998, p. 402). It is bound up with the 'self-concept', or the picture an individual builds up of himself or herself (a picture that is created by experiences at school, at home, with teachers, family and peer group).

During adolescence, which can be a shaky time for the most successful of individuals, having a positive self-concept or high self-esteem can be crucial to the teenager's wellbeing. Repeated failures at school or at home, however seemingly minor, can devastate self-esteem and lead to problems in all areas of life. Many studies have linked poor self-esteem with juvenile crime or experimentation with drugs (Coopersmith 1967). For many students it will destroy their willingness to try any new task for fear of failure. In fact some research has suggested that, unlike others who tend to attribute success to their own ability and failure to outside causes, dyslexic students get into the habit of identifying any success as due to extreme hard work on their part and any failure to their lack of ability (Osmond 1994).

Other research linked with the Pentonville Prison Dyslexia Project suggests that a high proportion of illiterate prisoners are in effect dyslexic, possibly as many as 30% of the prison population. This is not to suggest that people with dyslexia are any more prone to crime than anyone else in the population at large but merely to focus upon the damage that can be done to their lives if their needs are not met. There is certainly room for more investigation into the true nature of the difficulties of many of the children who end up in schools for students with disordered behaviour.

Dyslexia in adults

Is there any difference between the difficulties experienced by school-aged dyslexics and their adult counterparts? The latest research into brain processes (Grigorenko 2001) takes us beyond the discrepancy definition, which states that dyslexia simply involves weaknesses in the processing of symbolic material, and therefore beyond any suggestion that, once literacy problems have been sorted out, the individual ceases to be dyslexic. Longitudinal studies cited by Frith (1997) show persistence into adulthood of underlying problems linked mainly with phonological processing but also subtle impairments in visual ability and a wide range of abilities involving motor control (Nicolson and Fawcett 1995). Frith also describes Paulesu et al's 1996 brain-imaging study of five well-compensated adult dyslexics, which showed that, although they were capable of performing a set of simple phonological tasks, the brain activity involved in performing these tasks was abnormal.

Recent developments in techniques for the investigation of the underlying neural systems within the brain suggest that, although many adults with dyslexia master literacy, the brain activity involved remains different from those without dyslexia and that it will become possible to establish the patterns of brain function typical of the dyslexic student for the purposes of diagnosis and educational support.

Frith emphasises the fact that, even though dyslexic children usually master reading, they become dyslexic adults: 'dyslexia is not a disease which comes with school and goes away with adulthood' (1997, p. 8).

Most of the research that has given rise to the developments outlined so far has involved children under the age of 16. Research into dyslexia in adults or higher-education students is rarer in comparison (see Miles 1993, Miles and Gilroy 1986, Riddick, Farmer and Sterling 1997) dyslexic children grow up into dyslexic adults and many move on into higher education. The National Working Party on Dyslexia in Higher Education (Singleton and HEFC 2001) surveyed 80% of higher-education institutes and stated that 1%-2% of students in higher education present as dyslexic although there must be more dyslexic students who have not been identified. They are scattered throughout the range of subjects, particularly in areas such as the visual arts.

The majority may have overcome their reading problems, although many still report that their reading remains slow and arduous. They also report that they continue to find written assignments, organisation and note-taking very hard (Miles and Gilroy 1986) and need support in various areas of work if they are to fulfil their potential. Klein (1993) lists the most persistent difficulties she commonly encountered in dyslexic students:

- memorising names and facts
- remembering sequences (e.g. alphabet, instructions, procedures)
- rote memory tasks in maths, including times-tables and basic number facts
- right-left discrimination
- problems with telling the time, time-keeping and estimating time scales
- concentration difficulties and being easily distracted
- severe expressive writing problems even when orally competent
- copying difficulties
- word retrieval – getting ideas down on paper, either as notes from lectures or in assignments

To these should be added a range of problems linked both to study and day-to-day organisation.

In the academic sphere, students will frequently still find the volume of reading required for many subjects more time consuming and exhausting than their non-dyslexic counterparts. They will also frequently find it hard both to decode new technical terms and then to assimilate them quickly into their working written vocabulary. Problems with automaticity lead to major difficulties with note-taking as the majority of dyslexic students find it very difficult to attend to the logic of an argument while simultaneously attempting to store it on paper even if they are not handicapped by slow handwriting and doubts over spelling. If they record lectures on tape, they then have to face the time-consuming process of listening and scribing later.

Inadequate notes obviously add to the pressure placed upon dyslexic students by written examinations, particularly in subjects where ability at the subject is not directly linked to the ability to write about it. Revision is made more difficult by slow reading and problems with time and planning revision schedules. Timed examinations are a nightmare to students whose handwriting speed may still be half that of the average student and who are aware that their spelling, even if readable, will give the impression to unsympathetic examiners that they are really too illiterate to be at university.

Essays and assignments also pose considerable difficulties as many of the essay-writing skills that seem second nature to a non-dyslexic person were never absorbed by the dyslexic student at school where he or she was too busy concentrating on basic writing and spelling to absorb concepts of punctuation or planning. Planning itself is frequently hard, as the dyslexic student's sequential memory may be weak, as is the ability to sort out and organise main ideas from the mass of detail accumulated about a subject that may be of consuming interest (Miles and Gilroy 1986).

Planning in general is often very difficult for dyslexic students whether it be assignments or simple day-to-day living. Problems with organisation, with concepts to do with time or with short-term memory can lead to a range of difficulties from forgotten appointments, lost phone numbers, lost library tickets or missed assignments. The dyslexic student needs far more support with organising life away from home for the first time than the majority yet is frequently reluctant to seek it out.

To general difficulties with day-to-day organisation is frequently added the emotional pressure of deciding whether to admit either to friends or tutors that one has a problem or might be dyslexic or else, for some dyslexic students who managed to cope well at school within the structured home-school environment, there is the shock of discovering within the first year of higher education that they are not coping, and they do not know why. A significant proportion of dyslexic students are not identified until they reach higher education.

Dyslexia, annoying, yes, inconvenient – only if we fail to change society's and the education system's attitude to dyslexia. Remember it is only the under-diagnosing and treating of it that causes dyslexia to be an inconvenience. If this was done properly, many dyslexics would have a head start over those peers who lack the problem-solving abilities that many dyslexics have. (David, dyslexic graduate)

Chapter summary

Chapter 4 looks at the pattern of difficulties experienced by dyslexic children and adults at home and at school. Dyslexia is not simply a weakness with literacy or numeracy in an otherwise able child. It affects memory and organisation and frequently language use and behaviour. These effects are felt both at home and at school and frequently result in the kind of damage to self-esteem that leads to a cycle of repeated failure, poor behaviour and emotional damage.

It outlines the other main learning difficulties that sometimes co-exist with dyslexia:

- speech and language difficulties
- dyspraxia
- ADHD

It examines the prevalence of dyslexia among higher education and describes some of the difficulties dyslexic students may encounter at university level. Dyslexia does not go away once a dyslexic student learns to read. Dyslexic children become dyslexic adults and carry their difficulties throughout their adult lives.

Chapter 5 looks at some of the strengths and talents displayed by many people with dyslexia.

CHAPTER 5

Strengths and talents

Introduction: Does dyslexia bring special talents?

I am a very LOUD PROUD DYSLEXIC THAT LEARNS IN A DIFFERENT WAY. I don't have a disability. I am different and wouldn't the world be BORING if we were all the same. (Nicky Woodward, adult dyslexia co-ordinator)

I'm dyslexic. That means that my brain works faster than I can write. (Jamie, A level college student)

I am currently a TV and video student. The more I see others struggle, the more I realise that I am gifted. What I lack in auditory memory I more than make up for in visual. All the other students plan their projects, storyboard them, etc. I can see the whole thing in my head and know how to edit and put it together. They all wonder how I can do that. I wonder how they cannot. (Lawrence Arnold, dyslexic student)

The previous chapter painted a gloomy picture of the many ways in which dyslexic people can struggle to cope with everyday life. This is, however, only part of the picture.

Question? What do Einstein, Gustav Flaubert, the writer, Richard Rogers, the architect, and Tom Cruise, the actor, have in common?

Answer: They are all (arguably) dyslexic.

To this list could be added Winston Churchill, Isaac Newton, the poet W. B. Yeats, the scientist Michael Faraday, the sculptor Auguste Rodin (Thompson 1969), the comedian Eddie Izzard, the racing-car driver Jackie Stewart, five-times Olympic gold-medalist oarsman Steve Redgrave, photographer David Bailey, the actress and singer Cher and still leave many other talented and successful dyslexic individuals unmentioned.

These people epitomise the other approach to dyslexia that has been developed and examined by those such as West (1991), himself dyslexic, and organisations such as the Arts Dyslexia Trust in England and the Newgrange Trust in America. This is to see the range of difficulties with memory, language and organisation endured by many people with dyslexia as a 'price' that may have to be paid for being talented in creativity and visual thinking. The difficulties experienced by people with dyslexia have been compounded by the tendency throughout most of the twentieth century to transmit information in a verbal, linear way, thus condemning many dyslexic learners to early and lasting academic failure. West's book (1991) had coincided with and encouraged the development of a timely shift in the attitude towards dyslexia that had for so long tended to focus research upon deficits in phonological processing and emphasise the deficits and difficulties associated with the condition.

West celebrates the creativity and visual talents that many dyslexic individuals seem to possess. He suggests that individuals such as Einstein and Michael Faraday seem often to recognise that they have achieved extraordinary accomplishments 'as much because of, as in spite of, distinctive combinations of difficulties and disabilities, disabilities that are themselves sometimes the obverse of special talents' (p. 102). He emphasises the role this type of 'visual-spatial' thinking has to play in the technology of a new century in which the visual image may well become the primary focus of analysis in detecting relationships rather than the verbal, logical or mathematical modes of thought. Thus individuals with the ability to visualise scientific concepts and manipulate complex three-dimensional information in a range of graphic displays may well become more useful than those skilled in words or numbers.

This new approach has been invaluable in the way that it has inspired many dyslexic people and their families to take pride in strengths rather than focusing upon weaknesses and given them both successful role models and the power to see themselves as making an original and significant contribution in a range of areas of work and study. It does, however, remain controversial in a number of ways.

The research background

The all-important question must be: Is there reliable, empirical research to support the contention that dyslexia may frequently carry with it high talents in spatial, mechanical or visual skills? West (1991) cites two types of evidence to support this:

- anecdotal evidence
- evidence arising from hemispheric specialisation theory
- evidence arising from handedness research
- evidence from psychometric testing of dyslexic individuals

Anecdotal evidence

West provides much fascinating information about a range of highly talented individuals in the fields of science and the arts, emphasising evidence of the presence of many of the classic signs of dyslexia, such as difficulty with processing written and sometimes spoken language, disorganisation and forgetfulness, along with a gift for using visual imagination. He includes a range of anecdotal evidence including comments from friends and historians such as Tricker's (1966, cited in West 1991) reference to Faraday and Maxwell's habit of 'thinking in terms of physical pictures' (p. 32). He also quotes extensively from letters, diaries and lectures including Einstein's own comments about his 'poor memory for words' and the 'ghastly disorder that reigns among my worldly goods' (p. 12).

Einstein, who did not talk until he was four or learn to read until nine, has also been quoted elsewhere (Richardson and Stein 1993) as stating that, for him, the essential features and tools in his thought processes were signs and images which could be voluntarily reproduced and combined – words being used laboriously only when ideas needed to be communicated to others. The work of the Arts Dyslexia Trust has also publicised and championed the work of dyslexic artists across eight professional art and design disciplines. In itself, however, this does not constitute hard, quantitative evidence for a strong and consistent link between dyslexia and creative visual thinking.

Evidence based upon hemispheric specialisation theories

This theory is also sometimes referred to as the 'Two Mind Theory', which arose from the work of Ornstein (1972). He suggests that the two halves of the brain deal with information in diametrically opposite ways. The right hemisphere will process any incoming stimulus as an integrated whole while the left hemisphere will analyses it in a sequential manner. Freeley (1987) describes the types of processing that are specific to the different hemispheres.

Left Hemisphere	Right Hemisphere
respond to verbal instruction	respond to visual, kinesthetic and demonstrative instruction
depend on words and language for meaning	depend on images and pictures for meaning
	prefer a step-by-step process where details and facts build one upon the other in a logical order
	prefer a wholistic overview so they know where they are going and then can learn by exploration and discovery

(Freeley 1987, p. 68.)

This was supported by others, among them Cane and Cane (1979) and Torrance and Rockenstein (1988). The last suggests that the right hemisphere is linked with non-verbal, wholistic, concrete, spatial, creative, intuitive processing while the left-hemisphere is linked with verbal, analytical, abstract, temporal and digital processing.

West (1991) suggests that these two modes are fundamentally incompatible and that it is therefore not surprising that an individual with highly developed abilities in one mode would find the alternative mode difficult, to the extent that somebody who has a propensity to think in images rather than words would experience actual difficulties with verbal communication.

This is an elegant theory, since it both helps to explain the often puzzling contrasts of ability and disability co-existing in many dyslexic individuals and presents the condition in a very positive light, almost as a gift. However, it does not satisfy everyone. It takes certain premises for granted, for example why should strength in one mode of processing automatically come at the expense of another mode? Why can't these two modes be mutually supportive? It can also undermine still further the confidence of that large group of people with dyslexia who do not seem to possess superior visuo-spatial talents. Furthermore, the validity of the scientific basis to this approach, *Two Mind Theory*, as popularised by Ornstein (1972), has come under attack from a range of neuropsychologists, including Coren (1993).

The Two Mind Theory arose out of Sperry and Gazzaniga's neurophysiological research (1970, cited in Coren 1993) on split-brained patients. These were people whose corpus callosum, which connects the two hemispheres of the brain, had been severed. This allowed Sperry, Gazzaniga and their associates to examine responses mediated by each hemisphere of the brain separately in the hope of coming up with some definitive answers as to whether there was any difference in the functions and abilities of the two hemispheres. Initially, results seemed to indicate that there was.

In short, the left hemisphere handles language functions and several other functions that are language like, while the right hemisphere handles functions that are not easily translated into language, including spatial abilities, music and, perhaps, emotion. So far so good, and it is at this point that Ornstein (1972) seizes upon and popularised the idea that differences in the function of the two hemispheres are responsible for clearly identifiable and characteristic differences in abilities and thinking styles that affect all aspects of everyday behaviour.

In its turn this theory was taken up by educators and counsellors as a basis for direct action and therapy including suggestions (Cane and Cane 1979) that one of the goals of education might be to develop equal cerebral functioning through activities specifically designed to target and stimulate whichever hemisphere seems to be less dominant in any student. Unfortunately, in research following their original work, Gazzaniga and Ledoux (1978) point out that there is, in fact, little evidence to indicate that tremendous differences in thinking styles are really characteristic of left and right hemispheres. Coren emphasises this and says:

> In other words, the Two Mind Theory ... is wrong, according to the conclusions of one of the very researchers whose data served as the starting point for the development of this new scientific myth. (Coren 1993, p. 125)

Since then there has been considerably more opposition (Zenhausern 1982) to the concept that there are individual differences among people to the extent that one hemisphere of the brain can be differentially aroused or that different activities can be attributed to different hemispheres of the brain to the extent that some researchers consider it a total misapprehension (Levy 1982, cited by

Keefe 1987). Levy's review of the roles of the two hemispheres in various aspects of language seems to show that, contrary to the hypothesis that the left hemisphere controls language, in the normal child or adult, both hemispheres contribute important and critical processing operations, making it impossible to allocate the final level of understanding or output to one hemisphere or the other.

Dimond's (1972) research goes further and suggests that it is an oversimplification to attribute particular functions to a particular hemisphere. Dimond poses the question 'Can hemispheres function as information receiving, learning, remembering systems without each other?' He suggests that the answer to this in the animal brain was yes and cites support from the work of Buresova et al (1966). Each hemisphere appears to be the identical twin of the other, for example a duplicate set of memory traces is imprinted in one hemisphere by the action of the other although sharing seems to enhance performance.

Despite the fact, however, that each hemisphere possesses its own mechanisms for perception, learning and memory, information available in one hemisphere may not be available to the other, particularly if the linking function of the corpus callosum becomes inhibited. Hence the distortions of perception accompanying damage in a particular hemisphere. However, Gazzaniga's work on the bisected brain (1970b, cited in Coren 1993) indicates that, even when the corpus callosum ceases to operate, compensatory mechanisms will activate midbrain transit pathways in an attempt to maintain brain function.

Galaburda's work (1993) indicates that two-thirds of normal brains are asymmetric, larger to the left in the planum temporale, an area vitally important to language processing and comprehension. Dyslexic brains, however, show an abnormal symmetry. He also notes (pre-natal) malformations in the cellular architecture of the left hemisphere. Using Magnetic Resonance Imaging, Hynd and Heimenz (1997) found links between extreme phonological processing problems and symmetrical plana. These deviations, originating between the fifth and seventh month of fetal gestation, do not disappear with age. Geschwind and Galaburda (1987) also found that twelve times as many left handers are likely to be dyslexic as right handers – evidence that a significant proportion of dyslexic people do tend towards right-hemisphere mediated functioning.

A range of researchers would support the contention that the left hemisphere is the favoured hemisphere for language processing. This is not to say that language processing cannot be carried out by the right hemisphere or, as West seems to imply, that students who favour right hemisphere processing for a number of reasons will necessarily have superior visual skills. The left hemisphere controls the functions of the right side of the body, while the right hemisphere controls the left. Children who use the right ear (linked to left hemisphere) for listening to speech sounds and the right hand for manual tasks tend to be better listeners and readers. Research by Rippon and Brunswick (1997) and Rippon, Brunswick and Garner (1997) attempting to find correlations between hemispheric laterality, handedness and phonology or reading and spelling skills was, however, inconclusive.

Following the development of neuro-imaging techniques to study brain function in living subjects, there is a definite feeling that real progress is being made in providing valid and reliable ways of examining the probable differences in brain function between dyslexic people and the wider population (Hynd and Hiemenz 1997).

However, to state that each hemisphere can only deal with specific functions and that strengths in one set of functions will necessarily lead to weaknesses in the other seems to be an oversimplification. The picture is of a far more complex and adaptable system. Thus the claim either that dyslexic people operate in a right-brained way or that they will thus necessarily have weaknesses in verbal or sequential processing is not borne out by research.

To extrapolate further and claim that those individuals who shine in such allegedly 'right-brain' areas as visual and spatial skills are *necessarily* likely to struggle with language and sequential analysis or vice versa seems, to date, to have little empirical research backing.

In fact current research is moving away from examining the possibility of hemispheric specialisation to examine the role of the corpus callosum in suppressing one or other of the hemispheres when processing for a particular type of task is going on. The only stable finding seems still to be that problems in the left-hemisphere pathways disrupt verbal memory, while right-hemisphere problems interfere with visual memories (Steffert 1996).

There is, however, interesting ongoing work that examines the incidence of difficulties with verbal comprehension and memory among art-school students (Steffert 1996) and compares the learning styles of dyslexic and non-dyslexic students in higher education (Mortimore 1998); so the jury could be said still to be out.

In general the picture seems to be considerably more complex and ultimately unclear than many advocates of hemispheric-specialisation theory seem prepared to acknowledge. So, to use this research as reliable backing for claims that people with dyslexia will have superior visuo-spatial skills is probably unwise.

Evidence arising from handedness research

Some research into whether the effects of right- or left-handedness seems to indicate a link between dyslexia and left-handedness. There is also some evidence of a link between left-handedness and visual spatial skills. Coren (1993) examines some characteristics of left-handers. At university level, left-handers perform better in tasks that involve the visualisation of objects and mental manipulation of images, an important part of certain scientific applications of mathematics, such as physics, chemistry, engineering and architecture. They do not perform quite as well as the right-handers in tests of vocabulary, arithmetic ability and certain types of problem-solving tasks. However, these results are not consistent and seem to be influenced also by the sex and the age of the individual as some differences do not make themselves reliably visible until after the age of thirteen (puberty).

Coren (1993) also cites Peterson and Lansky's (1974) research, which discovered that an unusually high percentage of architecture students are left-handed and that left-handed students appeared to do better. Other data relating to chess and the Chinese game of go, where good spatial skills are required, found evidence of an over-abundance of left-handers among masters. This must, however, not be taken to extremes or linked with other so-called right-brained strengths, as a range of research cited by Coren (1993) has found no link between left-handedness and creativity, musical ability or artistic success. Although still feeling that the evidence in favour of the Two Mind Theory is based upon distortions and oversimplification of the neuropsychological data, he does admit to some differences between right- and left-handed people, but he does goes on to state that these are usually small, that they tend not to hold up in systematic laboratory testing and many left-handers do well at supposedly left-brained tasks and many left-handers also turn out to be left-brained for language.

Hence there is some suggestion of a link between left-handedness and visuo-spatial ability and between left-handedness and dyslexia in students; although there is, as yet, no conclusive research evidence to link dyslexic students with increased visuo-spatial ability. A recent study by Winner, Von Karolyi and Malinsky (2000) compares the performance of dyslexic and non-dyslexic students on a number of visual-spatial tasks and finds no evidence of superior talents in the dyslexic group. These were, however, very artificial two-dimensional tasks, and there was no apparent attempt either to ensure that the dyslexic and non-dyslexic groups came from comparable skills and backgrounds (for example all scientists or all arts students) or to discount gender as a factor. There is, therefore, a need for further research.

It is also possible that the disproportionate number of dyslexic people allegedly found in visual or spatial professions, such as art, engineering or architecture (Geschwind and Galaburda 1987) may be there by default as individuals with difficulties in the verbal field might be likely to avoid professions that require facility with language or extensive reading.

Evidence from psychometric testing of dyslexic individuals

Despite the paucity of the research evidence reviewed so far, there are, possibly, some more supportive pointers from studies that compare IQ scores in tasks that measure visuo-spatial skills. It is not uncommon for the educational psychologists' reports for children with dyslexia to reveal sometimes dramatically superior scores in the visual/spatial non-verbal subtests of IQ assessment instruments (Chasty 1985).

Research collected by Whyte (1989) also suggests a link between an above-average visuo-spatial ability and dyslexia or reading difficulties. He also cites research suggesting that strengths in visuo-spatial cognitive functions are genetically more common in boys. There are, of course, many more boys diagnosed as dyslexic than girls. Gordon (1989, in Whyte), however, does not see these visuo-spatial strengths as necessarily a blessing and suggests that this preference for visuo-spatial skills can often be a factor in learning difficulties. He suggests that verbo-sequential phonological deficits may well be the consequence of a locking onto a visuo-spatial model of cognitive processing with insufficient flexibility to adapt to the requirements of different learning tasks. He does not address the causes of this rigidity. It may, of course, be due to difficulties with verbo-sequential processing, rather than a real talent for the visual. To date there is insufficient collected data to come to any firm conclusions about the predominance of high visuo-spatial scores among dyslexic individuals, but this would certainly be an interesting source of information.

Conclusions

Is there reliable evidence of a link between dyslexia and enhanced visuo-spatial skills? The answer to this seems to be: 'Evidence? Maybe. Reliable? Perhaps not.' West's evidence tends to be either anecdotal or based upon a theory of mutually exclusive modes of processing derived from the questionable and possibly superseded (Steffert 1996) scientific model of hemispheric specialisation.

As explained above, there may be evidence for underdevelopment in an area of the brain associated with language processing in normal individuals. However, this does not necessarily mean visuospatial skills must be superior in people with dyslexia. There is little research evidence so far to suggest this.

For the teacher's purposes it would, however, possibly indicate an anticipated preference within the dyslexic population for a visually based cognitive style, even if the student is not necessarily particularly talented in this area.

The great value of the approach of West (1991), Vail (1997) and many other champions of the cause of dyslexic people has been to highlight and encourage the talents many undoubtedly possess.

Edwards (1994) cites Vail's list of ten special traits and adds four more of her own. Professionals and parents who have lived and worked with dyslexic students will undoubtedly find many of them familiar:

- rapid grasp of concepts
- awareness of patterns
- energy

- curiosity
- concentration
- empathy
- vulnerability
- heightened perception
- divergent thinking (Vail 1990)
- talent in art and design
- multi-dimensional thinking
- originality and problem-solving (Edwards 1994)

However, it is dangerous and potentially destructive to assume that all or even a high proportion of individuals with dyslexia will exhibit these traits. Many do not and feel doubly disadvantaged if expectations are raised. Many non-dyslexic people also possess them, and it is obviously rash to attribute many of them to the dyslexic condition rather than to life experiences. However, if we are to teach to and reward strengths rather than focus upon weaknesses, a good starting point is to recognise that every dyslexic person is a learner with a particular style and that the added vulnerability of the dyslexic person in the learning situation makes it even more important that this should be recognised and supported.

> No two dyslexics are the same, and the gifts will be different, but it is our ability to use other methods to come to the same ends. For example, my organisational skills are not that great; so I have strategies to make sure I don't miss appointments or double-up meetings. People who come and see me say how organised I am. It is my gift to work out a system that makes this possible. A lot of people with dyslexia have skills they don't know about because it's what worked for them and they assume that everybody else does it the same. To explain this is difficult because of the different kinds of gifts. The simplest way would be to say we have creative ways of doing things. (Nicky Woodward, adult dyslexia co-ordinator)

Chapter summary

This chapter reviews the suggestion that, for many dyslexic individuals, considerable talents, particularly in the visuo-spatial field, accompany the pattern of difficulties (West 1991). This acknowledgment of the creativity and talent of many dyslexic adults was long overdue.

After considering the research evidence from the hemispheric-specialisation field, handedness and psychometric-test reports, it concludes that empirical evidence is currently less than conclusive, despite anecdotal evidence and the existence of many talented dyslexic people.

However, it is suggested that the effect of dyslexia on some people may be to make them tend towards visuo-spatial learning styles and professions in which they can then become very proficient. Educators should therefore be aware of this in the classroom or lecture hall, especially when working with students with dyslexia.

Chapter 6 looks at how the theories of different learning styles can be put into practice.

PART THREE
'It's No Use If You Can't Use It.'

Applying learning style theory to learning

I hear and I forget;
I see and I remember;
I do and I understand.
(Chinese proverb)

Introduction: Recap: learning style and dyslexia

The first five chapters of this book attempt to provide answers to the following questions:

What is cognitive or learning style?

Cognitive style is our characteristic and relatively consistent way of processing incoming information of all types from the environment. Learning style is this cognitive style applied to a learning task. It is likely that individuals develop learning strategies to cope with both task and situation and that these strategies are closely linked with the predominant cognitive style.

What are the different cognitive styles?

The clearest and most all-embracing construct seems to be Richard Riding's pair of continua:

Wholistic-Analytic – Verbaliser–Imager

An individual can be a holistic-imager, an analytic-imager, a wholistic-verbaliser or an analytic-verbaliser. There is no particular virtue attached to any of these ways of dealing with the world except that some approaches will be better suited than others to specific types of tasks. There is also, as yet, no reliable evidence that any particular learning style is more conducive to academic success than any other. Riding (1998) also suggests that analytic-imagers and wholistic-verbalisers have a more flexible learning style in that the two styles complement each other rather than being similar or unitary; for example, an analytic imager might not easily see an overview of a situation but might use the whole-view aspect of imagery to supplement it. The analytic-verbaliser would have less access to an overview as he or she would only have the analytic style available. In the same way, a wholist-verbaliser would have both wholistic and analytic modes, whereas a wholist-imager would only have access to the wholistic approach.

The more flexible the style, the more an individual is able to use strategies to maximise learning success in a range of situations.

Why is knowledge of learning style important?

Much evidence seems to indicate that most people learn best when the style of presentation harmonises with their preferred learning style. It is therefore useful for teachers to ensure that they do not persistently use one style of teaching or demand the same style of response from their students, as this will disadvantage any student whose style is mismatched, particularly if that student finds it hard to adapt learning style to situation.

If students can be made aware of their preferred learning styles, they will then be more able to recognise their strengths and become sensitive to their weaknesses. They can then take responsibility for ensuring that they either use their preferred style, or, if this seems impossible, they find strategies to compensate for the mismatch.

Why might this knowledge be particularly significant for people with dyslexia?

There is a range of reasons. There is some evidence that dyslexic students may tend towards:

- a wholistic or imaging style either because memory difficulties and weakness in processing verbal information force them to rely on the visuo-spatial channels or through innate strengths in these areas.
- a less flexible unitary style, which leaves them with difficulties responding to verbal detail. It may be because of problems with concentration, attention span, working memory or automaticity. It may be due to fear of failure and increased anxiety in academic situations. Whatever the reasons, without explicit help, this will make it more difficult for them to develop coping strategies when teaching presentation does not match their preferred styles.
- Both research and experience suggests that dyslexic students succeed when teaching is multi-sensory and uses all channels to reinforce learning.
- For many highly intelligent dyslexic people, education is already fraught with difficulties. If matching style of delivery with learning style and helping students to develop compensatory strategies can enhance success, it seems less than sensible not to give it a try.

Learning styles and learning strategies

What is a learning strategy? A learning strategy is not the same as a learning style. Learning style is the application of a particular cognitive style to a learning activity. It is seen as relatively fixed. The difference between a learning activity and a strategy is that the activity becomes a strategy when it is selected as particularly helpful to the individual. Therefore, a learning strategy is one of a repertoire of ways of dealing with learning tasks that an individual develops to facilitate performance.

Riding (1998, p. 79) terms this 'the cognitive tool-kit' and points out that, although individuals cannot change their styles, they can develop strategies which compensate for weaknesses by using their positive skills to enable them to deal effectively with a range of situations. He suggests that the processing load on the brain is heavier if the information is presented in a mode that is not preferred. We have already discussed the difficulties that many dyslexic students have with overload in the processing of information. This could well be one explanation for the problems many seem to have in generating a more flexible approach to learning.

How are these strategies generated and developed? A number of researchers have suggested that there is a hierarchy of cognitive processes involved in learning. This goes from lower-order or primary processes, such as reflex or intuitive actions, through conscious and deliberate actions to higher-order actions or strategies, such as monitoring and metacognition – 'knowing about knowing'.

Developing knowledge of one's own mental processes, or metacognition, is seen as a major part of personal development and essential to the acquisition of learning strategies. Flavell (1987) calls the ability to take responsibility for generating learning strategies 'planfulness'. These strategies emerge over time through the cycle of action, reaction and the conscious selection of the activities and approaches that lead to a successful learning outcome.

There is a consensus among researchers that those students who have developed this repertoire of strategies will be more successful learners than others. Weinstein and Van Mater Stone (1996) emphasise that knowledge and the use of the following three items is vital for students if they are to achieve their goals: the range of available strategies, their own learning styles and when and where their knowledge could be useful.

They also need to be able to evaluate their own performance and know when they are not coping.

It is important to remember that the development of a learning strategy involves three phases:

- being aware of preferences or styles
- selecting the mode of learning that is most comfortable
- extending the strategy to apply to a range of tasks

This third phase should involve a range of strategies, most of which are designed to reduce the amount of processing to be done. They all tend to involve adapting or translating information from an uncomfortable mode into one the student finds easier to handle, for example an imager may represent spoken information from a lecture as a diagram, a mind map or an analytical student, who finds it hard to make links, may well choose to create a diagram that gives an image of the whole of a topic.

Recap

Successful students will develop learning strategies that complement their learning styles.

To do this they must be aware of their preferences and be given the opportunity to use them to their advantage. They will also need to be shown ways of adapting information to suit themselves.

What theories underpin these strategies?

The main aim in the teaching of strategies is to reduce the amount of processing needed to absorb and retain information. The most commonly used techniques are based upon research from two main areas of education theory:

- schema theory
- memory function

Books giving a more academic and detailed analysis of memory function, schema theory, scaffolding and the role of metacognition in reading and other types of comprehension will be found in the further reading section at the end of this book.

Schema theory – its role in learning

A *schema* is a general representation of the typical structure of a familiar experience. It involves knowledge of both the typical elements of some familiar aspect of the environment and of the relationships or sequence of these elements. Very young children develop schema for all sorts of events, such as going to bed at night, the events of a birthday party and simple stories. They are like recipes or sets of general rules for particular experiences. They affect both how we take in information and how we direct our own behaviour. They are closely connected to memory in that they are both the product of memory and help in the process of memorising – we can predict from our schema what ought to occur in any general situation and match that with the reality of the specific experience.

What relevance do schema have to learning? Researchers, such as Nist and Mealey (1991), consider schema to be vital to such basic learning processes as reading comprehension and for the building of mental models of information gleaned from oral or written information for the following reasons:

- They provide ideal *scaffolding* (see below).
- They help in the selection of important information.
- They aid inference by allowing a learner to fill in gaps with their own pre-existing knowledge.
- They help to edit, summarise and select key ideas.
- They help to fill gaps in memory through inference.

A range of studies seem to indicate that learning new information is easier if one already has a mental model of the topic and if the knowledge contained in this can be activated, expanded and organised to include any new information – almost like hanging decorations on an existing tree. Helping students to construct and use schema effectively to develop new models incorporating previous knowledge seems to lead to success.

The other contribution that schema research can make to teaching and learning strategies stems from the fact that schema do not simply apply to everyday experiences and knowledge. There is increasing emphasis in today's curriculum on the need to analyse and write texts of different types or genres, covering a range of fiction and non-fiction writing. Genre analysis research cited by Lewis and Wray (1995) suggests that there are six main genres of non-fiction writing: recount, report, procedure, explanation, persuasion and discussion. These types are reflected in the range of writing types tested in English Language at 16 – GCSE level. Each type has a typical specific structure and uses particular vocabulary or connectives. Giving students an explicit schema to match each type will provide them with a framework. This will often give those for whom writing is a real challenge the confidence to start.

Ausubel (1981) coins the term 'advanced organiser' for what has also grown to be a family of pre-organising techniques rooted in the principal that learners will benefit from a general introduction to a topic. The theory suggests that providing a student with a brief generalised passage prior to reading a longer more detailed piece provides a bridge between the student's existing schema and the new information.

This is particularly relevant to the wholistic learner. Wholistic learners tend to gravitate towards frames and models. It is their strength. When they ask in advance what they will be doing next lesson, they are already preparing to activate existing schema in the hope that they will be helped to absorb and retain detail by having a previously organised mental model which they can then add on to. Giving them what are sometimes also termed *advanced organisers* makes them feel safer. It reduces anxiety and therefore allows them to focus upon new facts or details that they might otherwise overlook, secure in the knowledge that the schema is reliably available for them to refer to when they want to slot the new information in to an appropriate section for future use.

Dyslexic students are often used to feeling anxious at the start of a lesson, confused after a few minutes and totally lost by half-time. Giving them the security of a reliable framework reduces this anxiety and allows them to focus upon the more detailed aspects of the task, that they know they may find difficult, without losing the thread of the whole.

Schema theory – or the way in which we create stored mental models from experience – obviously has relevance for helping both dyslexic and wholistic learners. It also has strong links with the theories that underlie our understanding of the functions of memory and memory strategies in ways which are particularly important for dyslexic people.

Memory function – its role in learning

Chapter 4 contains a brief discussion of some of the difficulties with memory that dyslexic learners may experience. The field of research throughout the twentieth century into the functions and processes of memory is both wide-ranging and fascinating. Anyone with a particular interest in this aspect of cognitive processing is referred either to Vasta, Haith and Miller's (1992) chapters on the development of research theories or Gathercole and Baddeley (1993), Wood (1988) and Rose (1993).

Both dyslexic and wholistic learners frequently have trouble with remembering facts and details; it is therefore necessary to have a basic understanding of current thinking about memory processes so that a teacher can select the most useful strategies to help them.

It is an oversimplification to see memory processing in terms of the simple two-stage 'storage box' metaphor where information is shunted from a short-term memory store to a long-term memory store. Until the 1970s, however, this was the model; a distinction was made between short-term and long-term memory and the process was seen as a fixed sequence with information flowing from short-term to long-term. No account was taken as to the nature of the material being remembered – what about familiar material or material related to information already known? Neurological evidence and one's own experience suggest that there is much more going on. This model also does not attempt to explain such questions as to why people forget or have problems retrieving information – does information decay, does it get overwritten by new data or is it simply in store and inaccessible?

In the seventies, more attention was paid to identifying the different types of activity that might be going on during various stages of the memory process (Baddeley and Hitch 1974, Baddeley 1986). The activity during the first or 'experiencing' stage was described as *registration, trace formation* or *encoding*. The moment of 'remembering' something was termed *retrieval, recall, recollection, reactivation* or *utilisation*.

A variety of interesting questions and areas of study arose from this research.

- Are there different types of memory?
- Do different types of memory involve different brain functions?
- Does learning or remembering change the structure of the brain?
- Does memory change developmentally as a child becomes an adult?

Are there different types of memory?

Memory processing involves four major components or codes:

- the **audio memory**: this includes both environmental sounds and word-based knowledge of sounds (phonology)
- the **visual memory**: this includes both visual experience, images and the orthography or forms of words
- the **semantic memory**: this is the aspect of memory that deals with meaning rather than sound, shape or touch. It is sometimes

termed 'declarative memory', and it can be subdivided into two categories – episodic and semantic memory (Tulving 1983, cited by Rose 1993). By episodic memory, Tulving meant the memory of the events in one's own life; by semantic memory, he meant knowledge that is independent of one's own experience.

- **movement, procedural or skill memory.** Sometimes termed **habit memory**, this is the hardest form of memory to lose, for example an amnesiac may lose the knowledge of the name of a bicycle while being able to operate one perfectly.

Do different types of memory involve different brain functions?

Rose discusses (1993) whether different biochemical changes located in different areas of the brain can be associated with particular memory functions. Use of the latest developments in analysis of brain patterns such as Magnetic Resonance Imaging (MRI) seems to offer the possibility of answering all these questions about brain function and its relationship with mental processes. However, as Rose points out, showing that a particular brain region is active when a person is learning or remembering can perhaps show us only the location of the cortical activity for that specific task.

Most tasks, however, involve a sufficiently complex range of processes to make it hard to be certain exactly what type of memory is being used. If a task could be made simple enough to be clearly attributable to a particular type of memory processing, it would not be typical of most everyday activities or tell us anything much about meaning or about the motives involved in transfers between different types of mental activity. It seems likely that there are specific links between brain function and types of memory processing, but reliable forms of measurement are still in their infancy.

Does learning or remembering change the structure of the brain?

Biochemists have established the general principles of the cellular mechanisms involved in animal learning (Rose 1993). When an animal learns, specific cells in its central nervous system change their properties. These changes in the structure of the neurons and their synaptic connections can be measured in terms of localised change in blood flow or oxygen uptake or through other physiological changes. This means that brain cells change their properties adaptively in response to events in the environment. It is as though experience reprogrammes the brain and can affect critical parts of the brain, having a knock-on effect on other functions and conditions. Thus, in learning, it is likely that patterns of responses are set up leading to the tendency to utilise specific styles of processing and memorising. Hence, if we have a particular weakness in, for example, auditory processing, our tendency towards a visual style may well set up a type of brain structure that is particularly suited to this style and is therefore less flexible.

Does memory change developmentally as a child becomes an adult?

The answer seems to be 'yes' (Rose 1993). However, before we can investigate this, we need to look at the current accepted model of working memory – that of Gathercole and Baddeley (1993).

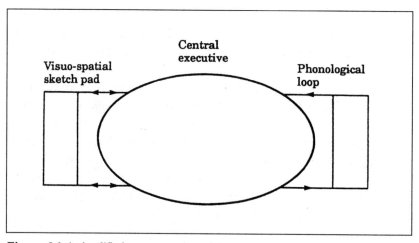

Figure 6.1 A simplified representation of the Baddeley and Hitch (1974) working memory model.

Gathercole and Baddeley are particularly interested in a functional approach. How is information held while it is being worked on? How do we combine information from the senses with knowledge held in long-term memory? They present a three-part model of short-term, or, as they describe it, 'working', memory. This involves:

- **a central executive**, which is seen as a supervisory attention system, served by
- **two slave systems**: first, the 'visuo-spatial sketchpad'. It encodes verbal material as imagery, generates and maintains images and spatial awareness. Secondly, 'the phonological loop', which includes a phonological short-term store that decays over time, an acoustic store and the articulatory (sub-vocal) rehearsal system that both renews phonological material stored in the loop and converts non-speech for storage. They term this slave system the 'phonological working memory'.

Does memory change developmentally as a child becomes an adult?

Memory seems to go through several stages. In **early infancy** it is visually based, non-selective and timeless. The focus must be upon the visuo-spatial slave system. Around the **end of infancy**, recognition is enhanced by some form of recall memory (Mandler 1988, cited by Vasta Haith and Miller 1992). At this stage the average auditory digit span – or number of sounds that can be recalled – is around two or three units, compared with the adult span of seven items, plus or minus two. By **4 years**, all three components of working memory are present. Phonological processes are strongly involved and auditory speech is retained through the second slave system, the phonological loop. During the **early school years** rapid development takes place, owing to a range of both environmental and internal factors.

The environmental factors include the increased opportunity for problem-solving and exploration and the variety of people around to provide models for imitation. Emerging literacy also has an enormous impact on memory function. Wood (1988) cites research (Perera 1984) which suggests that a skilled silent reader begins to use subvocal rehearsal rather than visuo-spatial processes for memorising even visual material and that this is a far more efficient way of recalling information. The relationship between reading and memory skills is so interactive that there seems to be a vicious circle operating between memory skills and poor reading development in that poor memory skills lead to reading difficulty and that below-average reading skills can impede the development of memory skills.

Many of the internal cognitive developments are closely linked to the functions of that supervisory attentional system, the central executive:

- A range of *rehearsal skills* come into action. These include articulation, or the use of internal speech.
- Children start to *develop landmarks, schema and rules*, which start very simply and then incorporate more information (Case et al 1988).
- Children start to *construct memory* – to use inference to build bridges between new information and what they already know (Paris and Lindauer 1976).
- Memory processes begin to involve *metacognition* or *the use of strategies* (Flavell 1987).
- The increasing efficiency of all three memory systems (Gathercole and Baddeley 1993) and of automatisation frees up operating space for new encoding or memorising, thus creating a loop of new automatisation, new strategies and so on.

After puberty, the *adult memory* develops ways of selection and filtering and becomes (particularly through the influence of literacy) linear, time-bound and more verbal. The processing therefore becomes more structural and relies more upon phonemes and semantics (the sounds and meaning of language.)

To sum up, the basic progression seems to be from the infant's timeless, non-selective, visuo-spatial system, through increasing development and reliance upon the phonological slave system for the rehearsal and construction of memory during early school years to the adult system, where the central executive plays a strong role in planning, focusing attention and developing strategies.

Dyslexia and memory

It has already been stated that memory problems are one of the most commonly quoted aspects of dyslexia, and there is a range of research into memory deficits and dyslexia. It is, however, essential to establish whether people with dyslexia really do show problems on memory tasks compared with others for there is, of course, as much variation in performance among the dyslexic population as there is amongst non-dyslexic people.

To study this, researchers always use a matched non-dyslexic group of people as 'controls'. They can match these controls in a range of ways – chronological age, gender or reading age are frequently used. Thus a dyslexic participant aged 12 with a reading age of 9 can either be matched with a non-dyslexic of 12 with a reading age of 12 (chronological match) or with a non-dyslexic of 12 with a reading age of 9 (reading-age match). Bearing in mind the link between poor reading and memory skills, comparing a dyslexic person with a same-age non-dyslexic will usually mean that the dyslexic has a lower reading age. Therefore any poorer memory performance by the person with dyslexia may be due to the lower reading age rather than the dyslexia. It is therefore common to eliminate this possibility by using the reading-age match. Obviously, with this pairing, researchers are still not comparing like with like as factors linked with the age difference are ignored; therefore one must always exercise caution.

Currently, research into dyslexia and memory has established some interesting links. The most significant must be between dyslexia and phonological impairment.

Dyslexia and phonological processing

A number of researchers, including Snowling (2000) and Stanovich (1988), emphasise the links between phonological or sound-based processing skills, vocabulary development and the acquisition of reading skills. Baddeley and his associates (Pickering 2000) have to date carried out a range of further studies into the dyslexic experience and come to the following conclusions:

- People with dyslexia have particular problems with the phonological code in working memory. They appear to use it less efficiently. They have problems translating visual information into phonological form. In terms of reading development, they are less able to store new words in the phonological loop before moving them into a permanent position in the lexical/semantic system – thus their ability to learn new words is limited.
- Dyslexic individuals have difficulty with phonological repetition – for example repeating multi-syllabic or nonsense words.
- Dyslexic individuals do not seem to use phonological mnemonics

(memory strategies) as readily as others. They have difficulty maintaining phonological information using rehearsal or repetition. They do not spontaneously attach verbal labels to pictures, and they have difficulties with lists.

All indications are that the difficulties lie in the phonological area of memory processing. However, it must be emphasised that, so far, research has focused upon the phonological slave system of memory, and very little work has yet been done on the relationship between the visuo-spatial sketchpad or the central executive and dyslexia.

There is some evidence (Stanovich 1990, cited in Torgesen 1990) that, given these phonological-processing weaknesses, dyslexic individuals develop strong compensatory processes. Many may come to rely more upon visual codes for memory processing. This is an idea that has been mentioned before in the context of the alleged link between dyslexia and superior visuo-spatial skills.

Other dyslexic students may develop the kind of skills mediated by the central executive. These would include context skills or the use of meaning (semantic codes) to support recall. However, there is some suggestion that there may also be some impairment of the central executive function in at least some individuals with dyslexia (Pickering 2000). This gives rise to the question of whether teaching strategies might be able to provide support for the central executive.

Dyslexia and automaticity

As discussed previously in the chapter dealing with the difficulties encountered by dyslexic individuals, many have problems in any situation that involves the combination of a number of subskills. The work of Nicolson and Fawcett (1994) investigates the possibility that, owing to some deficit in the cerebellum area of the brain, people with dyslexia have difficulty in making a range of basic skills automatic, whether motor or cognitive. Therefore, continual concentration and effort is required to maintain basic subskills reducing the efficiency of other simultaneous ongoing processes. In terms of memory, children will have difficulty maintaining material in temporary memory storage while carrying out another skill. For example, a dyslexic person may need to focus upon decoding or working out letter-sound links while reading, thus reducing the potential attention available for the processes of understanding the material. Most problem-solving involves several elements, Chasty (1991), cited in Pumfrey and Elliot (1990), identified ten subskills for reading. An inability to automaticise subskills and to weld them together into a complex automatic schema is a true disability that will have implications for the simultaneous processing involved in memorising.

To sum up, dyslexic students may well have difficulties in two areas of memory function: phonological processing and automatisation. There is some further suggestion that there may be difficulties in the 'organising' department – the central executive. They are likely therefore, to need support in three fundamental areas:

- compensation for poor auditory or phonological skills
- the kind of support that will reduce the possibility of overload
- encouragement in the use of thinking strategies

What are the most effective ways of providing this support for a vulnerable student?

It seems likely that the use (whether consciously or automatically) of thinking strategies or metacognitive skills enhances study, whatever the learning style of the student. Much research has been carried out into the nature (Weinert and Kluwe, 1987) and developmental aspects of metacognition (Nelson, 1992). The inter-related activities of this monitoring system include:

- prediction
- planning
- monitoring
- testing
- revising
- evaluating

The consensus is that the most successful learners are those people who develop a sense of themselves as active thinkers, those who are able to influence the course of their learning. Research into success and failure in reading comprehension suggests that the main differences between skilled and unskilled comprehenders are the extent to which they are able to use:

- inference to create efficient mental models
- schema to aid the creation of mental models
- working memory to store ongoing information
- automatic decoding skills
- metacognitive strategies

However, there is less consensus over whether it is possible to teach these strategies. Some programmes, such as Feuerstein's (1979) Instrumental Enrichment programme, have attempted to teach students to use cognitive strategies and have claimed that these skills can transfer to other learning situations, but there is a lack of empirical evidence to back these claims, and many researchers have strong reservations as to the effectiveness of teaching general skills in isolation (Quicke 1992).

The most effective programmes seem to be those that involve two approaches – they are firmly grounded within 'real' tasks that need to be accomplished and, secondly, they follow the social-learning apprenticeship model advocated originally by Vygotsky (1978) (sometimes termed the scaffolding, modelling or apprenticeship approach). He observes that children learn in collaboration with 'experts', parents, teachers or older children. Initially, they watch, then they begin to imitate and take increasing responsibility, relying on the expert only when problems arise. Finally, they take full responsibility for the activity. Nist and Mealey (1991) express this as an eight-step process:

1. focus attention
2. give a general overview
3. introduce new terms
4. go through the procedure step by step
5. model the process – think aloud – introduce new frameworks of thought, the students also discuss the processes and teach each other
6. guide the practice – students repeat the instructor's strategy with support
7. independent practice
8. re-demonstrate the practice, if necessary, to reinforce

This is a three-stage process moving from the first stage, where the responsibility falls on the teacher, to the second, where it is shared and, finally, to the third, where students become responsible for their own learning, and at this stage transfer occurs. The external scaffold modelled by the teacher must be internalised by the student's own spontaneous use of the techniques.

For any student, dyslexic or otherwise, whose confidence is shaky, an apprenticeship or scaffolding model of this type offers fewer opportunities for failure. It also gives the opportunity to learn by doing, rather than purely listening, in an atmosphere where everybody is a novice and the expert is on hand to offer support where needed. There is scope for reinforcement through repetition and also the possibility for the student to become an expert and support others.

This approach can be used and adapted to a range of strategies suited to all learning styles

Chapter summary

This chapter provides a recap of information about the nature and importance of cognitive style, focused upon Riding's Wholistic-Analytic/Verbaliser–Imager continuum. It introduces the idea that students with a more flexible learning style have an advantage over those whose style is more unitary and suggests that some dyslexic students may tend towards a wholistic or imaging style, which can be less flexible.

It makes a clear distinction between learning style and learning strategies and examines both how these strategies are generated and the two major areas of education theory underlying learning strategies:

- schema theory
- memory function

It outlines the difficulties dyslexic people may encounter with memory and suggests that these probably originate from deficits in the phonological processing aspects of memory, although research is now investigating the role of the visuo-spatial sketchpad and the central executive. Other difficulties may arise in the area of automaticity.

It introduces the most effective strategies available for supporting students and helping them to develop awareness of their own strategies. These 'scaffolding' strategies are based on the work of Vygotsky (1978).

The following four chapters offer a selection of practical techniques aimed at helping teachers and students to develop and utilise learning strategies based upon a sound knowledge of their own preferred styles. They come from a wide range of sources and have been used successfully by a number of colleagues and mentors to whom I am indebted.

Chapter 7 explores the experience of wholistic learners; Chapter 8 does the same for analytics.

Each chapter follows the same structure:

A brief description of the kinds of behaviour typical to each type of learner and reminder of the theories that underpin the suggested strategies.

A three-part section describing teaching and learning strategies.

Each part corresponds with one of the three stages of learning:

- Getting the information in – modes of presentation
- Processing the information – storing and retrieving
- Getting the information out – modes of expression

PART FOUR
Strategies for Wholistic and Analytic Learners

CHAPTER 7

Wholistic approaches

Introduction: What types of behaviour and approaches to learning might be characteristic of a wholistic learner?

Riding and his associates have carried out many studies investigating the differences in behaviour between individuals with contrasting learning styles. Some of their work measuring mental activity during information processing (1993) established that there are clear differences between wholists and analytics both in location of activity within the brain and in intensity of activity. Cognitive style affects the way in which anyone relates to and represents incoming information from the environment. It must, therefore, have a strong influence upon behaviour in a range of situations. Riding's group has also attempted to establish what effect these differences may have on behaviour.

The Cognitive Style Assessment package (Riding 1994) contains the Personal Style Awareness (PSA) booklet, which describes the behavioural attributes associated with each cognitive style. It must, of course, be emphasised that cognitive style is only one of a range of physiological and environmental factors that shape our behaviour. Although many students do recognise the different types of behaviour in themselves, others inevitably declare that they are nothing like that! Whatever the response, however, this is yet another way of getting students to think about their behaviour and its implications for their learning.

113

It must be remembered that a student's behaviour is likely to be affected by two important factors:

1. The student's position on the scale between wholistic and analytic. This will determine how flexible his or her approach will be.
2. Whether the student tends to be a visual or verbal learner. A strongly wholistic approach may be made more flexible if the student has skill in processing verbal information.

It has already been established that wholistic learners would tend towards taking an overview of any situation. They also would tend to absorb information from a number of environmental sources simultaneously, often in a random order. They tend to find performing in any linear fashion constricting. Their strengths reside in their tendency and ability to make links between aspects of any situation – their intuitive, answer-orientated approach. Their weakness lies in the lack of detailed analysis and, frequently, their inability to deal with sequences or lists or to spot sequential processes.

Extreme wholists, with their ability to see the broad perspective of a situation, may very well also be more indecisive. Riding and Rayner (1998) also provide more behavioural detail. They suggest that the Wholistic-Analytical dimension affects an assertiveness-shyness dimension. Socially, wholists seem to be more open, aware and people orientated than analytics, being realistic and flexible in their relationships with others. They can also be spontaneous, generous and caring. The negative side, however, is that this urge for social integration can lead to a lack of independence; flexibility can become inconsistency, and in social life, as well as study, their responses may be shallow, rash or superficial.

What are the implications here for learning behaviour?

Wholistic learners prefer to deal with the whole before focusing in upon the parts. They would, therefore, find this chapter easier to absorb if it had a brief overview at the start as well as a summary at the end and would be well-advised to skim any chapter before reading to spot any overviews or summaries provided. They are more confident when given the context and a framework within which to work. Since they find analysis and retention of detail less easy, they need to be given the opportunity to link or chunk pieces of information together to facilitate comprehension and memorising. The wholistic learner may well be the student who drives the teacher mad by cornering her during the lunch hour and asking what they are going to be doing in the lesson that afternoon. It isn't simply that wholistic learners have so little going on in their lives they are already longing for the lesson, it is more likely that they realise instinctively that they have more chance of understanding it if they are fore-warned and can begin to predict what will come up.

From a longer-term perspective, some research from the University of London (cited by Rose and Goll 1992) suggests that the most successful students are not necessarily the ones who seem most able on entry, but those who had consciously related their subject to their long-term life goals. This crucially raises their motivation. There is obviously a lot to be gained by focusing any student's attention onto both the short- and long-term 'big picture'. Wholistic learners will tend to want to do this automatically; so educators should take advantage of it!

Making use of the students' social preferences can greatly enhance successful study and research. Wholists are considered to be more people-orientated than analytics (Riding and Wright 1995). There are implications for the educator in terms of the organisation of working methods. The wholists in the group may prefer the chance to work collaboratively, sharing ideas and tasks with others and be good at summing up the contributions of others. They may, in fact, be good facilitators, strongly and spontaneously empathising with others, helping to draw out and support the students who find social interaction more difficult. However, just because they may flourish in a group situation, it does not necessarily mean that they are particularly articulate or linguistically competent. As stated earlier, some dyslexic students also experience difficulties with speech and language. They may be wholistic imagers who sponta-neously gravitate towards the visual in a range of forms both for learning and expression.

The learning implications for people with dyslexia

Further research needs to be carried out to confirm any suggestions that many people with dyslexia could be wholistic learners.

However, they frequently have trouble in the following areas:

1. memory, short-term and, particularly, sequential memory
2. academic self-esteem
3. social self-esteem

1. Dyslexic undergraduates reported less confidence in their ability to retain facts than their non-dyslexic counterparts (Mortimore 1998). It is likely that they would be inclined to focus more successfully upon the outline of any topic rather than its details or sequences of information. This may well lead by default to the adoption of a wholistic learning style across a range of study activities. The central executive function of memory may well need strengthening; so dyslexic students will probably need to be shown explicitly how to organise strategies and construct schema so that they can both relate new information to previous experience and lay down strong foundations for memory.

2. As discussed earlier, people with dyslexia frequently do not see themselves as successful students and suffer from higher anxiety levels in academic situations. Being able to predict what will occur in a lesson or lecture and having a framework into which they can slot new information will decrease stress levels and therefore lead to more successful learning. A wholistic dyslexic learner with low academic self-esteem may well find group work within a supportive group allows him or her to gain confidence from collaborative work and provides a less exposed situation in which to try out ideas before they come under the scrutiny of the teacher or the whole class. Approval or respect of peers can begin to rebuild students' confidence in themselves as learners with opinions that deserve attention.

3. Some people with dyslexia fall into the group of students who have not been happy in school, have become withdrawn or socially inept as a result of negative classroom experiences and may well need careful support to rebuild confidence and social skills. Virtually any subject area can provide opportunities for productive and absorbing group work to which a wholistic learner will respond. Providing an interesting and challenging task that has to be completed co-operatively takes the emphasis away from general socialising where students may have

developed destructive behaviour patterns. Experience of carefully structured pair or group situations where appropriate social behaviours, such as turn-taking, are articulated and practised should result in many spin-offs, such as the development of the ability to listen to each other and the mutual respect and friendships that can arise out of shared success. Some sources for ideas for group work can be found in the additional reading section of this book.

What strategies can teachers use to help wholistic learners?

Many wholistic learners discover through experience that they need a big picture of the whole of a writing task before they start. Without this, they can be blocked, they can panic and, when they do start, they scatter and lose information before they can write it down ... and this is without being dyslexic!

Figure 7.1 shows the big picture used to plan this section of the chapter.

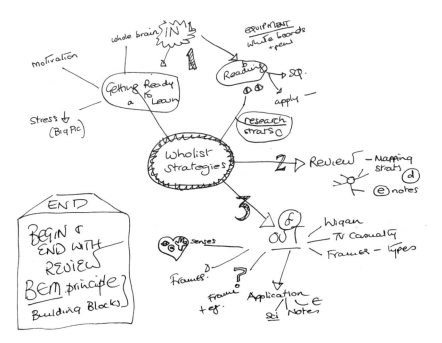

Figure 7.1 Concept map.

Wholistic learners respond to the 'whole' picture rather than making a detailed analysis of the parts. Many dyslexic students may tend towards this approach. They may be naturally wholistic thinkers, or they may have perceived or existing limitations in memory for detail or difficulties with automaticity. An extreme wholistic thinker will have trouble finding the facts or details to support overall assumptions and may well struggle to remember lists of facts. Strategies to help wholists will include:

- schema or overviews to aid prediction and comprehension
- memory aids to help link information
- scaffolding frames to support the oral or written expression of information
- co-operative learning techniques to develop and make use of collaborative strengths

Getting students ready to learn

Learning style seems to make no difference to the following premise. It seems to be true that people learn best:

- when they **want** to learn
- when they feel **challenged** but not stressed
- at the **beginning** and **end** of a session rather than in the **middle**
- when the **whole** brain is involved

Motivation

> When students can't see the point of learning – when they don't want to learn – they almost certainly won't. (Hughes 1999, p. 5)

Motivating students has to be the key – how to do it keeps teachers awake at nights. There are no miracle solutions here – all suggestions gratefully received! However, here are a few contributions:

Goals or the 'What's in it for me?' factor seem to be crucial. It is probably wise to forget about love of learning for all but an eccentric few. Goals are as personal as learning styles and probably unrelated! The general principle must be that students need to be helped to identify and set their personal goals at the start of the learning experience. Try asking students.

Here are a few goals that have worked. They can be long- or short-term and frequently bear little relation to the expectations of the teacher.

- Long-term goals – sometimes, obviously, students are motivated because they want to do well in GCSE exams, but, frequently, dyslexic students have had little belief in their ability to get reasonable grades and therefore find it safer to disparage exam success than to allow themselves to try for something they fear they won't achieve. It is often more successful to look beyond GCSEs and to focus on the rest of their lives. Either, 'OK, if you want to join the army to get their mechanics training, you'll need a C in this subject.' Or: 'If you're going to do media studies at college, you don't want to waste time retaking English there.'
- Short-term goals – some dyslexic students are so unused to success in the classroom that they are desperate for some form of positive feedback, whether it is a report going home or just a smile and a positive word. Others will do anything for a jelly baby or the promise of a video later or for a chocolate bar if they earn enough plus points. The only essential is that they should know both what they'll get and how to win it. This is, of course, very Pavlovian and unashamed bribery.

Control seems to be highly significant. If students feel in control both of their learning and their goals, this reduces stress and increases involvement and security.

Challenge – not stress

All teachers will know the student who bursts into their lesson furious about something that has happened in the recent or not-so-recent past. This individual is usually burning up and unable to focus on anything you might want to teach him or her. Educators obviously cannot be responsible for the emotional baggage students bring with them, but they can try to ensure they don't fan the flames. Stress is not conducive to learning. People are all programmed in such a way that stress turns on the fight or flight mechanisms of the brain, which override any other processes. Many dyslexic students find that class-rooms and teaching situations can automatically trigger these responses despite their best intentions and motivation.

People learn best when in a state of restful alertness. The class-room can consciously be turned into an environment that puts people at ease. There are a range of things that can be done to promote this:

- welcoming students
- establishing routines

> *Welcoming students* The way in which a teacher welcome students creates a mood. For any students entering anxiously, the sight of the teacher actually smiling can make them relax and return a smile. It can also change the teacher's mood if the last lesson was stressful. Making eye contact individually with as many students as possible also sends out the message that it's all right, you're OK here. Classroom greetings reduce tension and provide security right from the start.
>
> *Establishing routines* Many dyslexic students need the confidence of routines. This does *not* mean turning to page 10 in the same textbook and boring them to death with the same stale old format but giving them a stable framework for new experi-ences. Knowing that there are unlikely to be any nasty surprises makes dyslexic students far more willing to take risks and move into new areas of learning.

Once students are relaxed, how can educators be sure they are alert?

Seizing the best moments for learning

The start and the end of sessions are the golden moments. They should not be wasted. This is where the wholistic learner will partic-ularly respond to a frame showing the direction the lesson will take. This could be either verbal, visual or preferably both. The wholistic learner will often want to know the big picture into which it fits:

> It's a bit like a train. If I'm in a carriage, it helps to know what's in front and behind and where we're going. (John, 16, dyslexic wholistic learner)

This can be done in the form of a flip chart, a chart on the wall or reproduced in the students' files or books at the start of a topic so that students can see where today's lesson fits in with the whole. Don't forget to refer back to the previous session. Focusing attention on this big picture reduces the stress of uncertainly and allows the student to start to use prior knowledge. It can also be used at the end of the session to reinforce new learning and help the memory process (also to mop up bits that have had to be left out if time has run out too soon!).

Figure 7.2, a topic web with a You-are-here pointer, shows that it doesn't need to be particularly fancy. Since each group will need a different chart, a series could be kept on a flip chart a smaller display board can be kept on the wall for this purpose rather than taking up space on the main board.

The **start** of the lesson is also the point at which relaxed students are ready to respond to challenges, particularly if goals and rewards have been spelled out. Hughes (1999) suggests the following types of challenge and phrasing:

- I bet you can't think of three reasons...
- I bet you can't think of a really hard question for me to answer...
- I'm setting you a real challenge in asking you to do this in ten minutes, but I know you're good enough...
- This is really challenging. I wonder if you can do it...

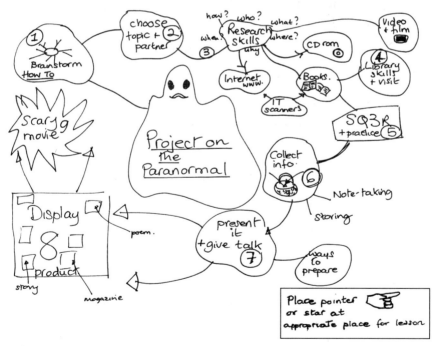

Figure 7.2 Numbered topic web with (movable) pointers.

Obviously, educators need to be sure with dyslexic students that they **can** do these things! The session is then structured for rewards and success. The students should be relaxed; they may even be alert. However, it's good to remember that secondary-age students of all sorts can rarely concentrate for more than 15 minutes at a stretch, even adults tend to drift off after about 20 minutes (Hughes 1999). For dyslexic or ADHD students, the timespan is usually shorter – often much shorter – and the signals that their attention is wandering may be that bit more disruptive. Some may really need a couple of minutes' break, to switch off completely, chat, even move about. This can be used to everyone's advantage if the session has been structured as a series of varied but linked activities. It gives teacher and students alike the opportunity for several new starts, where focus is re-established, plus several endings with the chance for a sum-up and rewards for goals achieved.

So, the students are in the mood for learning. They're restful but alert and they know what's in it for them. The teacher has provided the group with a 'picture' of the lesson and located it within the 'big picture' of the topic. What next?

Teaching and learning strategies to help wholistic learners

This section is divided into three parts. Each one corresponds with one of the three stages of learning:

- Getting the information in – modes of presentation
- Processing the information – storing and revising
- Getting the information out – modes of expression

Getting the information in – modes of presentation

How do students get new information in?
- reading
- listening
- watching
- doing

Whatever the medium may be, the wholistic student will value the big picture and will be helped by focusing on it in advance.

Helping the wholistic learner with reading for information – using SQ3R

Try asking most students in most classes why they are reading a text and the most likely answer will be, 'Because you told us to.' Try asking them how they started and the answer (with a pitying look) will usually be, 'At the beginning.'

Fair enough (possibly) if the students are highly competent readers who will dash through the text with a minimum of effort and recall and regurgitate all the salient points. Unfortunately, this is not typical of the majority of mainstream adolescents, let alone any student who struggles in any way with reading, comprehension or memory. One of our main aims has to be to provide dyslexic students with compensatory strategies and shortcuts, and why shouldn't other students use these too?

SQ3R is a method that has proved useful to all sorts of students, whatever their learning style or degree of difficulty. It does, however, complement the wholistic approach. Versions of this method occur in a range of sources, including accelerated learning texts and Science Research Associates (SRA) materials, which were, allegedly, originally devised to help American service personnel improve their reading skills. It is soundly based upon the schema and comprehension skills theory cited in earlier chapters.

SRA called it SQ3R (Survey, Question, Read, Review, Respond) Using an acronym like this and sticking it on the classroom wall can serve as a memory cue and remind students to use it, see Figure 7.3.

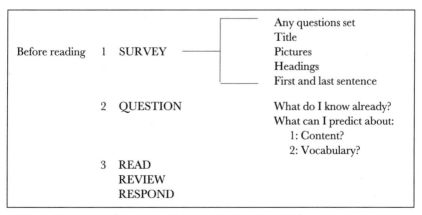

Figure 7.3 Information finding system SQ3R.

However, it isn't enough simply to suggest that students use it. A bit of groundwork has to be done first to demonstrate why it might be worth giving it a try. One way is to take the group through this process:

1. Provide the students with a text – use any short newspaper article or short section of a textbook that is within most students' reading level. (For ways of assessing reading level of texts, see the Fogg Index in Appendix 1.) It is useful to have a text with a couple of comprehension questions set at the end.
2. Offer the students a prize for the first one to come up with the correct number of times the word 'that' is used.
3. Ask them to work either individually or in pairs to answer the comprehension questions. Ask them:
   • How did you do the comprehension questions?
   • How did you find the 'thats'?
   • Did you use the same method to do these two tasks?
4. Ask them, again individually or in pairs, to come up with the best summary of the main point of the article in fewer than twenty words.
   • How did you do this?
   • Did you use the same method as before?
     You'll find a range of strategies will come up.
     Then a challenge, 'I bet you can't work out why we're doing this!' – someone always does.
     Answer: (Just in case!) Different tasks require different types of reading.

FOCUS the students' attention upon this fact
Different tasks require different types of reading skill. Don't waste time. ALWAYS ASK YOURSELF WHY YOU ARE READING A TEXT. Choosing the right strategy will save lots of effort.
ONCE YOU KNOW WHAT YOUR TASK INVOLVES – WHY YOU'RE READING, USE SQ3R

Look at Figure 7.3 and follow the instructions

Through using this strategy, a teacher has followed apprenticeship procedures recommended by a range of research studies in guiding the students through two ideas.

a) that different purposes in reading necessitate different approaches
b) that it is essential to identify the purpose of each reading task prior to starting to read

Why is this technique so helpful for students with dyslexia? Most of these students are bad at decoding; comprehension is hard because so much mental energy is used up in simply working out what the words say. Trying to hold on to meaning takes real effort. If you've staggered to the end, the idea of going back to the beginning to find answers to questions or key points for notes is the last thing you want to do. You want to find a way of cutting down the amount of reading you have to do. This technique makes use of the dyslexic student's strengths. How?

- **Surveying** The wholistic learner is beginning to get an overview of the content of the text. The analytic is forced to start to consider the gist of the material before getting caught up in detail. The visual learner can make full use of any graphic clues here. The verbaliser will be tuned into headlines, main statements and keywords.
- **Questioning** What do I know already? This is the really strong area for many dyslexic students. It is vital that readers should be asking themselves questions about their own knowledge as they survey. Dyslexic students often have a real fund of general knowledge picked up from the environment in a range of ways that do not depend on the written word. They are used to piecing things together and making assumptions. Telling them that their own knowledge is both valid and useful in this academic task is a real boost for their self-esteem and a chance for them both to show their knowledge and to use it.
- **What can I predict from this?** Dyslexic students habitually make use of context (Stanovich 1988). They should be able to predict in two ways: What is the text going to tell the reader? What kind of vocabulary will come up? Prediction reduces the demand made upon exact decoding and increases the likelihood that context

supported guessing will be accurate. Often students will read the text to discover that they have predicted most of the contents.

- **The 3 Rs: Read, Review, Respond** Students now read, review and respond in the way most suited to the task and questions set. They should always have access to highlighters and often find small whiteboards and dry-wipe pens useful for collecting information. If there is a time constraint, as is often the case in examinations, dyslexic students will want to avoid lengthy re-reading so they can use highlighters to mark key points and information as they go.

Five minutes spent using this technique will save far more time that could be wasted in having to reread to understand. This cannot be repeated often enough for dyslexic students. *This is what is in it for them!*

Helping wholists to review information

This type of reviewing involves the ongoing process of checking that the text has been understood. Strategies for revising and memorising will be dealt with in the second strategy strand of this chapter – which deals with processing.

Wholists often have difficulty following the sequence of an argument. They need to be shown how to monitor their understanding and practise sequencing. They can review in the following ways, either working alone or with a partner:

- After reading a paragraph, find the main topic sentence – frequently the first – and highlight it or write it on a separate slip of paper. At the end shuffle the slips and work with a partner to reconstruct the whole passage orally.
- As you go through, stop at the end of each paragraph and answer the question: 'What have I learnt?' If you're not sure, go back and check.

Helping the wholistic student with research reading

Wholistic students need the security of a frame or big picture. Without this, they won't know where to start on an open-ended task such as: 'Find out all you can about ghosts for a talk next week.' Frequently, students preparing for school-leaving examinations can find themselves thrown in at the deep end and be expected to collect information independently. This is really hard without support.

One excellent way of doing this is to use what it sometimes termed a **brainstorm**. As with all other reading, students should start off with what they know already. So they should collect this information at the start. Here is a rough one about the paranormal collected by a dyslexic group of 13-year-olds and recorded from the whiteboard.

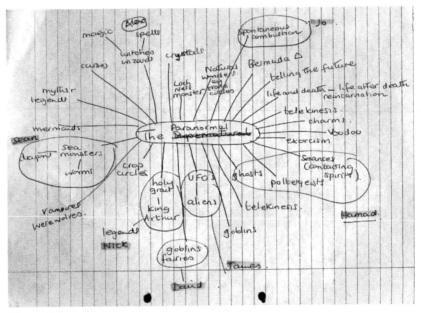

Figure 7.4

The students' names showed which topic each had decided to follow up.

This is how this stage was reached:

1. Each student turned a piece of A4 paper landscape and wrote the topic 'The Paranormal' in the centre.
2. The group had five minutes in which to collect as many paranormal things as possible and either write words or symbols to store them round the centre point.
3. Everybody's ideas were collected on the whiteboard where they were printed as simply and legibly as possible. The teacher can

then make neat copies by hand or computer and give them to the group. Of course, the teacher's work is halved if the classroom is equipped with the sort of interactive whiteboard from which copies can be printed! A less high-tech way of doing this is to write on an overhead projector transparency and then photocopy it.

There are two main ways of brainstorming: random or structured.

- *Random*: This paranormal brainstorm is a random brainstorm. The students are given no more support than the topic heading. A fluent verbaliser would find this relatively easy. Someone with difficulties retrieving vocabulary or ideas might need more support.
- *Structured*: Here are two ways of creating a structured brainstorm using question words. Again, it is sometimes easier to turn the page to landscape.

For students starting on a search for information, this question-based brainstorm (Figure 7.5) is a great springboard. As they answer the questions, they discover what they don't know and need to find out. They now highlight or stick their personal 'find out' symbols on these parts of their brainstorm. They can always leave gaps on the brainstorm to fill in with keywords or page number references as

Figure 7.5 Structured question Word Brainstorm.

they find them. The more analytic learner may well prefer to make a grid here for the topic using a sheet of A4 divided into columns. See chapter 8, p. for an example.

Figure 7.6, Conquest, was compiled on a whiteboard by the teacher while using the question words to help the student create a piece of writing about her experiences helping out at a riding stable. It was then photocopied onto a sheet of paper.

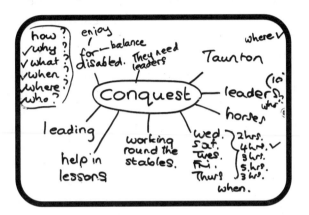

Figure 7.6 Conquest question Word Brainstorm.

Holloway (1995) also gives step-by-step guides to brainstorming aimed at the 8 to 13 age group.

The basic principle to follow is that of giving a wholistic learner a frame within which to collect the information at the outset. The type of frame depends rather upon the sort of information collected.

Whenever possible, it is really helpful to communicate with teachers in other subject areas when teaching students how to use these techniques. That way, students can be encouraged to try them out in real situations across other areas to see how useful they can be.

RECAP

Strategy strand: Getting information in

Wholistic learners need the big picture before they start.
Use strategies to help them predict and organise.
Use SQ3R for general reading.
When setting out on a research project, provide frames for them to fill with information.

Strategies for processing, storing and revising

Once students get the hang of using these reading and comprehension strategies, the next stage is to help them process and retain information – whatever medium it may be obtained from.

The key to successful processing has to be organisation. Dyslexic students find this particularly hard. Their thinking and learning life is frequently chaotic, and they need to be able to see themselves as active thinkers in control of their learning. There are two types of 'storing' – physical and mental.

A few simple measures should help deal with the physical aspects of storing. Any teacher of dyslexic students is likely to be familiar with the phenomenon of the exploding file. This usually erupts all over several desks and students, frequently at a point when its owner has been asked to produce a particularly vital piece of home or coursework. The fallout is usually discovered to contain anything from last year's biology notes (crumpled) to that please-don't-confiscate-this-picture-of-Britney-Spears/Brad Pitt/that-20lb-pike-I-caught/that-skateboard-I-want etc. By the time everything has been gathered in, you've possibly forgotten what it was the student should have given you (they hope). Either way several minutes of the lesson and the group's concentration have been lost.

Two basic principles emerge from this:

- Decide what students need to keep. The minimum.
- Help them organise it on a regular basis. To this end you can provide file dividers (transparent plastic envelopes or plastic dividers – cardboard usually disintegrates) with headings (e.g. Shakespeare, poems from other cultures).

Be prepared to collect in and store any information they may need later for revision. Dyslexic students have real problems with organisation. Anxiety at approaching exam or coursework deadlines will increase this. It can be argued that the teacher shouldn't take responsibility for organising older students, because they won't get this kind of support in further or higher education. There are, however, two counter-arguments to this: one is that, without this kind of help, they won't get the grades they need to get into higher education; the other is that teachers should be helping students to develop strategies to use independently later on and that the best way to do this is by example. For further suggestions on how to help organise work physically, see the further reading section at the end of this book.

To be organised mentally is a real advantage. Most students need guidance as to how to organise incoming information effectively. Dyslexic students, in particular, are likely to need to be taken through the most user-friendly techniques. One way of doing this is to help them to practise frameworks to organise incoming information. These are an excellent way of storing mental representations of information that will be needed for exams later. Dyslexic students should be helped to organise these and keep the physical records safely.

How can this be done? Here are two ways:

- mapping and imaging
- using structures

Mapping and imaging

This technique develops from the brainstorms previously described and has the added advantage of involving both hemispheres of the brain. It comes from the work of Tony Buzan on mind-mapping and also Levy's brain-imaging programme (1993) and has been given a range of titles. Students must be led through the technique and given the chance to practise it before deciding whether it is useful to them. Wholists will usually take to it quickly; analysts may be more reluctant, but even they may get to like it eventually.

> I hate it. It's useless. I won't do it. I like lists. (Tom, 13, dyslexic student)
> Oh, go on – *trying to hide his concept map* – you've caught me at it. I suppose it works for me really. (Tom, 16, at public examination time)

Mapping is also a great tool to use to boost listening comprehension and should stand students with dyslexia in good stead way beyond school. If students are expected to map from written text, it is best to start with very simple information for those with dyslexia or any kind of reading difficulty as they will also have to focus on decoding.

How to do it

The teacher's knowledge of the group will help to decide how many sessions to spread this work over. Dyslexic students will, however, need a brief recap of the previous stage each time.

First stage
Discuss and model the idea of creating a brain image or concept
map.
Tell the students that they will:

1. Identify the main concept or idea of a passage.
2. Build a concept map around this main idea.
3. Take a simple, short passage of information such as 'the dangerous dingos' from Levy's brain-imaging programme (1993).

> The Dangerous Dingos
> Dingos are wild dogs that live in Australia. They were brought there by the first
> people to live in Australia called Aborigines.
>
>   Dingos are farly large dogs that have yellowish-brown fur. They rarely bark
> and mostly howl. If Dingos are caught as puppies, they make good pets.
>
>   Dingos' most important food is a small kangaroo called the wallaby, but they
> also kill sheep. Because of this, the Australian Government has spent a lot of
> money to catch and poison them.

- Read the passage out to the group once.
- Issue students with a blank concept map (Figure 7.7)
- Tell them to identify main idea and write it in the central circle.
- Tell them to fill in as many ideas as they can remember –
  keywords or pictures.
- Tell them to put their pens down while you read the passage to
  them again.
- Immediately tell them to add more information to their brain
  images.
- On the board create class brain image (sometimes called a
  concept map) taking ideas from the students.
- Issue completed concept map (Figure 7.8) and discuss why theirs
  is better!

Next stage
Chunking and labelling information to help the memory
Chapter 11 provides a range of sources and suggestions to help
with memorising).

- The main aim of this process is to help the students to organise
  the information into categories, which they can memorise and
  use as hooks upon which to hang details.
- Use the completed concept map. (See Figure 7.8.)

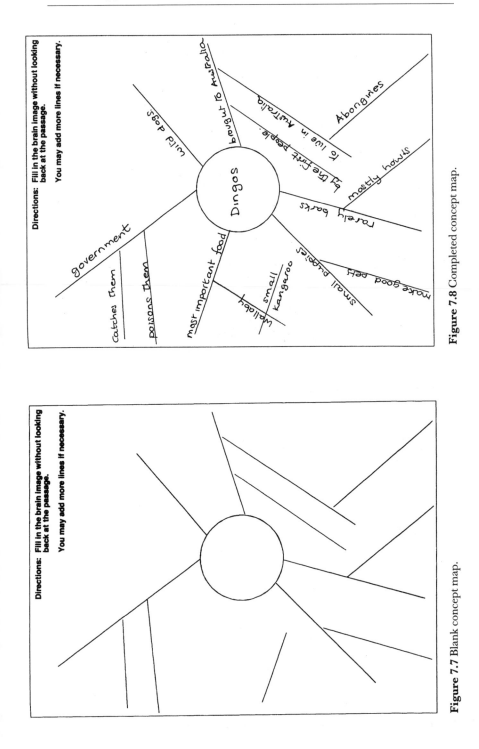

Figure 7.8 Completed concept map.

Figure 7.7 Blank concept map.

- Ask for suggestions as to how all this information could be organised into 'boxes' for storage. A range of methods will come up, possibly linked to different students' learning styles. These could be answers to questions such as where? when? who?; 'meaning' or semantic categories, e.g. food, controlling dingoes, uses for dingoes; visual symbols used to express these semantic categories.
- Different students will choose different approaches and individualise their maps (e.g. Visual Figure 7.9).
- Count the number of main categories – dingoes has six – and try to find a way of remembering the number, e.g. six letters in dingoes, a cartoon or mind's eye picture of a dingo in a number-six football shirt.

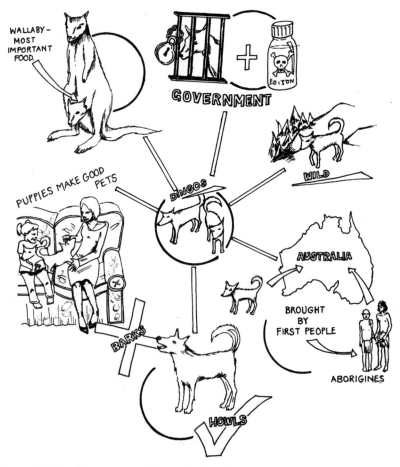

Figure 7.9 Visual concept map. Illustration by Elly Wdowski.

- Finally – issue a challenge. A prize for anyone who can fill out a completed dingo concept map next lesson!
- Third stage, testing out the strategy. Next lesson, issue a blank concept map. Set a time limit (optional). Check the key number of concepts and see how well their memories work. They will mostly be surprised by how much they can remember!

Further steps

Concept maps are useful in a range of situations, particularly when listening to information or watching film or video. It is usually helpful to practise this strategy as a group with a particular video related to a topic they may be researching. A3-size wipe-clean whiteboards and board writers are an invaluable tool here. Students can jot down a concept map of keywords or pictograms and then, at a later stage, develop these into more storable notes on paper either individually or in pairs.

It is important to give individuals the opportunity to explain their maps to the group and to explain how they developed them. It is an opportunity for those individuals with dyslexia who take everything in to gain some status and for others who are less fluent to practise developing expressive language within explicit boundaries. They usually like to compare their maps, and it's often positive for the teacher to attempt one too, particularly if it gives students a chance to do something better than the teacher! It's also a good way of validating the use of symbols and pictures as a storage tool. There are also some students who are more receptive to advice from their classmates than from their teacher.

Most research suggests that strategies are far more likely to be internalised when used in a practical situation where students can see why they're doing things and how useful these strategies could be. Every method from bribery to coercion should be used to get them to try them out but with the understanding that it is experimental. If any strategy really isn't working for a particular student, it can be dropped and something else put in its place.

There are two obvious and related ways of putting concept mapping into context:

- Introduce concept maps as a way of reviewing information. Time this as part of a revision strategy a couple of weeks before examinations, and set specific topics to be revised and checked with the rest of the group.

- Make sure that every student selects a lesson from another curriculum subject, such as science, history or geography. Suggest that he or she makes a concept map of the lesson. Then review these maps with the group. These self-generated concept maps can then be used as revision-test aids where the information is blanked out and the students have to recreate them, checking accuracy with the original and highlighting areas they find hard to remember. It can be helpful to let other staff know that the students are doing this.

The aim of this supported work is to enable students to create their own maps independently and then spontaneously. The amount of support needed will vary from individual to individual. In either of the above tasks, teachers will have to choose how much support they give the students, ranging from a sheet of blank paper to a half-prepared map with category headings.

Using structures

Concept maps or brain images are an all-purpose tool that can be applied across the curriculum. Other subject areas or situations may require other frameworks. Students should be encouraged to try out a range. For example:

- Time-lines: In history, or any other chronological narrative, students often find time-lines useful. Figure 7.10 shows a simple time-line of the events in John Steinbeck's *Of Mice and Men*. Buzan and Coleman's excellent series of literature study books (1998) uses a range of these methods.
- In science, cycles can be helpful where they can be used clearly to show such pieces of information as how to test for starch (Figure 7.11, page 138) but also for studying subjects, such as literature. Figure 7.12 is taken from a study book (ILEA 1990) on J. B. Priestley's *An Inspector Calls*.
- English literature – character study. Figure 7.13 (see page 139) shows a character icon for an imaginary character created by a dyslexic student; visual learners will probably prefer icons and

Events in 'Of Mice and Men'

Day	Time	Place	People	Events
Friday	Evening	By the river	George, Lennie	Camp near ranch before job. Dream of owning land. G looks after L.
Saturday	Morning	Ranch bunk house	G, L, Candy, Boss, Curley, C's wife	Meet others. G tells L to keep away from Curley's wife.
Saturday	Early evening	Bunk house	Candy, G, L, Carlson, Slim, Curley, etc.	Carlson shoots Candy's dog, makes G and L's dream possible. Curley attacks L. Fist crushed.
Saturday	Night	Crook's room	Crook, L, Candy, Curley's wife, G.	L visits Crook. Talk about land and loneliness. Crook offers to join dream but humiliated by C's wife.
Sunday	Afternoon	The barn	C's wife, L, later G, Candy.	L kills his puppy then C's wife. Manhunt starts.
Sunday	Later	By the river	L, G. Later Slim, Curley and others	G shoots L to save him from Curley.

Figure 7.10 Vertical time-line.

like to draw their impression of the character. This is obviously useful as a memory or comprehension aid while reading or listening to a story.

Students preferences will vary:

- some like seeing events as a series of boxes
- others like to be given a set of blank squares
- others like boxes with lines
- some like unlabelled diagrams that can be prepared easily by photocopying any relevant diagram and deleting headings

Some of these structures, such as time-lines or sequenced boxes, may

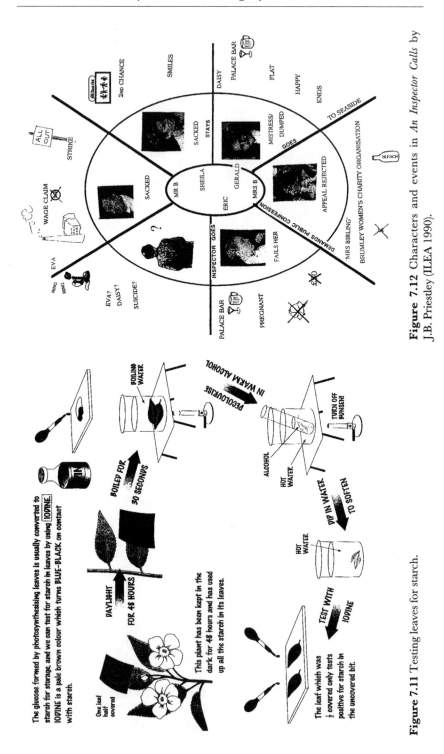

Figure 7.12 Characters and events in *An Inspector Calls* by J.B. Priestley (ILEA 1990).

Figure 7.11 Testing leaves for starch.

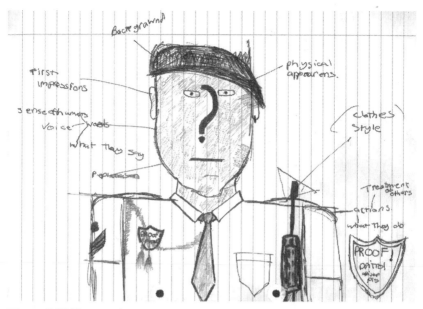

Figure 7.13 Character icon.

well appeal more to those analytic students who are happier with sequences.

Any of these frames can be suggested as a way of collecting information from any visual or verbal text and students can generate their own or be provided with them.

The 'I See What You Mean' series (Kilpatrick et al., 1982) is a really excellent resource for a variety of frames and activities enjoyed by students and teachers alike. It is particularly useful as it is targeted at the middle-school years but can be used successfully until around the age of 13. These middle years are an ideal time to develop students' awareness of their learning style, as they are mature enough to deal with the concepts and responsibility yet young enough to develop useful strategies before hitting the GCSE years.

Whatever type of frame used, the eventual aim is that the students should decide which is going to be best in each situation and should be given the skills to devise their own.

Revising

Once students have mastered using maps and structures, they should be encouraged to use them to review newly learned topics regularly.

The more students process information, the more they will remember each time. They should be shown how to convert information from one mode of presentation to another – for example from a graph to a mind map, a recipe to a flow chart or a set of instructions to a diagram. Doing this both develops flexibility of learning style and reinforces information in a multi-sensory way. It also caters for the full range of learning styles. The Headwork series of books (Culshaw & Waters, 1984) is a really excellent resource for practising these skills. It is aimed at the middle-school age range and contains light-hearted material of high-interest level at a lower reading age. Mason (1990) provides other opportunities.

Converting new information from a lesson into another mode is a really useful homework task for any subject. For example:

- Provide a squared page like a storyboard. Ask students to write a key new point in each square.
- Provide a time-line. Ask students to fill in the events leading up to a particular event.
- Ask students to write up an experiment in the form of a cartoon flow chart.
- Ask students to use the full range of question words to set a quiz on a new topic.

Another advantage of this for dyslexic learners is that it minimises the amount of language they will need to generate or revise from.

Recap

Strategies for processing, organising and revising

Dyslexic students need help with ORGANISATION.
Wholistic students naturally take to the use of FRAME-WORKS.
Try out MAPPING and using STRUCTURES so that students can make a choice.
Practise using a range of types across the curriculum.
Encourage students to CONVERT information from one type of structure to another.

Getting the information out – modes of expression

Many students with dyslexia seem to fall into one of two categories when producing written work. Either they have so many ideas they don't know where to start or their minds go blank when presented with the empty screen or sheet of paper. Either way the result can be the same – total blockage. What is needed is the trigger that can set them off and free them. Here, as in other situations, different people will need different solutions. It is crucial to experiment with different methods and to be sensitive as to when to press students to persevere with a method and when to let them go in their own direction. Sometimes making an unwilling student stick to a particular way of planning for a couple of tasks actually forces him or her by default to discover his or her own best method and stick to it, even if it is only to show you that you were wrong!

Wholistic learners also often have trouble starting to write because their ability to see the whole picture prevents them from knowing where to start. They need to find a starting point that can unlock the whole structure for them and show them the path to follow.

The most successful solutions to this problem come in the form of writing frames. Ideally, students will eventually begin automatically to be able to transform the concept maps that they use for collecting ideas into writing frames to help them express them. There are a range of different types of writing frame and students will discover by experience which they prefer.

Writing frames – a three-stage process

Many students quickly become adept at writing in two stages – straight from mind maps or brainstorms to written text – once they are used to ways of organising and sequencing ideas into paragraphs. (Chapter 9 describes how to structure and adapt mind maps or brainstorms in this way.)

From brainstorm to text is a two-stage process.

brainstorm ⟶ text

The majority of students will, however, certainly need to be taken through a three-stage process.

brainstorm ⟶ writing frame ⟶ text

The question-word brainstorm shown in Figure 7.5 is a good example of the first stage of a three-stage process. The brainstorm can easily be transformed into a writing frame for factual writing where each paragraph answers a particular question. (see Figure 7.14) This can also obviously be provided very easily as an IT template. Here is an example of a writing frame used to help a dyslexic student write up information acquired from a video. It may seem almost ludicrously simple for those of us who are used to organising our ideas, but it can be a lifeline for a panicking dyslexic student.

A writing frame is a bridge between ideas and text that provides an organised shape for a student to follow. Most brainstorms can be transformed into a simple frame structure.

There are basically two types of frame:

1. **blocks**
2. **chains**

Writing frame

Victorian factories

Paragraph 1
When did factories develop?

Paragraph 2
Who started them? worked in them? profited from them?

Paragraph 3
Where were they? (and why?)

Paragraph 4
Why did they start?

Paragraph 5
What did they do? was the effect on people's lives?

Paragraph 6
How did they produce goods?

Figure 7.14 Writing frame.

Both types are based upon schema theory and discourse analysis and aim to make students aware of the way different types of text are usually structured and to enable them to use these structures to help organise their own thoughts and writing. This also builds their confidence in the predictability of pattern in texts. Both types can be applied both to narrative and non-fiction. **Blocks** may appeal more to wholistic students while **chains** are more sequential and are dealt with in detail in chapter 8.

Blocks

Lewis and Wray's (1995) work on writing frames offers the basis for the block system of organisation. Their book of templates for the six non-fiction genres of writing is invaluable. Although designed for children, they can be used successfully at all levels, most recently seen in action on a Masters in Education course! They follow the same scaffolding approach of:

demonstration → joint activity → scaffolded activity → independent activity

Lewis and Wray provide block frames for six types:

- recount
- report
- procedure
- explanation
- persuasion
- discussion

Figure 7.15 shows examples of Lewis and Wray's basic frames. They can obviously be adapted to suit different situations and subjects, for example a frame can be structured to reflect the stages of a scientific experiment or created as an IT template. The frames also provide phrases and connectives appropriate for each type of genre. A range of these phrases and connectives is provided in chapter 10. These are particularly helpful for strongly wholistic learners who have difficulty creating sequences, dyslexic learners whose sequencing skills are weak, visual learners who often have difficulties with expressive language or learners with speech and language difficulties.

(a)

Goal
Equipment and materials required
Action plan (step 1, 2, 3, 4, etc.) Step 1. Begin by Step 2. Then
Evaluation How well has the goal been achieved? Any further action to be taken?

(b)

Although I already knew that ...
I have learnt some new facts from our trip to I learnt that ... I also learnt that ... Another fact I learnt ... However, the most interesting thing I learnt was ...

Figure 7.15 Basic frames. (a) Proceure frame. (b) Report frame.

Teachers sometimes forget that these abstract connectives do not come naturally to many students and that it is therefore safer to provide them and model them. Those students who already use them will make use of the spelling and generate more of their own.

Figure 7.16 shows a Lewis and Wray explanation frame.

How to

You will need

1. First you

2. Then you

3. Next

4.

5.

6.

Figure 7.16 Explanation frames.

Another strong point is the help these frames give to those many students whose work is usually a single, several-page paragraph. The simple recount-genre frame forces a student to use five paragraphs and provides an opener for each paragraph. This can easily be adapted to provide a framework for independent coursework. Once students are familiar with the process, they should be able to use it at any educational level, generating their own openers.

Fig 7.17 shows how Lewis and Wray's (1995) discussion frames were adapted and used for postgraduates on a module at Master's level (University of Birmingham 1999).

Writing Activity

Discussion

This activity should help you to plan the discussion of the main points of your argument. It could help you organise your sections and your paragraphs.

There is a lot of discussion about whether . . .

The people who agree with this idea, such as . . .,
claim that . . .

They also argue that . . .

A further point they make is . . .

However, there are also strong arguments against this point of view.
They believe that . . .

They say that . . .

Furthermore, they claim that . . .

After looking at the different points of view and the evidence for them I think . . .

because . . .

Figure 7.17 Lewis and Wray discussion frames.

Chapter 10 examines how this block-frame structure can also help students to develop detail.

Frames for adults with dyslexia

Block frames can easily be adapted for use in the workplace by utilising the conventional frames of the business world, for example agendas or minutes.

Frames for narrative writing

Persuading any student to plan a story is heavy going. Many talented writers say that they don't know how the story ends until they get there. This is obviously fine in any situation except the typical exam where there is a time limit and the candidates are expected to provide a crafted piece. The 'and then I woke up' ending usually means that the writer has lost the plot, run out of time or both! Examiners have rumbled this. Not making a plan also makes life difficult for students who get lost, forget where the story is going or dry up. The wholistic student may well have an overall idea of a story but will then frequently have difficulty articulating it as a coherent narrative and incorporating detail. The analytical student will frequently focus on detail but get stuck when it comes to structuring an overall plot.

It is, arguably, almost impossible to structure a story without a combination of wholistic and analytical approaches. Most stories, particularly at a simple level, tend to be analytical – a linear structure with one event developing from another. However, before developing this sequential narrative, it is usually necessary to have an overall idea of the whole. This is a situation where approaches from both this chapter and chapter 8 have to be combined. It is possible, as Figure 7.18 demonstrates, to express the wholistic and analytical natures of a story as a frame.

The situation–problem–solution–outcome chain represents the sequential narrative while the wholistic elements are shown in the lower half of the frame.

This is one way of making the wholistic learner think about the separate ingredients that must be examined when writing up an idea for a story. It is, of course, equally useful given in advance to students as an aid to memory, attention or note taking while reading or listening to a story. Chapter 8 describes in more detail the story-chaining or storyboarding techniques that can be used to structure the sequence of the narrative.

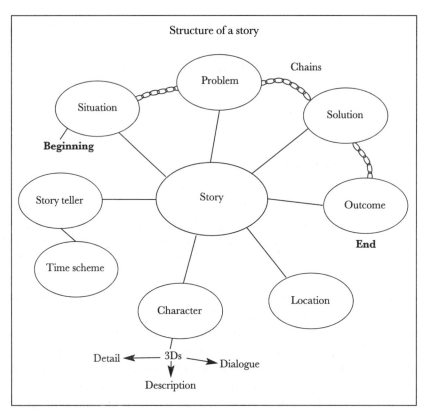

Figure 7.18 Story as a frame.

Recap

Strategy strand – modes of expression

Creating written work is a three-stage process

brainstorm ⟶ writing frame ⟶ text

A writing frame is a bridge that helps the student organise ideas into text. It follows the structure of the type of text written – factual or fictional.

Any learner is likely to be helped by the provision of frames.

A dyslexic learner is particularly likely to need a frame.

Wholists and analytics are likely to need different types of frames. Wholists may prefer blocks or maps, while analysts may respond to chains. Stories often require both types.

Examination and revision techniques for wholists

Revision is a headache for everyone, but it is often a nightmare for dyslexic students. They frequently state that they haven't the faintest idea how to revise and that they can't read their notes anyway; so what's the point? This chapter has already suggested ways of using the transfer from one type of frame to another as a way of processing and revising information. Writing frames can be used in a range of ways for exam support. Here are two approaches:

Preparation

Students need to interact with any material they are trying to learn. For most dyslexic people, reading through notes is hard, because the effort expended in reading interferes with memorising. A way of getting beyond this is to take a discrete section of notes and read it through with the purpose of extracting keywords and main points and building a grid or mind map from this. Wholists will probably want to create a graphic map, analysts may prefer grids or sequenced lists – either way the aim is to personalise the material and make it manageable. Once the map is ready, the student can start to memorise the shape and the detail, to count how many arms it has, to see the shape in the mind's eye. At this point, he or she should prepare an unlabelled version on a separate piece of paper and see how much information can be filled in from memory, going back to the original to retrieve forgotten details and filling these in in a different colour. The aim is to be able to produce the map spontaneously (ideally, the next time the student sits down to revise this topic).

Using keywords

Students who lack confidence in their memories or organisation often feel as though they are swirling in a sea of evaporating information during the run-up to an exam. They often need help in structuring and reducing information to the essential. They need simple structures that they can store and use to build on. The most practical way to create these is to use the examination papers as the starting point. Exam papers in all subjects are structured around keywords. These fall into two types:

- subject specific (e.g. metaphor, industrial revolution, erosion, etc.)
- test specific (e.g. compare, contrast, evaluate, etc.)

Chapter 10, which deals with ways of strengthening the verbal channels, describes more work with keywords.

There is a finite number of types of question that can be asked about any topic, and all teachers are familiar with the concept of question spotting and preparation of trial answers. For wholists or both wholistic or analytic dyslexic students, however, these answers will be more user-friendly if they are placed within a frame hung upon keywords. Here is an example taken from an English GCSE paper where students have been studying a group of poems for the exam:

Question: **Compare** the ways in which **two** poets from this selection explore the idea that your own **identity** is closely **linked** with the **language** you use.

The keywords are written in bold. The students will have practised identifying keywords and their meanings. They will also have created a grid showing which poems deal with which themes (see chapter 8). They will have practised using a comparison grid (see Figure 8.13). They are, therefore, ready to create either a grid or a concept map to frame their answer

Students should be able to create a basic frame within minutes. Dyslexic students find writing onerous. Practising full exam answers takes up time and often provides them with revision material they can read only with difficulty. It is frequently more useful for them to practise creating frames like this and then to discuss the details with a partner using keywords or images as memory joggers. They can then cover a range of possible questions and store the frames or concept maps they have created in a file for later revision.

Helping wholists to identify detail and sequential structure within a topic

A useful technique is described by Race (1992). It is called a Question Bank. He suggests that all students should devise a set of questions for every topic they study. They should decide exactly what questions they would need to ask someone to get them to show that they understood the topic. Students should write these questions down to build up a bank of questions to accompany all topics that they need to revise.

Exam technique

Getting started on exam questions under time constraints is often a major problem for dyslexic students. Frequently, they will have to produce a full example in as little as thirty minutes, and they can waste half that time staring at a blank sheet of paper. If they have practised producing quick keyword frames, they will have an automatic procedure to follow. This security will often provide the push start that they need.

Working with an amanuensis

It is now possible for students with dyslexia to apply to the examination boards for concessions and to gain up to 25% extra time in all GCSE and further-education examinations. Further concessions such as 50% extra time, use of IT, transcripts of written papers, readers and amanuenses for all examinations except English Language and some foreign language papers can be applied for.

(For further information see the annually revised *Regulations and Guidance for Candidates with Particular Requirements from the Joint Council for General Qualifications* and Backhouse (2000) or Vivian (1998)

If a student is allowed an amanuensis or writer, it is obviously essential that some training in this skill is provided. Although many dyslexic students are fluent orally, dictating essay-length exam answers is a particular skill which involves organisation and memory. Using a concept map and writing frame before starting to dictate is a proven method. For more visually orientated students or those whose verbal processing is slower, this device allows them to anchor ideas in a shaped form that they can then elaborate upon while dictating. Figure 7.19 is an example of practice in GCSE English Language by a dyslexic student. He needed organisation time to retrieve the language he wanted to use. It shows his three-stage plan from which he dictated a more developed B-grade answer to an amanuensis. He has stuck closely to the keywords in his brainstorm (A) and made a clear paragraphed frame (B).

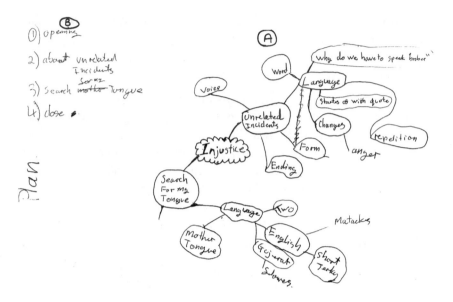

Figure 7.19 Exam planning

Chapter summary

This chapter describes the types of learning behaviours typical of wholistic learners and many dyslexic students. It introduces the optimum conditions for learning. People learn best

- when they want to learn – motivation
- when they feel challenged but not stressed
- at the beginning and end of a session rather than in the middle
- when the whole brain is involved

Strategies for getting the information in – modes of presentation

Wholistic learners need the big picture before they start.
Use strategies to help them predict and organise.
Use SQ3R for general reading.
When setting out on a research project, provide frames for them to fill with information.

Strategies for processing, storing and revising

Dyslexic students need help with organisation.
Wholistic students naturally take to the use of frameworks.

Try out mapping and using structures so that students can make a choice.

Practise using a range of types across the curriculum.

Encourage students to convert information from one type of structure to another.

Strategies for getting information out – modes of expression

Any learner is likely to be helped by the provision of frames.

A dyslexic learner is particularly likely to need a frame.

Wholists and analytics are likely to need different types of frames.

These techniques will be particularly helpful to students under exam pressure either when revising, in the examination or working with an amanuensis.

Chapter 8 introduces strategies to help students with an analytic learning style.

CHAPTER 8
Analytical approaches

Introduction: What types of behaviour and approaches to learning might be characteristic of an analytical learner?

Analytic learners tend naturally towards a linear, sequential style of learning. They tend to prefer to progress in a step-by-step fashion, focusing upon each piece of information in turn and gradually building towards a conclusion. This is a logical, problem-solving approach to learning, *content* rather than *context* based. Given an overall picture, the analytical student will want to take it apart to study its components.

An analytic's strength resides in the ability to focus upon details and move from one to the next. Conclusions are reached through the steady and thorough accumulation of detail rather than through flashes of lateral insight or intuition.

The weaknesses of this approach are a tendency to be unable to see either the overall structure of any topic, the relevance of its context or the ways in which different aspects relate to and complement each other. Once something is taken apart, an analytic may have trouble reassembling the whole. Extreme analysts may well be very indecisive, as they become so immersed in detail that they are unable to see any overall picture which might enable them to make a decision. Frequently, a quick solution is staring them in the face, but they are unable to see beyond whatever they are immediately concerned with. They also often find it impossible to consider more than one piece of information at a time and feel bombarded if expected to deal with more than one task or idea at a time or asked to work in a random fashion. At this point they may well forget the detail they had so carefully analysed only seconds before.

Socially, analytics tend to be far more self-reliant, consistent, idealistic and organised than their wholistic friends. They are often perceived as more shy and less people-orientated, more detached and less active in social situations (Riding 1994).

What are the implications here for learning behaviour? Overview or step-by-step?

It is important not to forget that the Wholistic-Analytic continuum is only half of the learning style picture. Every individual also falls somewhere along the Verbaliser–Imager line. Analytic imagers are said to have a complementary style in that they can use the whole-view aspect of imagery to help supply themselves with an overview of a situation. Analytic verbalisers, however, have a more unitary style in that verbalisers are also prone to linear ways of processing. They will therefore need more support in developing the ability to see a broader picture.

Many accelerated learning approaches to study emphasise the importance of presenting all students, regardless of learning style, with the big picture or an overview of a topic before embarking on the step-by-step approach. The research findings do not really present a clear picture, as results are complicated by gender and whether students have unitary or complementary style combinations (Riding and Rayner 1998). The 'try it and see' approach seems to be the best way forward here. Analytic learners do not naturally tend towards an overview and may, as a result, be disadvantaged in various ways. For some analytics, the overview methods described in chapter 7 may enhance their learning and retention. Others may simply find themselves overloaded and prefer to stick to a linear progression leading to a conclusion. Chinn and Ashcroft (1998) would probably call these students the 'Inchworms'. The only way to discover preferences is to experiment.

Analytic learners are comfortable with logical progression. They will, therefore, be more able to follow the kind of academic work that is carefully structured in this way. For example: a science practical lesson that is organised and presented from the outset as a clearly seen progression of activities will be better received than one that asks students to consider a range of possible combinable activities. In design and technology, verbal analytics will do better following a set of instructions for assembling a bookshelf in a way that moves from the parts to the whole rather than having to improvise their own method from looking at a finished example. In history they are likely to respond to time-lines and lists rather than overviews of a topic.

Retaining the details

Analytic learners are likely to enjoy detail. They are good at analysing and teasing out meaning. For example, they may be good at putting together utterances in a foreign language as they find it easy to analyse the syntax of a sentence, locate the meaning and reproduce it (Banner and Rayner 1997). Research will be thorough. Written work may well be focused in depth on a narrow area. This is obviously an excellent skill for generating texts of all kinds. Difficulties can arise, however, when analytic learners need to retain and memorise, as they are likely to be faced with material that has large numbers of individual pieces of detailed information without a clear framework upon which to hang and group them for storage. They are not natural 'chunkers' of knowledge, and this places a heavier demand upon memorising skills. This is an area where they will need support.

Connecting topics

Analytics are less likely to see connections between ideas other than simple links. This may be the case within subject topics. In history they will not automatically see the relationship between increasing scientific knowledge about the solar system and the decline of unquestioning obedience to the church. Straightforward cause-and-effect links will be easy, but more creative links or parallels may pass them by. In literature they may find it harder to pick up on a theme in a novel and realise that it is also being dealt with in a play. In the secondary school where a day is divided into lessons in a range of subjects, taught by different teachers in separate rooms, analytics are likely to compartmentalise the knowledge they are gaining. As a result an analytic can go straight from a lesson on Wilfred Owen's poetry to a history lesson on trench warfare without making any connections. Once the connection is made for them, they will then be able to use their funds of detail to deepen their understanding, but it is fairly vital that the connections are made explicit.

Social preferences

Analytics may be less comfortable with group work, preferring to absorb themselves in individual research. It is obviously up to the teacher to decide at what point to encourage group work, but combining a wholistic with an analytic can be really productive as the analytic is likely to produce the detail that may be lacking in the wholist's big picture. The wholistic learner's group skills can also serve to bring out the more introverted analytic.

Managing group work

It can be very appropriate to group students according to their style. There are two ways of doing this:

- same-style groups
- mismatched groups

> *The advantages of same-style groups:*
> A teacher can use teaching methods matched to a particular style with a particular group and know that they will all respond. Students sharing a similar approach to a task will tend to work harmoniously and boost each other's confidence.
> They can also reinforce successful working strategies.
> Reinforcing new information in a similar way helps retention.

> *The advantages of mismatched groups:*
> Grouping students in same-style groups can lead to reinforcement of less appropriate approaches to study.
> Students working with complementary styles in tasks that demand a range of activities can help to develop new approaches and also to produce a 'team' outcome which utilises all the group's strengths.

The learning implications of an analytical style for people with dyslexia

Sequencing

The analytic approach focuses on the parts rather than the whole. It is sequential and gathers detail. This causes two main types of difficulty for people with dyslexia:

Dyslexic people frequently have difficulty with sequencing of any sort. They will have trouble both with following the order of any sequence and with retaining more than two or three items in a sequence in their memory. Many sequences are not automatised.

Some dyslexic people have weaknesses with language, which include difficulties with the language of time, cause and effect or prepositions. This sometimes means that they cannot access the verbal labels that would help them to operate effectively in a sequential way. This will arguably suggest that, by default, few dyslexic people with accompanying language difficulties are likely to be analytic verbalisers, but there will be a minority. Beyond primary school, much information continues to be presented primarily in a linear-verbal mode without wholistic or visual reinforcement. This may suit analytic verbalisers but is unlikely to be helpful for the majority of dyslexic students.

Memory

People with dyslexia frequently have difficulty with memory and organisation. Focusing on detail rather than on structure puts a greater load on memory processing, as one is less able to group ideas into bigger clusters that can be remembered more easily. This means that more processing is needed to retain this type of detailed information. Dyslexic students also have less confidence than others in their ability to retain factual information. They find this kind of memorising stressful, which further reduces performance.

What are the social implications of an analytic style for dyslexic students?

The analytic is reputed to be more self-reliant and less sociable than the wholistic learner. Although most dyslexic individuals are neither more nor less sociable than the rest of the population, there is a small sub-group that suffers from language disorders. This can mean that they have problems with receptive language, either because their vocabulary is impoverished for a range of reasons or because they have difficulty with an interpretation of language or social signals. Equally, some struggle with expressive language.

This can be linked with vocabulary or phonological deficits, retrieval difficulties or slowness of processing. A third group may have pragmatic weaknesses, which means that their grasp of the social use of language is uncertain – they have trouble with the conventions of conversation (elements such as turn-taking, sticking to a topic, humour, word play or taking another person's point of view and knowledge into account). All these areas can lead to failure in social situations and can either make a student choose, or be forced, to work alone. If that student is also strongly analytical, this may exacerbate any tendency towards isolation. There may well be a need for carefully structured social-skills group work for these particular students.

Between the ages of 11 and 15 adolescents tend to move away from the family group and to forge strong links with their peer group. They begin to depend far more upon the good opinion of their friends. The increasing importance of conversation with peers and social inclusion for the personal wellbeing of adolescents has been well documented (Rawlins 1992, Nippold 2000, Coleman and Hendry 1989). Some people find that, for a range of reasons, which may include semantic or pragmatic language difficulties, the kind of social and conversational skills that gain acceptance do not come automatically. These students will benefit from explicit practice in social-skills groups. The necessary skills include:

- staying on topic
- asking relevant questions
- making supportive comments
- interrupting appropriately
- turn-taking
- shifting the topic gracefully
- using humour and figurative expressions skilfully
- exercising discretion and good judgement with personal information concerning the self and others
- employing body language and facial expressions that enhance interactions

The majority of students need only limited support in these areas. For further suggestions and reading on speech and language difficulties, see the further reading section at the end of this book. Rose and Goll (1992) also provide some very practical structured work to help set up co-operative learning groups, Csóti (2001) suggests practical strategies to develp social awareness. Holloway (2000) emphasises the important part played by listening skills in social interaction and learning and provides a range of suggestions for activities and classroom management to enhance these skills.

Mathematics and dyslexia: do dyslexic students prefer analytical methods in maths?

The study of mathematics combines both linear processing and intuitive problem-solving. Chinn and Ashcroft (1998) produce valuable insights into the role of cognitive style in mathematics, exploring the differing approaches taken by inchworms and grasshoppers, two categories of learner that seem to correlate loosely with analytics and wholists respectively.

They suggest that, despite the strain placed upon memory and processing by the inchworm style, when it comes to mathematics there are still more inchworms than grasshoppers among the dyslexic population, although they point out that any individual student may use both styles. They speculate that this may be linked with the possibility that a lack of confidence in themselves as mathematicians prevents dyslexic students from following what might seem a more risky intuitive approach and makes them stick to a more step-by-step procedure, despite the overload on memory and processing (Chinn et al., 2001). They state that inchworms with poor memory for basic facts are at risk in mathematics and that for some students this lack of ability to remember basic facts (for example the times-tables) could contribute to the adoption of a grasshopper style, where a student overviews data because he or she cannot remember the facts necessary for a step-by-step approach.

Their invaluable book suggests both the difficulties dyslexic learners face in this subject and a range of ways of helping them with mathematics, using both types of approach.

Getting students ready to learn

It is suggested in chapter 7 that people learn best

- when they **want** to learn – motivation
- when they feel challenged but **not** stressed
- at the **beginning** and **end** of a session rather than in the **middle**
- when the **whole** brain is involved

This obviously applies to both wholistic and analytical learners.

Teaching and learning strategies to help analytical learners

This three-part section corresponds with the three stages of learning:

1. Getting the information in – modes of presentation
2. Processing the information – storing and revising
3. Getting the information out – modes of expression

As stated earlier the picture is less clear with analytical learners than wholists. It seems that analytics process in a linear, parts-to-whole, sequential way. Some find it hard to grasp the whole of a topic, others have difficulty in making connections. Arguably they should benefit from being given overviews and structure in the same way as recommended for wholists, as this should help them to create links and memorise the detail that they gravitate towards. However, some analytics are really uncomfortable with this approach and state that being forced to take an overview simply overloads them. There are two ways of dealing with this. One is to use the strategies suggested in chapter 7, but to emphasise that they are free to discard them if they find them of no help. The other is to stick to the idea that analytics do need to be helped to see the big picture, but to find more sequential, linear ways of expressing this.

Strategies for getting information in – modes of presentation

When reading for information, both analytical and wholistic students will benefit from being taken through the SQ3R procedure described in chapter 7. SQ3R is universally useful. It allows prediction and encourages links and the use of context.

With research reading, analytics, like wholistic students, will benefit from collecting what they know about a topic before they start to gather more information. However, they may well find the exploding shape of the brainstorm hard to cope with. They are also more likely to need help with knocking some sort of shape into the random facts and details they do ferret out. The way around this is to provide them with a fill-in structure that is more linear or list based. A question-word grid or set of columns, is shown in Figure 8.1.

Grids – Question words: UFO		
Things I know Roswell incident	**Find out** When? _____ Where? _____	**Facts** _____
UFOs seen in England *and so on*	When? _____ Witnesses?	_____ (*UFO* magazine p. 22) UFO letters page

Figure 8.1 Grids – Question words.

After they have found their information, this structure will allow them to consider the big picture of the topic and how their collection of facts hangs together at the end of the research process.

There are several ways of doing this:

• Separate lists: some students will need to generate keywords or questions to start themselves off. Figure 8.2 shows some science prompt sheets.

SCIENCE PROMPT SHEETS

Planning Experimental Procedures

1. Write down a title that says what you are going to do or find out.
2. Write a plan of how you are going to do it.
   • Have you explained how you will make your method safe?
   • Have you used scientific knowledge to help you make the plan? If so, have you explained how you have used it?
   • Have you written down the names of any books or other material to which you have referred?
   • Did you try out any preliminary experiments first? If so, have you written down what these were and what you found out?

3. Write down a prediction, if it is appropriate.
   • Have you written down what you think the result will be?
   • Have you written down why you think this will happen?
   • Have you used scientific reasons to explain what you think will happen?

4. Write down what it is that you are going to measure or observe.
   • Have you explained how you will make sure that it is a fair test?

Figure 8.2 Science prompt sheets.

- Have you said which things you are going to keep the same?
- Have you said which things you are going to change?

5. Write down a list of the equipment that you are going to use.
   - Have you said why you have chosen this particular equipment?
   - Have you been specific? For example, have you just written down 'an ammeter' or have you written ' a 0 to 10 amp ammeter'?

6. Write down the range and number of readings you are going to take.
   - Have you written down how many readings you will take? Have you said why this is a suitable number?
   - Have you said what are the first and last readings that you will take? Have you said why you are not going to record outside these limits?
   - Have you said how accurate the readings must be? For example, are you going to measure to the nearest millimetre of the nearest centimetre?
   - Have you planned to repeat any of the measurements or observations? If so, have you said why you think this is necessary?

Evaluating Evidence

1. Write down how successful you thought the investigation was.
   - Have you explained whether your prediction, if you made one, turned out to be right or wrong?
   - Have you used scientific knowledge to explain your results?
   - Have you said whether all of your results support your decision? Have you pointed out any results that do not fit the pattern? (These are called *anomalous* results.)
   - Have you tried to explain any anomalous results that you got?
   - Have you tried to estimate how accurate your results are? For example, do you think your measurements are to within 1%, 10% or 20% of the true value?

2. Write down any changes you would make if you had to repeat the investigation.
   - Have you said whether it is the method or the equipment that you would change?
   - Have you explained why these changes would make the investigation better? For example, would it make the results more accurate or would it make the evidence more reliable?
   - Have you said whether it really was a fair test?
   - Have you made a note of any difficulties that you met during the investigation?

3. Write down anything that you could do to get more information, if you had time.
   - Have you made any suggestions for other ways of getting extra information about the topic?
   - Have you said how this extra work might make you more sure about your conclusions?
   - Have you made certain that this extra work would give you new information, and not just more of the same?

Figure 8.2 Contd.   (Contd)

Analysing Evidence and Drawing Conclusions

1. Process the information that you have collected.
   - Do you need to re-group the information, perhaps into another table, in order to show a pattern?
   - Do you need to carry out any calculations on your results? If so, have you shown clearly how you have done this?
   - Do you need to draw a graph of the results? If so, should it be a bar chart or a line graph? If it is to be a line graph, should you draw a line of best fit?
   - Have you labelled clearly, with units, any tables, pie charts or graphs that you have drawn?

2. Write down what you have found out.
   - Have you described what you have found out? For example, can you see any pattern in your results?
   - Have you said whether this is what you thought the result would be?
   - Have you used scientific knowledge to *explain* your findings?
   - Have you thought about any other ways of explaining your results?

Figure 8.2 Contd.

- Box sequences – allow one keyword per box
- Question word columns (Figure 8.3)
- Grids – Figure 8.4 (page 166) shows a poetry example; these are useful for collecting information for revision. They appeal to wholists and imagers.
- Time-lines – see Figure 7.10. Some wholists will like these, but they usually appeal more to analysts.
- Visual hierarchies (Figure 8.5, page 167)

Strategies for processing, storing and revising

Any dyslexic student is likely to need help with organisation. Although analytical dyslexic learners are good at disembedding the main points of an argument from surrounding information, they may in fact be at more of a disadvantage than wholists for two reasons:

1. their linear approach can put more strain upon their memory
2. they do not spontaneously work towards fitting pieces into a whole so that links and schema can be formed

Who	What's happening	Where	When	Moods Atmosphere	Memorable lines Dialogue Voice	Message
	1.					
	2.					
	3.					
	4.					

Figure 8.3 Question word columns for writing or summarising fiction.

	Main subject	Poet's voice (tone)	Themes	Main images	Form rhyme?	Metaphors? Similes?	Students own suggestion
Stealing	Feeling of a thief (thief, people)	Thief speaks Dialogue conversation	Isolation	Snowman cold unexpected			
When you were mine	Feelings for and about mother (poet, people)	Poet as adult looking back with affection					
War photographer	War photographs (people)	Poet describes photographer's job painful		Priest visual (photos)		M Priest	
In Mrs Tilscher's class	Growing up (poet, people)	Poet as adolescent talks to Mrs T memories					
Valentine	Pain of love (poet, lover)	Poet to (painful) lover			Irregular No rhyme	M onion extended met. S onion – like the moon	
Carol Ann Duffy							

Figure 8.4 Poetry grid.

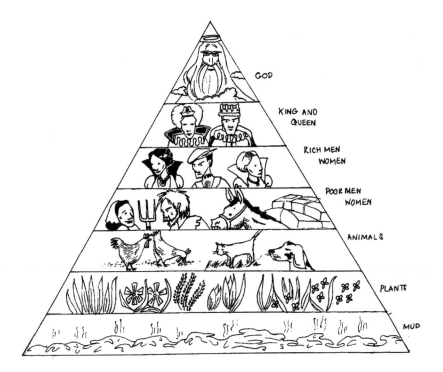

Figure 8.5 Visual hierarchies. Illustration by Elly Wdowski.

RECAP

Strategies for getting information in-modes of presentation

Some analytical learners may benefit from having the big picture before they start. Others will prefer to have help pulling it together at the end.

Strategies, such as SQ3R, that encourage them to think about the context of a text and to predict both vocabulary and logic will be useful.

They may well find linear frames useful at the start of a project. Most will find them helpful at the end for seeing an overall picture of their results.

The solution to this for a wholistic thinker is to provide techniques such as the brain mapping and imaging described in chapter 7.

Analytics, however, although needing help, are more likely to be resistant to this kind of support if it is presented in this visual wholistic form They may be more comfortable with other structures, such as grids, boards or trees.

One way of storing and processing information, particularly from visual or auditory sources, is to issue the students with dry-wipe A3-size boards and pens. Paper can, of course, be used, but marks cannot be removed once they are on paper! Wholistic students are likely to be happy with the suggestion that they turn the board or paper landscape, place a topic title in the centre and then create a concept map of visual or verbal key points as they pick them up. Analytics may be happier to divide the board into a grid of between 12 and 18 squares and to collect one key point per square as they go. They should be allowed no more that three or four words per point! They can, of course, experiment with different shapes – one student used to like working outwards from the centre of a spiral!

This is a useful way of developing listening skills and providing a focus for those students whose concentration span is short. Students can then be asked to present and explain their boards to mixed- or same-style groups, which allows them to add in points they have missed and either encourages them to try other methods or reinforces a particular approach. Students are often interested to see how different structures suit different people. This helps them to realise that there are really no completely right or completely wrong ways of working with information. It is just a matter of identifying the right method for the student and for the task. Some students also find that stopping to capture information at suitable breaks, such as paragraph or section endings, enhances their comprehension while reading.

Converting information from one mode to another

As with the wholistic techniques described in chapter 7, analytics should be encouraged to convert information from one mode of presentation to another. For example, they might like to try turning a section of a history textbook into a time-line either using actual dates or numbers or time-concept words such as 'beginning', 'middle' and 'end'. Some analysts will find that simply turning a page of text into a numbered list or a flow chart helps to internalise the information. Analytical imagers will like cartoon-type storyboards with the minimum of text, visual hierarchies or ladders to express concepts, such as food chains or social structures. Again, the series 'I See what you Mean' (Kilpatrick et al., 1982) provides a range of ideas and material for practising.

Helping analytics to identify structure

Being able to create or spot the structure or schema of a text or series of notes is important for a range of reasons. It will help with memorising. It helps students to predict content and shape and it will help an analytic to make links within one text and connections between several. Arguably, many analytics may prefer retrospectively to identify the structure of the information they have accumulated.

Analytics tend to work sequentially. They tend not to like the wholistic type of frame where all aspects can be viewed simultaneously. The **chaining** system developed by the Wigan Language Project (Mason 1990) may be more helpful to them. Mason (1990) cites Micheal Hoey's work on discourse analysis, which looks at the common patterns within types of text. Like the block systems described in chapter 7, it is useful for both stories and academic texts. It is usually easier to introduce its use through stories, as students are often more comfortable with stories than academic texts and are later relieved to discover that academic texts do actually follow a similar structure.

Story chains
The basic links of a story are:

- **Situation**
- **Problem**
- **Solution**
- **Outcome**

Familiarity with these links will help an analytic both to extract the basic narrative line and to plan a story. For any age group, oral story telling is a good way of introducing the concept and links. Here is one way:

1. Start telling any simple story, for example:
   It was Monday morning. Jane woke with a start. For a moment

she lay, feeling comfortable, then three horrible truths slowly dawned on her. Today was the day of The Test; a terrible fate awaited those who failed; she would be one of those people!

2. Stop here, ask the group to suggest what Jane should do.
3. While the group are thinking, write on the board:

Situation	**Jane wakes on Monday**
Problem	**The Test! She will fail!**
Solution	_____
Outcome	_____
Final Outcome	_____

4. Ask for the Solutions to Jane's Problems and add some to the chart.

Figure 8.6 shows a simple story chain with no Final Outcome. One outcome will actually provide Jane with more problems and further episodes to her story. To finish the story off in a satisfying way, the group will need to choose one that finishes the story conclusively. It is important to discuss the basic steps of the story with the group, ensuring that they understand why each stage differs from the other, before you focus on the Final Outcome.

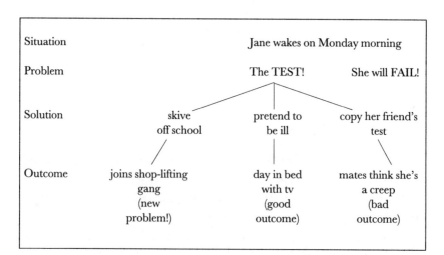

Figure 8.6 Story chain.

This is a simple, single-chain story.

5. At this stage it is sometimes useful to either collect some more simple story chains from the group or provide some jumbled four-part stories and ask students to arrange them correctly and read them aloud to each other to check that they sound right.
6. Once you are certain this concept is clear, return to Jane and her Problem. Ask the students to develop one Solution from Figure 8.6 (perhaps, a). For example, Jane's Solution to the test has given her an even bigger Problem.

   Problem – she's caught up with the shop-lifters
   Solution – she decides to wait at the door hoping to slip away
   Outcome – the security man catches her – this is another Problem
   Solution – she tells the security man what the others are doing
   Outcome – the gang are caught and Jane gets a reward
   This could make a satisfactory Final Outcome or the story could continue as long as the tellers like with new problems to solve, such as the gang getting revenge on Jane.
   This is an extended story chain, which would look like this:

Situation	Jane on Monday morning
Problem	The test – fail!
Solution	Skives off
Outcome – Problem	Pulled into shop-lifting gang
Solution	Waits at door
Outcome – Problem	Caught by security man
Solution	Tells on gang
Outcome	Gang is caught (Final Outcome – reward) or (New problem - gang's revenge)

A chain like this would give a student an eight-part story, which could then be developed with detail and atmosphere.

7. Students should then be given the opportunity to turn a range of stories into their chains. It is often helpful to provide a frame with the links.

Figure 8.7 is an example that can be adapted to suit students. Stories can be told, read or watched from video or television. Groups often like to look at soaps at this stage for an example of how more complex stories are formed from a number of separate but closely connected chains. *Neighbours, Eastenders* or *Brookside* or any standard soap are useful. However, series such as *The Bill, Casualty, ER* or *The Simpsons* add another dimension, as each episode contains final outcomes, frequently for several temporary characters; yet there is an ongoing group of regular characters with storylines that continue across separate episodes. Students can be asked to spot particular characters and their storylines and map how the chains interconnect. Again, printed frames, such as Figure 8.8, which shows a completed story chain, can be useful.

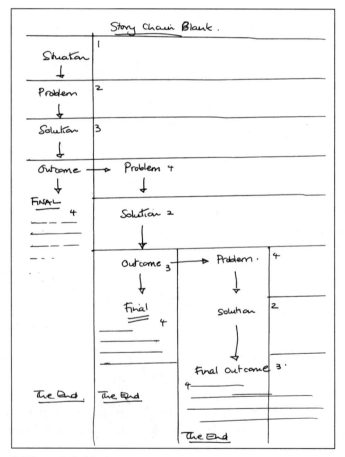

Figure 8.7 Story chain blank.

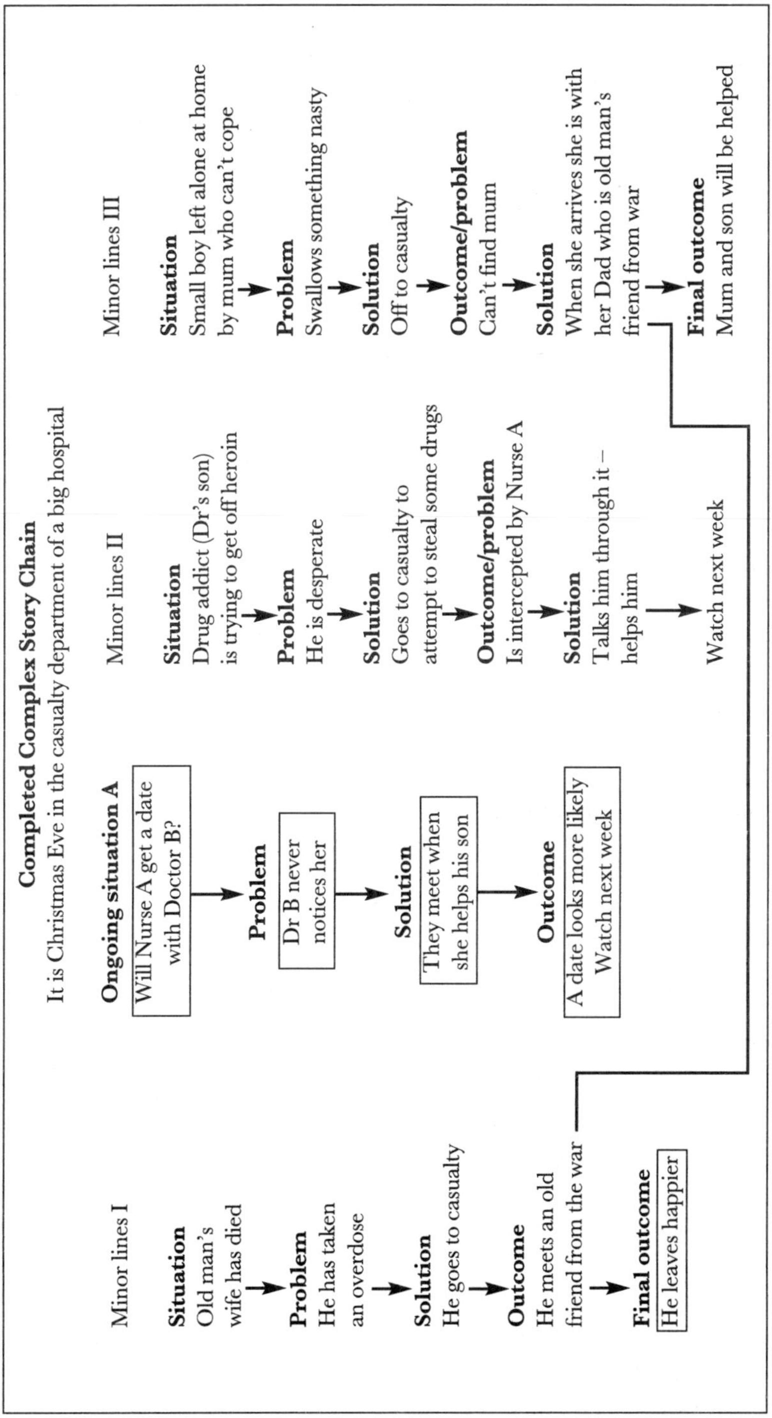
Completed Complex Story Chain
It is Christmas Eve in the casualty department of a big hospital
Minor lines I
Situation
Old man's wife has died
Problem
He has taken an overdose
Solution
He goes to casualty
Outcome
He meets an old friend from the war
Final outcome
He leaves happier
Ongoing situation A
Will Nurse A get a date with Doctor B?
Problem
Dr B never notices her
Solution
They meet when she helps his son
Outcome
A date looks more likely
Watch next week
Minor lines II
Situation
Drug addict (Dr's son) is trying to get off heroin
Problem
He is desperate
Solution
Goes to casualty to attempt to steal some drugs
Outcome/problem
Is intercepted by Nurse A
Solution
Talks him through it – helps him
Watch next week
Minor lines III
Situation
Small boy left alone at home by mum who can't cope
Problem
Swallows something nasty
Solution
Off to casualty
Outcome/problem
Can't find mum
Solution
When she arrives she is with her Dad who is old man's friend from war
Final outcome
Mum and son will be helped

Figure 8.8 Complex Story Chain.

This kind of analysis can be applied to any story – including a Shakespearean one – and this leads on to students planning and writing their own and also analysing stories for literature criticism. There is obviously scope here for a wide range of activities, including group work devising characters, situations and scripts for soaps or group serials where each student carries on from the last problem. This is also a good memory aid for students who have difficulty keeping track of and remembering a storyline. They can be provided with a story-chain frame and use keywords or symbols to mark the main events as they read or listen to the story.

Chains in academic texts

Although the subject matter of academic texts is different from stories, the structure is basically the same across the curriculum.

Situation
Problem
Solution
Outcome
(or SPSO) still applies
For example:

Control and design technology

Situation	We have a dog, and he loves going out in the car. It is an estate car, and we put him in the back.
Problem	This isn't safe, as he tries to get on to the seat with us.
Solution	I decided to design and build a barrier, which keeps him in the back of the car.
Outcome	This works well. He knows he can't get at us and settles down.

History

Situation	Japan wanted to take the whole of southeast Asia.
Problem	The only obstacle to the plan was the American fleet.
Solution	They bombed Pearl Harbour
Outcome	After this they were able to start to take southeast Asia.

Chemistry

Situation	Two solids, salt and sand, are mixed.
Problem	How do we separate them?
Solution	We have to dissolve them in water.
Outcome	One dissolves in the water, and the other does not. This separates these two substances.

In academic texts, however, other phrases are sometimes more accurate than SPSO.

> Situation could be:
> State of affairs, Starting point, Background, What things were like when we started.
>
> Problem could be:
> Task, Need, Difficulty, Question, Purpose, Gap in knowledge, What we had to do
>
> Solution could be:
> What we did about things, Action, Method
>
> Outcome could be:
> Result, Answer, Response, Success

For students with a weakness in language, it would be important to establish this vocabulary.

The above examples are all taken from Mason (1990). Her highly recommended book provides a thorough range of activities to give a grounding and practice in text analysis. These activities include:

- dividing academic texts into their component parts
- unjumbling mixed parts
- looking at several problems that can be solved with one solution
- looking at one problem that might have several solutions

This is a useful way for analytics to process information that they need to retain. It manages to combine a sequential approach with a developing awareness of the patterns that appear regularly in different academic activities. It makes students think about the stage they might be at in any process and about how that process hangs together without insisting, at this stage, that they take an overview.

Strategies for getting information out – modes of expression

The three- or two-stage process described in chapter 7,

brainstorm ⟶ writing frame ⟶ text

is equally relevant for analytics. Analytical learners are just as likely as wholists to become blocked when trying to express their ideas. Working sequentially will quite frequently give them a writing order if the task provides a logical progression, such as writing up an experiment or a chronologically ordered story. However, they will often get into difficulties halfway through the text when they realise they don't know how to end their story or their account.

RECAP

Strategies for storing, processing and revising

Although analytics prefer to work in a linear way, they will benefit from being helped to see the overall structure in a text.

They may prefer to generate the structure *after* going through the process.

They may respond to some of the methods suggested for wholists but prefer more linear frames, such as text chaining, time-lines, columns or lists.

Like wholists, they should be encouraged to convert information from one form to another.

Stories often cause considerable difficulty. Reluctant to plan in advance, some will need the push of an opening sentence or situation to start them off and then not know where to go. Others will ramble on happily, only to lose their way completely and get bogged down in inconsequential detail. Five hundred words and an hour later, their hero still hasn't got out of the door. This is where an overall picture of the whole is really necessary, preferably presented as a sequence. They will need some organising structures.

- Here is a storyboarding technique, devised by LePage.
   1. Fold an A4 sheet to make 8 sections.
   2. Number each box 1-8.
      Box 1 – Beginning of story – the opening line
      Box 2 – Location
      Box 3 – Main character(s)
      Box 4 – Character's main problem
      Box 5 –
      Box 6 – Solve the problem in three steps

Box 7 –
Box 8 – End the story – final sentence

Students can choose to use pictures or keywords; if using words, set a *strict* limit on the number per box.

The example in Figure 8.9, the Mad Sid storyboard, was provided by a dyslexic student who, although an excellent oral storyteller, preferred images to words when attempting to capture his stories on paper. He then went on to write an entertaining, well-structured story, complete with paragraphs! The storyboard kept him focused.

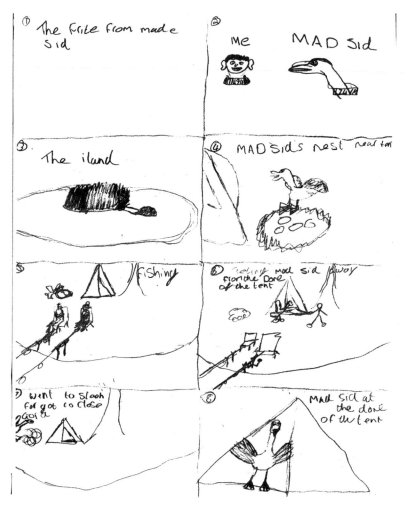

Figure 8.9 Mad Sid storyboard.

Fugure 8.10 is another example from a much younger student who had difficulty both with generating ideas and with logical outcomes. We had worked on the use of who? where? what? and why? structures, which she had internalised and used to create this storyboard. She particularly liked pictures to jog her memory.

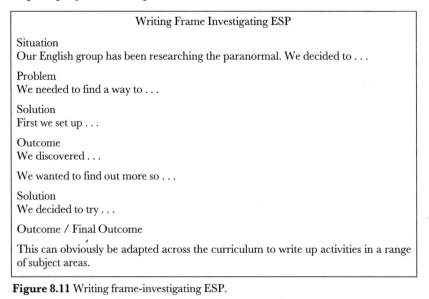

Figure 8.10 The Easter egg story.

Writing frames for academic texts (see Chapter 7) are also adaptable for analytics. Figure 8.11 shows how story chains are adapted to use to plan project write-ups.

Writing Frame Investigating ESP
Situation Our English group has been researching the paranormal. We decided to . . .
Problem We needed to find a way to . . .
Solution First we set up . . .
Outcome We discovered . . .
We wanted to find out more so . . .
Solution We decided to try . . .
Outcome / Final Outcome
This can obviously be adapted across the curriculum to write up activities in a range of subject areas.

Figure 8.11 Writing frame-investigating ESP.

Figure 8.12 shows a question word frame with sentence starters.

	Using question words to compile a writing frame The Shelter **who?** **where?** **when?** **what?** **how?** **why?**
Why?	We needed to build a shelter for ...
How?	To make it we needed to ...
What?	Inside it has ...
Where?	It would be built ... To hide it, I ...

Other sentence starters
'I decided to'
'The shelter consists of'
'It contains'
'We needed to'

Don't forget
defence
camouflage
air
drainage
shelter from the rain

Figure 8.12 Question word frame – The Shelter.

A particularly useful frame is Lewis and Wray's comparison grid. Secondary-school students are expected to be able to compare activities, ideas, places, people and texts. Many find it very hard indeed. Here is how it works. This is a blank comparison grid (Figure 8.13).

Compare _____ and _____. Which do you prefer?

	a. Victorians	b. Present day
c. Play		
d. School		
e. Work		
f. Housing		
Conclusion	Would prefer… because…	

1. Write the items to be compared at *a* and *b*. For example, 'Life for a child in Victorian England' and 'Life for a child today'.
2. Decide aspects that they have in common. For example, housing, work, education, leisure.
3. Write these in at *c*, *d*, *e* and so on.
4. Collect keywords in the grid. Each box will form the basis of a paragraph.

Figure 8.13 Lewis and Wray's blank comparison grid

This is a very simple task, but the same structure can be applied to far more sophisticated areas of study. This form is likely to suit both wholists and analytics, as it combines sequential and unitary structures.

Although most students, whatever their learning style, benefit from trying out writing frames, some do find the block style too rigid and are more comfortable with something curvy. This is where the **chains** described in the second set of strategies come into their own as writing tools or frames.

These more fluid structures are useful across the curriculum to help students write stories or academic text, to write up practical lessons, analyse new information and revise previous information at exam times. As with block writing frames, many students are really helped by the provision of chain frames with terminology appropriate to the particular subject. For disorganised dyslexic students, regular practice with a predictable form will build confidence and help the students to analyse and remember the steps they have to go through. Collaboration with colleagues across the curriculum can develop a resource bank of appropriate chains that can then be reinforced or used at exam times to enhance revision. Chains can incorporate verbal cues, visual cues or both.

Recap

Strategies to help get information out – modes of expression

Readers are referred to chapter 7 where the following points were explained. This is all equally relevant to analytical learners.

Creating written work is a three-stage process

brainstorm ━━▶ writing frame ━━▶ text

A writing frame is a bridge that helps organise ideas into text. It follows the structure of the type of text written – factual or fictional.

Any learner is likely to be helped by the provision of frames.

A dyslexic learner is particularly likely to need a frame.

An analytical learner is likely to be more comfortable with a sequential, step-by-step type of frame. This chapter introduces the use of storyboard techniques for narrative writing and chains for both narrative and academic writing. A chain would consist of situation, problem, solution and outcome.

The linear approach taken by analytics does, of course, place a particular type of burden upon the memory. Chapter 11 suggests some techniques for improving memory strategies.

Examination and revision techniques for analytics

Those sequential readers who started at chapter 1 and have worked their way through will recognise much of this section from chapter 7. Revision is a headache for all dyslexic students. They frequently state that they haven't the faintest idea how to revise and that they can't read their notes anyway; so what's the point? Sequential processing imposes a considerable memory load.

Analytical students will need help with structuring material to reduce this load. Chapter 11 provides techniques to help with this.

The strategy of transferring information from one type of frame to another as a way of processing and revising information is as valid for analytics as wholists. The types of writing frame that appeal to analytics can be used in a range of ways for exam support.

Preparation

Students need to interact with any material they are trying to learn. For most students with dyslexia, reading through notes is hard, because the effort expended in reading interferes with memorising. A way of getting beyond this is to take a discrete section of notes and read it through with the purpose of extracting keywords and main points and building a grid or mind map from this. Wholists will probably want to create a graphic map, analysts may prefer grids or sequenced lists; either way the aim is to personalise the material and make it manageable. Once the map is ready, the student can start to memorise the shape and the detail, to count how many arms it has and to see the shape in the mind's eye. At this point, he or she should prepare an unlabelled version on a separate piece of paper and see how much information can be filled in from memory, going back to the original to retrieve forgotten details and filling these in in a different colour. The aim is to be able to produce the map spontaneously – ideally the next time the student sits down to revise this topic.

Using keywords

Students who lack confidence in their memories or organisation often feel as though they are swirling in a sea of evaporating information during the run-up to an exam. They often need help in structuring and reducing information to the essential. They need simple structures that they can store and use to build on. The most practical way to create these is to use the examination papers as the starting point. Exam papers in all subjects are structured around keywords. These fall into two types:

- test specific (e.g. compare, contrast, evaluate, etc.)
- subject specific (e.g. metaphor, industrial revolution, erosion, etc.)
  Chapter 9 provides more work with keywords.

There is a finite number of types of question that can be asked about any topic, and all teachers are familiar with the concept of question spotting and preparation of trial answers. For analytics and students with dyslexia, however, these answers will be easier to memorise if they are placed within a frame hung upon keywords. Here is an example taken from an English public examination where students have been studying one of Shakespeare's plays: **How far** do you consider **Friar Lawrence** to be to **blame** for the **tragedy** of *Romeo and Juliet*? **Give reasons** for your answer.

The keywords are written in bold. The students will have practised identifying keywords and their meanings. Figure 8.14, page 184 is an example of practice in answering English literature examination questions from Tom, a 16-year-old dyslexic student. Although he is an analytic with a penchant for lists, he eventually began to like and succeed with concept maps, but his is structured in a more sequential way and is therefore a different shape from the standard, wholistic concept map, which is likely to radiate out from the centre. He planned to use this for revision and put more detail in each of the boxes than he would have done if organising a plan in the actual examination.

Students should be able to create a basic frame or chain within minutes. Dyslexic students find writing onerous. Practising full exam answers takes up time and often provides them with revision material they can read only with difficulty. It is frequently more useful for them to practise creating frames like this and then to discuss the details with a partner using keywords or images as memory joggers. They can then cover a range of possible questions and store the frames, chains or concept maps they have created in a file for later revision.

Exam technique

Getting started on exam questions under time constraints is often a major problem for dyslexic students. Frequently, they will have to produce a full example in as little as thirty minutes, and they can

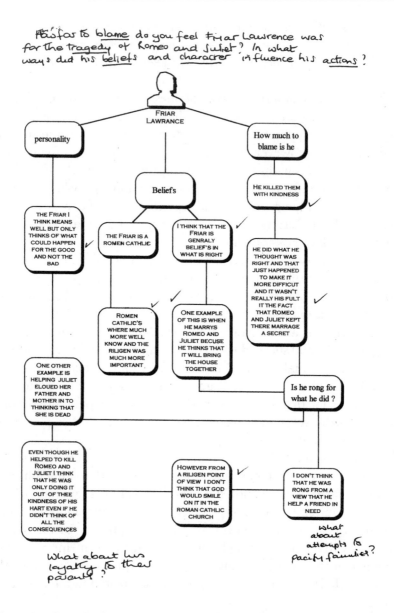

Figure 8.14 Example of practice in answering English literature examination questions.

waste half that time staring at a blank sheet of paper. If they have practised producing quick keyword frames, they will have an automatic procedure to follow. This security will often provide the push start that they need.

Working with an amanuensis

It is now possible for students with dyslexia to apply to the examination boards for concessions and to gain up to 25% extra time in all GCSE and further education examinations. Further concessions such as 50% extra time, use of IT, transcripts of written papers, readers and amanuenses for all examinations except English Language and some foreign language papers can be applied for.

If a student is allowed an amanuensis, it is obviously essential that some training in this skill is provided. Although many individuals with dyslexia are fluent orally, dictating essay-length exam answers involves organisation and memory. Using a concept map and writing frame before starting to dictate is a proven method. For more visually orientated students or those whose verbal processing is slower, this device allows them to anchor ideas in a shaped form that they can then elaborate upon while dictating.

For further information about exam concessions for students with dyslexia, see Backhouse (2001) and the annually revised *Regulations and Guidance for Candidates with Particular Requirements from the Joint Council for General Qualifications*.

Chapter summary

This chapter describes the types of learning behaviours typical of analytic learners and many dyslexic students. It introduces the optimum conditions for learning.

People learn best

- when they want to learn – motivation
- when they feel challenged but not stressed
- at the beginning and end of a session rather than in the middle
- when the whole brain is involved

Strategies for getting information in – modes of presentation

Analytical learners tend to operate in a step-by-step manner. They will need to be helped to make wider connections and see where details fit into the whole. Some analytical learners may benefit from having the big picture before they start. Others will prefer to have help pulling it together at the end.

They may well find linear frames useful at the start of a project.

Most will find them helpful at the end for seeing an overall picture of their results. Strategies, such as SQ3R, that encourage them to think about the context of a text and to predict both vocabulary and logic will be useful. When setting out on a research project, provide columns, grids or chains for them to fill with information.

Strategies for processing storing and revising

Dyslexic students need help with organisation. Analytical students do not automatically see the big picture and so need help with creating frameworks that reflect their more linear preferences. Try using structures and chains so that students can make a choice. Practise using a range of types across the curriculum. Encourage students to convert information from one type of structure to another that suits their mode better.

Strategies for getting information out – modes of expression

Any learner is likely to be helped by the provision of frames. A dyslexic learner is particularly likely to need a frame. Analytics are likely to need different types of frames.

These techniques will be particularly helpful to students under exam pressure either when revising, in the examination or working with an amanuensis.

Section 5 suggests ways in which to develop students' visual and verbal modes of processing.

PART FIVE
Words or Pictures?

Introduction

Part 3 explores the different ways in which similar organisational strategies for dealing with information can be adapted to help wholistic or analytical students. The Wholist-Analytic continuum is, however, only half of the learning style picture. All individual students also fall somewhere along the Verbaliser–Imager continuum.

Their positions on it will determine whether they prefer to deal with words or images and thus the types of strategies they will find most helpful. This will not change their tendency to prefer sequential or wholistic learning, but it means that simple factors, such as whether information is presented to the ear or the eye, will affect the outcome.

People at either extreme of this continuum are likely to be consistent in their preferences. Others are more flexible, choosing to mix words and images or varying in their preference according to the task. Wholists who are also imagers are more likely to be uncomfortable dealing with words than analytics who are imagers. Conversely, analytic-verbalisers are less likely to find images helpful than wholistic-imagers. In general, analytic-imagers and wholistic-verbalisers are more flexible learners. Any teaching group is likely to contain a mix of styles. It is always tempting for the teacher to stick to his or her own preferred style, but it is clear that this is risky. Bringing a multi-sensory element into any teaching situation can avoid difficulties. For people with dyslexia, where the weak channel for information is, arguably, likely to be so very much weaker, this multi-sensory approach has already been tested in work with literacy. It is, however, also invaluable across the curriculum.

A range of researchers and teachers suggest that developing flexibility in any learner will increase success. There are always many learning objectives in any teaching session. Here, the focus is upon just two:

- getting information across successfully (teaching the content)
- helping a student to strengthen weaker channels (teaching the strategies)

Ideally, both should be able to be addressed simultaneously, but, when working with students who have difficulties with a particular mode, a decision has to be made as to what the specific focus will be at a particular time. Is the aim to build up the weaker mode or are we hoping the student will learn a specific topic successfully? Evidence shows that teaching to a weaker mode may not be as successful as teaching to a stronger. However, not all tasks are suited to a purely visual or verbal approach; so it is necessary to put aside time for building up the weaker mode to give students more flexibility of approach.

For this reason, part four of the book has been divided into two chapters:

- Chapter 9: visual approaches – methods that can both develop and match *visual* or *imaging* skills
- Chapter 10: verbal approaches – methods that can both develop and match *verbal* skills

Depending on the teaching goals, these methods can be appropriate for any learning style, for dyslexic or non-dyslexic students alike. This may seem a less helpful structure than separate chapters dedicated respectively to verbalisers and imagers. Busy practitioners may understandably hope to use the index to cherry-pick and match strategies and techniques to particular learning styles. The danger of this is that it can give a partial picture of a learner's needs, which may vary from task to task. The important factor is to give students a choice from a variety of strategies that stimulate and use different senses to enable them to become familiar with what is most likely to work for them in a range of situations. To this end, it is essential to be aware of both visual and verbal possibilities.

CHAPTER 9

Images and visualisation

Introduction: The power of images

> The words or the language, as they are written or spoken, do not seem to play any role in my mechanism of thought. The psychical entities which seem to serve as elements in thought are certain signs and more or less clear images which can be 'voluntarily' reproduced and combined. (Albert Einstein, cited by Thomas West 1997)

> I hate words. They mess up the pictures. (Ed, dyslexic student)

Everyone knows the power of a picture. Einstein actually stated that he visualised the theory of relativity – it was his use of imagery that produced the breakthrough. Visualisation is undoubtedly a powerful tool for learning and inspiration, which can be undervalued in some school systems. It is believed that babies think in pictures before they develop the ability to think in words, and this visual memory remains strong and vivid. Some research has suggested that up to 40% of gifted adolescents and adults are visual and fewer than 30% of the school population prefer the auditory mode (Milgram et al., 1993). It is also the preferred approach of many, but not all, dyslexic students. Here a note of caution must creep in. Many dyslexic students do not have superior visual skills and can easily feel doubly disadvantaged and dejected if they are expected to succeed in this area:

> I'm dyslexic. I'm supposed to be good at this! (James, dyslexic student, frustrated by a diagram)

Many, however, do use their mind's eye to create 'mental movies' as they listen to information or search for inspiration. However, even if students do not spontaneously use visualisation, they can be taught to do so and to make use of all the senses to bring anything they are learning to life. This will produce the strongest possible traces in the long-term memory.

How to develop the power of imagery

This six-stage process has the double benefit of both developing the power of the mind's eye and also calming students. Guided visualisation can, of course, be a really useful relaxation technique. Often used in drama sessions, there is no reason why it should not be transferred to other classrooms when a dose of tranquillity would be helpful. Students can be taken through a process like this. (The actual instructions are here written in italics to distinguish them from the linked commentary.)

1. *Sit comfortably upright and relax.*
2. *Breathe steadily and deeply for at least six inhalations.*
3. *Close your eyes if you like.* (Optional: some students feel vulnerable closing their eyes unless everyone else, including the teacher, does. This isn't always practical!)
4. *Bring your subject gently into your mind.*(If this is purely for relaxation, then the teacher can suggest somewhere, for example lying on a beach, sitting under a tree in a cool garden. If it is to develop the mind's eye, the students should be given a particular image – perhaps a perfect rose, a bowl of strawberries, a bonfire, a sleeping cat – preferably something that will engage all the senses.)
5. *Create a **detailed** picture of your subject using all your senses. What colour rose is it? Do the strawberries have cream on them? Sugar? Is the cat purring? and so on.* The students should be helped to see it, taste it, smell it, feel it, hear it, etc. It is also helpful to place it in context and relate it to yourself. Are you about to eat the strawberries? Touches of humour also help. If you're thinking about the industrial revolution see Heath-Robinson-style spinning machines huffing and puffing and wrapping the workers in metres of thread.
6. *Open your eyes. Capture the image by drawing it, making a mind map of it, describing it to your neighbour.*
7. *Spend a few moments quietly finalising and adding any other suggestions that may come to mind.*

Anyone can develop the ability to use images. Visual learners are already proficient. Some verbalisers are surprised and delighted by the results when they are guided into it. It is also a useful technique for developing any form of creative writing, whether it be generating poetry or adding descriptive detail. It can also be adapted to any subject you are learning, from science to literature.

Kate, a dyslexic teenager with listening difficulties, was trying to make sense of some information about how beaches are covered with sand. She listened to the process – starting with mountain rocks, going via rivers to the sea and ending up as sand on beaches. When asked how the sand got from the sea to the beach she said, 'The rivers take it.' She had not thought through that this would involve rivers running backwards from the sea and all manner of unnatural phenomena! When, however, she was asked to start in the mountains and visualise the streams, broadening into rivers and carrying the sand downhill to the sea, she realised immediately that her answer was illogical. It was as though her difficulties with the listening process had turned off the 'common sense' side of her mind. Once she was helped to **be** there and experience the situation, it became clear to her. Practice in visualising the reality of information in her subject areas has helped improve her understanding and confidence.

One of the roles of a teacher is to help any subject topic to become **REAL**. It is useful and often fun to practise these visualising skills. Always start by breathing calmly and focusing. Always try to imagine the mind as a cinema screen. Here are some ideas:

- Picture a toy car; add another and another. Are they all the same colour? Look at each one. What model is it? Look at all three. Are they the same size? Are they parked in a row? Arrange them how you want them. When they are really clear, open your eyes and draw them.
- Imagine a ginger cat; change the colour to black. Put a white bib and four white paws on the cat. Make the cat lie down. Put a red cushion under it. Change the cushion to green. Turn the cushion into a blue mat. Now imagine the cat stands up and walks out of your picture leaving the blue mat.
- Play with abstract shapes. Create a line. Move it around to form a circle. Fade half of the circle out. Join the ends to form a crescent.

Colour the crescent silver. Place the silver crescent in a black sky ... and so on.

The pictures can be as vivid as the students want them to be. Some students particularly enjoy visualising and eating plates of food or conjuring up *Baywatch* girls or pop idols. The possibilities are endless!

Psychologists and therapists also use guided visualisation to help develop confidence and assertiveness in situations that people find threatening. They will encourage individuals to build up a picture of an ideal performance in an activity that intimidates them. They then vividly see themselves going through all the steps towards a successful conclusion. They replay the images over and over until they flow. This provides an automatic performance framework and builds confidence. Many adults with dyslexia find a range of academic and employment situations threatening and can be greatly helped in this way before interviews, presentations or any challenge. Dyslexic students are frequently skilled visualisers with vivid imaginations. This strategy helps them to use these skills to bolster their confidence and performance.

> At the age of 59 I have yet to write a letter and still write figures the wrong way round. At school I was put in the class for the stupid. The British denigrate the visual as something to do at the weekend, not realising that visual people are luckier than verbal people; they are not limited by their vocabulary. And who's to say what's normal? Maybe dyslexics are the clever ones. (David Bailey, photographer)

Teaching and learning strategies to help imagers

This three-part section corresponds with the three stages of learning:

Getting the information in	–	modes of presentation
Processing the information	–	storing and revising
Getting the information out	–	modes of expression

Getting the information in – modes of presentation

> I was bright enough to pass my 11-plus exam, but the grammar school was a disaster for me, and I was expelled. I couldn't spell, and I couldn't learn from

the way they were delivering the curriculum, which was to do with teachers talking a lot and writing quickly on the blackboard. We were expected to take notes, and that's the aspect of school life I found the hardest; so I cheated and lied and became destructive. (Elizabeth Henderson, head teacher of Oldfield Primary School, Maidenhead, cited in *TES* 1999)

For imagers, well-presented visual material is vital. Use images – that much must be obvious. Make sure, however, that the material is well spaced, clearly printed and, ideally, uses colour to differentiate subject areas. It is also helpful to break up extended information visually either with horizontal or vertical lines or by using different colours. Many dyslexic students – even imagers – will have difficulty with complex, detailed or extended visual arrays, especially if they are densely packed. Empty spaces are reassuring. Too much information will cause anxiety. Highlighting or underlining keywords, either previously or as the material is presented, will also help. Suggesting that dyslexic students highlight and underline with you will also improve their interaction with the material. Nearly all subjects, including predominantly verbal areas, such as languages, can be enhanced by visual presentation.

Use charts, diagrams, graphs and film. The Film Education website on www.filmeducation.org suggests ideas. They also have a teachers' centre with resources and offer workshops and training sessions for teachers.

Use well-presented instruction manuals to back up verbal instructions: 'Teach Yourself Visually' in the three-D 'Visual Series' by IDG books is highly recommended.

Use symbols to back up verbally presented information. Give students regular breaks from either reading or listening to information, and either sum up graphically yourself or ask students to do so for you. When presenting new vocabulary or words to be learnt for reading, allow students to represent these with their own visual memory joggers either beside the words or on the backs of cards.

Three years ago, I would do a bit of this, that and the other, willy-nilly, ending up feeling utterly frustrated. The turning point was the creation of a ginormous 16-square-foot time-line mind map with my past events, present state and future aspirations. If anyone had told me then, while I was carting filthy second-hand fridges round south London, that I would be studying multi-media, I would have sent them to a shrink.

I try to make time for a healthy lunch before setting off for my afternoon lecture armed with my mind map pad and Dictaphone ... to keep the old concentration going if the lecture seems dull, and there are no visual aids to look at. (Why can't lectures be presented in a multi-sensory way?) I jot keywords down in bright colours. I often add notes after listening to the tape. (Toby Burt, dyslexic student, University of Kent, cited in Brenneker 2001)

'Physical' aids to offer imagers

Just because a student is an imager does not necessarily mean that eyesight will be flawless. Students who depend upon visual strengths may be putting a lot of strain upon their eyes. Students with dyslexia sometimes suffer from the glare of a white paper page or from seeming blurring or movement of print on a page. It is often surprising how much the removal of glare can help. The following things can be done:

- Non-reflective transparent coloured overlays of the reader's colour preference can be placed over documents. Wilkins (1995 and Wilkins et al 2001) has carried out and reviewed research into the effect of coloured lenses on reading.
- Documents can be printed on coloured paper.
- Some students find the use of Irlen-prescription tinted glasses or overlays a noticeable help (Irlen 1991)
- Text size, colour and background colours on computers can be changed.
- When reading, students with visual-processing difficulties will frequently lose their places in the text. They can be helped by a range of text maskers that can be placed either over or under the text. There are some commercially produced maskers that incorporate magnification or a range of coloured overlays. For example, the E.Z.C. Reader (available from reallygoodstuff.com) combines an opaque masker like a horizontal bookmark with a coloured transparent edge that can be placed over the line being read. Obviously, it is also easy to create these for individual students. Arguably, it is better to encourage the student to mask above rather than below the line being read. Covering up the next part of the text can discourage scanning ahead to aid comprehension.

Teachers should always be alert for signs that a student is suffering from a visual processing overload or problem. Straightforward signs like headaches or uncomfortable eyes should be followed up. Any combination of reading problems such as losing the place, rereading or skipping lines, missing words out or needing to use a finger or marker to keep the place may be suspect. Some aspects of visual difficulties in dyslexia may, however, not show up in a standard eye test. A list of optometrists who specialise in dyslexia can be obtained from:

Cerium Visual Technologies, Cerium Technology Park, Appledore Road, Tenterden, Kent. Tel: 01580 765211

Strategies for processing, storing and revising – turning words into pictures

I hate thinking about poetry. The words get in the way. (Ed, dyslexic student)

All imagers will fall somewhere along the Wholistic-Analytic continuum. They will therefore prefer wholistic mind-mapping strategies or more sequential approaches. Imagers, however, are going to respond more strongly to the use of images and symbols to enhance their structures and are also going naturally to want to use visualisation as a way of processing and revising material. It is in the processing phase of learning that the development of visualising skills and the ability to turn words into mental pictures will be most helpful. Students should be reminded of their experience of television documentaries and encouraged to create documentaries in their minds for any subject. How can this be done?

- Students can be encouraged to view scientific, natural or historical processes as if they are the directors of a newsreel 'seeing' events unfold.
- Students can be filmmakers, filming at points of interest, such as the formation of volcanoes or from a plane flying high over coastal defences.
- Students can be TV reporters interviewing characters, uncovering motives and emotions.
- Students can look through the eyes of characters or – for that matter – atoms or blood cells! Some groups of students, even at GCSE level, will find it easier to learn the order of the planets in

our solar system by being these planets. This is obviously linked too with the ideas of kinesthetic learning or learning by movement and experience.

Students should always be encouraged to create concept maps. These are all techniques encouraged by visualisation strategies. As with these, spending a quiet few moments at the end drawing a mind map and consolidating what has been learn will be invaluable.

A caution

Some students can really be thrown by working in this more 'creative' way. One subgroup of dyslexic students can be very 'literal' in their interpretation of information. They can be very puzzled and confused if analogies are introduced or if they are asked to pay attention to something that does not seem directly linked to what they are learning about. If it is suggested that they might like to think of the Blitz as though they are making a documentary, they will start looking for the video camera and moaning when there isn't one! These may be the same students who encounter difficulties with language and pragmatics, who are thrown by figures of speech, cannot spot inferences and are totally oblivious to sarcasm. (A highly destructive tool at any time!) They may well be imagers by default but need to be supported carefully if these types of visualisation techniques are going to work for them.

These students, however, should usually be happy with the concept map. By this stage in this book, the idea of a concept map or the similar mind map, as pioneered by Buzan, should be really familiar. Chapter 7 gives a step-by-step procedure for generating one. Tony Buzan's books and video are widely available from the Buzan Centres. Svantesson (1998) also explores a range of types and takes the reader through the process of creating them. This book gives examples of mainly verbal maps using words. However, a concept map is, by its nature, a visual tool and can be ideally adapted for imagers. Students go through the steps outlined in chapter 7 but they focus on the visual:

1. Start with the central idea.
2. Decide what shape map to do. Will it be a cluster? a family tree? a fishbone? (see Figure 9.4 and 9.5)

3. Use one big branch for each main idea. Use a separate colour for each branch. This helps memory in that a student in an exam can visualise the separate colours and thus link the ideas.
4. Use symbols or images wherever possible. When using words, use one or two and add an image.
5. Draw pictures that sum up a number of concepts.
6. Use mnemonics to remember lists, e.g. a picture of an acronym to remember items, e.g. cat = coal, aluminium and titanium
7. Use symbols and signs to show connections.
8. Make important points three-D.

ABOVE ALL, BE AS CREATIVE AND INDIVIDUAL AS POSSIBLE.

THIS IS YOUR MAP

Here are some examples of concept maps created by students. Figure 9.1 shows all the elements explained above, except the colours. Figure 9.2 shows a concept wheel and Figure 9.3 shows how a student used pictures to plan an oral presentation.

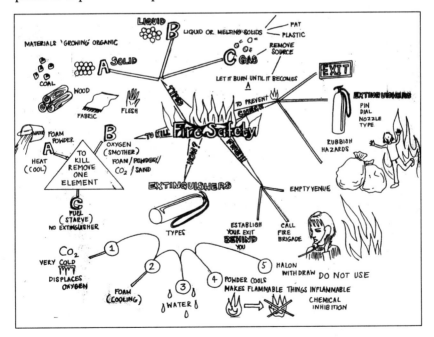

Figure 9.1 Visual concept map.

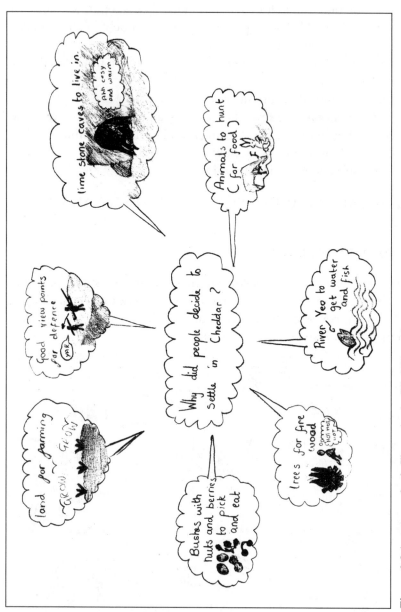

Figure 9.2 A concept wheel. Illustration by Elly Wdowski.

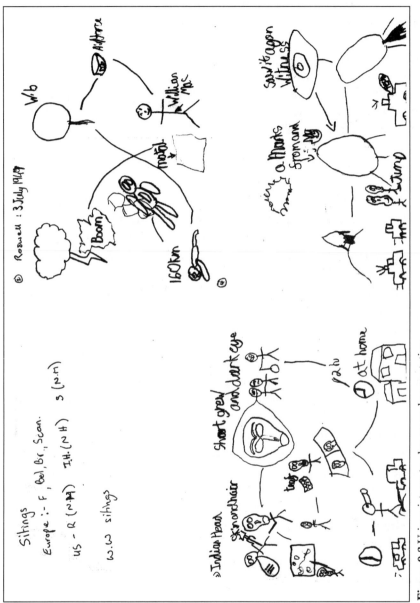

Figure 9.3 Using pictures to plan an oral presentation.

There are also some useful computer programmes available to help make concept maps. Inspiration is one of them. It is a visual mapping tool that enables the user to create a visual map of ideas similar to Tony Buzan's mind mapping but using a computer. The software has a library of 1,250 coloured shapes and pictures accessible from a palette on the screen, This means that every concept map can be unique and that text can be added to either symbols, pictures along arrows or not at all. A number of different icons from the toolbar provide additional help:

- The 'outline' key can turn words to diagrams or flow charts or chains to text formats, offering a real facility to move information from one mode of presentation to another almost instantly. Ideas can be organised visually on the screen and then transformed by outline into a linear form to guide the writing of any student who prefers to work sequentially at this stage.
- The 'arrange' key places the final touch by ensuring that the diagram is orderly and equidistant. In the latest version (version 6) a spell checker is also provided.

Inspiration has a number of different templates that provide starting frames for those who need this extra support. It also provides guides for teachers including lesson suggestions for such activities as concept mapping, brainstorming or analysing events. There is a trial version available from the website at www.inspiration.com. Inspiration can be used on both PCs and Macs; www.eMindMaps.com or www.MindManager.com also provide a good, though somewhat similar, system for PCs.

Imagers and many dyslexic students are likely to have difficulties absorbing and retaining information from text, even if it is read for them. Even fluent readers need to be persuaded to interact with the text. This turns them from passive into active learners. There are various ways of interacting:

- The effectiveness of the Survey and Question section of the SQ3R strategy is discussed in chapter 7.
- Some less-confident readers find it helpful to generate a frame in advance of reading. This can be done either in a sequential or wholistic way. The simplest way is to count the number of

paragraphs to be read and then create whichever structure the student prefers. For example, draw the correct number of boxes for a storyboard headed with the title of the passage or create a blank concept map with the appropriate number of spokes around the central concept.

- Many dyslexic readers are easily daunted by the length of even a comparatively short passage. They should be encouraged to divide the text visually into a series of short bursts, even by simply drawing lines between paragraphs. (This is one reason why it is often more practical to use photocopies of the original text with dyslexic students!) They should also be encouraged to keep a physical grip on where they are, either with a marker, a pen or finger down the margin. Some people find that drawing their finger along the line ahead of themselves speeds up their reading. When they need to take a break, they should mark the spot either by highlighting or placing a tiny post-it at the stopping point.

- Readers who are insecure about their comprehension or memory could try pausing at the end of each paragraph to rehearse the main points that it contains. Visual learners can be encouraged to create an image that can be noted on a reading record or to visualise themselves into the situation described – to be there. If they are uncertain, they can reread the paragraph highlighting a few keywords and then store these, or related images, as a guide through the text.

- Track while listening. The unreliable reading skills possessed by many dyslexic students will mean that they will be relying on their listening skills when the teacher reads a text to them. It is not always helpful for them to be expected to follow the text while it is read to them. Some will find that this is best for them and that they can highlight keywords happily and take away a good picture of the content. Others, however, find it impossible to decode the text at the speed at which it is read and the added fear of losing their place prevents them from absorbing the content. For these, it is probably better to accept that they should listen competently and track the information on a whiteboard or rough paper either in the form of a mind map or a storyboard. It is obviously helpful if they have had a chance to survey and prepare this frame in advance.

Even when using the previous techniques, imagers or dyslexic students may well have difficulty dealing with words in two particular areas:

- vocabulary deficits
- taking in new technical terms

   Vocabulary deficits. Some imagers may have vocabulary deficits and need support to extend their vocabularies, both of everyday words and technical terms. Chapter 10 suggests a range of strategies for developing vocabulary. However, for imagers, it is important to try to build pictures into this process. They will be more likely to remember both new vocabulary and information if it is made visual or physical. This is particularly true in subjects such as maths where concepts can be so abstract. For example, if talking about weight, link it with something tangible for example 'as heavy as a bag of sugar'. If looking at cones, think of ice-creams, traffic cones or make some out of paper.

   Taking in new technical terms. When trying to learn new terms, try to associate them with pictures or stories. Bartlett and Moody (2000) cite the example of learning the bones in the ear: the hammer, the anvil and the stirrup. Try imagining a blacksmith hammering at a stirrup on his anvil. Then you can either place it within a huge ear or just make the link with the ear by making it really noisy. Dyslexic students are frequently brilliant at coming up with associations like this.

Recap

This section introduces a range of strategies all aimed at utilising and developing the visualising skills that imagers, and many dyslexic people automatically possess and use. Educators should:

- encourage students to create documentaries in their minds for any subject
- turn concept maps into pictures
- generate keywords and link these words with images
- develop 'umbrella' concepts in a range of subjects and express these as images
- help students to interact with the text and provide visual markers for verbally presented information.

Getting information out – modes of expression: oral and written

Whenever possible, find visual ways for students to present their information. They could, for example, compile a poster display or make a video film.

Oral presentations

Oral presentations may well be challenging for imagers. They may have difficulty with word finding, particularly when put on the spot. For people with dyslexia, their problems with concentration and short-term memory can mean that they get lost and forget what they want to say. In a more informal discussion it will be important for them to establish beforehand what points they really must get across in case the conversation moves off into unexpected areas. Dyslexic people are unlikely to organise themselves automatically; so there are ways in which they can be taught to develop these oral skills:

- Ensure that they plan their presentation carefully. They could prepare a large colourful visual mind map or numbered storyboard of the whole thing for their own reference and tape this to a table.
- Some students like to work with the support of numbered cue cards, each with a separate symbol to jog their memory. These can also include reminders as to when illustrations need to be produced. It is important that these cards are not cluttered and that the student practises using them so that they don't get dropped at the wrong moment. In a more informal discussion, they can write the main points they need to express and then refer to the card at the end to make sure nothing has been left out. This can actually give an impressive air of efficiency!
- In a more sophisticated presentation, this cue-card summary can be produced for the whole audience on an overhead projector or computer projection. This will benefit the dyslexic and usually goes down really well with the imagers in the audience who will think that the student has done this for their benefit rather than his or her own! If the presentation is being graded, this is usually seen as evidence of excellent audience awareness and worth lots of extra marks!

- Many students can find that structuring their presentation around a series of visual aids gives them the support they need to talk fluently.
- Reducing anxiety. The best way of reducing anxiety is to be really well prepared! Try to give students the opportunity to practise their talks with feedback from supportive friends until they feel confident.

As is suggested earlier in the chapter, visualising themselves going through the activity successfully is an excellent way for to dyslexic students to get to grips with their anxiety. It is helpful to experience the fear and to visualise themselves passing through that fear to a successful conclusion.

> I have trouble word-finding, and, as far as I understand, the reason is that when I first think of a thing I see a picture of it and the picture suffices for the internal explanation of the thing I have in mind. I know what it is, there's no deficit there, I merely have to translate that knowledge into language, which involves a long-term memory seek. A bit like doing a search on a slow hard disk really. My Mum and I used to communicate about a plethora of thingummies and whatsits because she was as bad as me at it. (Lawrence Arnold, dyslexic video student)

Bartlett and Moody (2000) give a range of helpful ideas for dyslexic adults coming to grips with oral presentations. They also suggest that dyslexic students should check the way they actually speak to avoid the kind of aggressive mannerisms that often spring from anxiety. They provide suggestions for assertive speaking:

- neither too loud nor too soft
- steady, even pace
- regular eye contact but not a fixed glare
- open relaxed facial expression or expression matching words
- short pause between sentences but no overlong pauses
- use of assertive statements such as: 'I'd like...', 'My view is...'

It is well worth giving people this kind of training in oral presentations at school or college. These strategies will be useful throughout their working lives.

Writing

Imagers may be either wholists or analysts. Either way, dyslexic imagers will benefit from the use of writing frames in either a wholistic or sequential form. (See chapters 7 and 8 'modes of presentation' sections). The only real difference is likely to be that they'll find visual cues, diagrams or even pictures more useful than words. Reid (1994) provides some excellent examples of using visual representations tied in with mnemonic devices to develop sequencing skills. Figure 8.9 presents a storyboard for Mad Sid the swan. This is also a very visual approach. Imagers may well find it comparatively easy to structure a text with this kind of support. The area where they may well have difficulty is in finding the words and detail to expand their outline into a convincing extended piece. Everything seems very flat and uninteresting. They need a bit of 3D!

The 3D technique was introduced by Mason (1990) as an adjunct to her work on story chains. The three Ds are:

- Detail
- Dialogue
- Description

All English teachers have their own favourite ways of encouraging their students to flesh their writing out; this chapter therefore only contains two suggestions, both of which were demonstrated on inset courses and both of which have been particularly successful with dyslexic students. The first is a technique for using the senses and guided visualisation to produce detail and atmosphere within a writing frame. The second big-sheet cut-and-paste technique provides a way of expanding a first draft.

Using the senses

Students usually find this fun and produce descriptive writing with a minimum of pain. Strong imagers are often particularly good.

Here is how to do it:

1. Each student divides a sheet of paper up until it looks like Figure 9.4 (this is a fishbone structure).

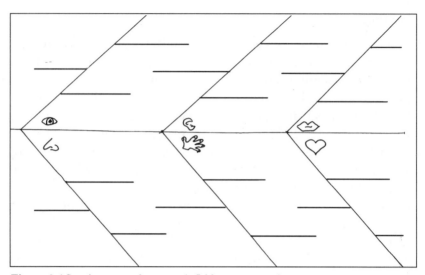

Figure 9.4 Starting to use the senses (a fishbone structure).

2. They draw in the symbol for each of the senses and the heart for feelings.
3. On the line at the left they write the name of a place and a mood, for example the *graveyard at night, scary*.
4. They must then visualise the graveyard. On each line of the eye rib they write one thing they can see in their graveyard.
5. When they have finished this, move on to the ear. Listen to the sounds around you. Write what you hear on each line of the ear rib.
6. They carry on to do this for each sense, finishing with their emotions on the heart.
7. The students then share their ideas with each other in whatever way seems best.
8. Some students will inevitably still be producing nouns and be low on adjectives. This is now the chance to take them back to their graveyard and ask them to think about the details. You saw a tree? Was it in leaf or bare? Was it tall? Was it stunted? By the time they have fleshed these pictures out, the frame will look a bit like Figure 9.5.
9. They now have a writing frame to take away and work on to produce a complete description. It is sometimes interesting to take contrasting situations, such as the beach in high summer or mid-winter, and create a frame for each to savour the contrasts.

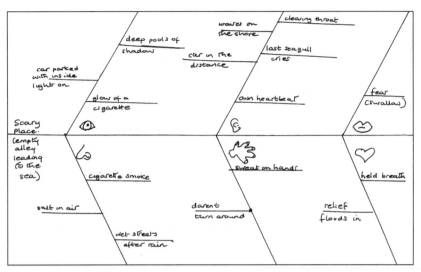

Figure 9.5 Senses frame.

The cut-and-paste technique

Despite using writing frames successfully, imagers can frequently end up with a complete but very short first draft. At this stage the big-sheet technique can give the writer a break and produce a bit of extra inspiration. It's very simple.

1. Go through the draft with the student and divide it into paragraphs if it isn't already done.
2. Take a sheet of A3 paper, portrait or landscape depending on how long the first draft is.
3. Glue the draft onto the middle of the A3 sheet so that it looks like Figure 9.6.
4. Go through the text paragraph by paragraph using question words or 3D techniques to add extra detail, which you write in note form onto the A3 sheet linking each extra idea to the appropriate section of the original.

This technique works well for some dyslexic learners. It is a separate activity from the first draft with a set procedure the student can follow. It provides measurable results and what is, in effect, an expanded frame for the final draft.

The finished draft will look something like Figure 9.7.

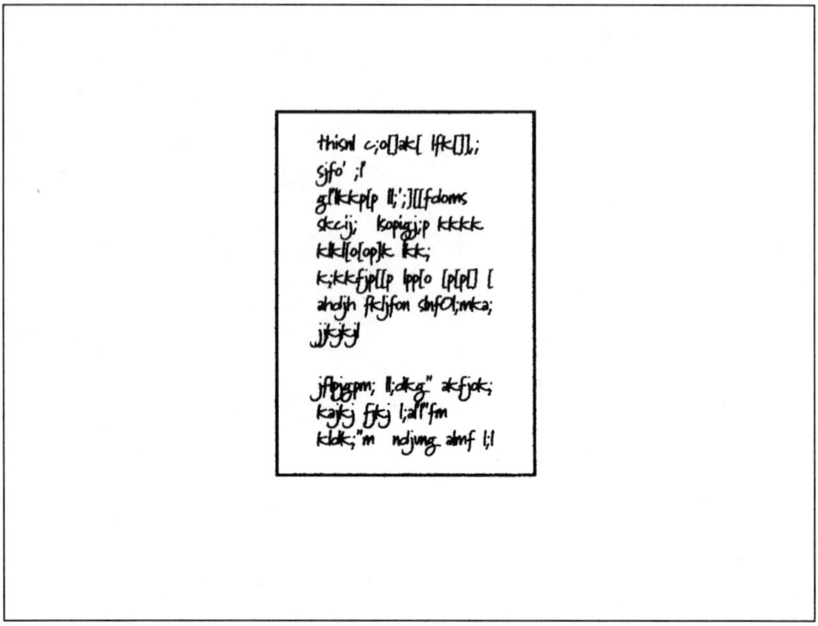

Figure 9.6 Starting cut and paste.

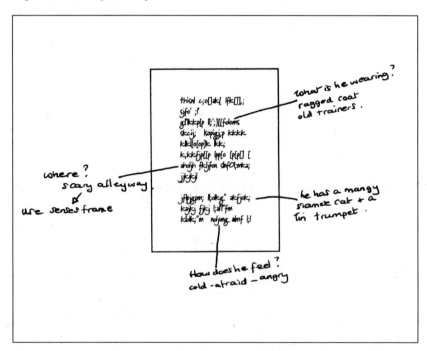

Figure 9.7 Finished cut and paste.

Recap

This section provides ways of supporting imagers with both oral and written tasks.

For oral tasks, educators should reduce stress levels by providing much opportunity for visual reinforcement and practice.

For written tasks, help students to use more visual frames and to build in detail and description by using the senses.

Examination and revision techniques for imagers

Understanding exam keywords

It is essential that students are really clear about the precise meaning of key terms used in examination questions. Bearing in mind that many dyslexic candidates have difficulties with language, the precise meanings of these should be discussed explicitly, rather than taken for granted. For example, to **compare** two things a student must look at each one's qualities and see in what way they are similar or different. As suggested before, these words should be identified as keywords and then they can often help to form the skeleton of an answer plan. A list of test vocabulary is provided here:

Test vocabulary

argue	give reasons
circle	grammar
circle the best answer	identify
compare	illustrate
complete	interpret
comprehension	investigate
conduct	issue
context	justify
contrast	list
criticise	multiple choice
define/definition	opposite
describe	outline
differences/similarities	punctuate

differentiate	relate
discuss	select
distinguish	source
draw up a table	state
evaluate	summarise
explain	trace
fill in the blank	true or false
give evidence to support	underline
vocabulary	

Use keywords and link them with images

Most dyslexic students are likely to find memorising for examinations difficult. Here, along with imagers, they should be encouraged to use keywords and images across the curriculum. The ideal approach for them is one that combines the use of a small number of concepts as 'umbrellas' for related ideas with vivid ways of fixing these concepts into the memory. Visual learners will welcome support in using images to 'fix' ideas.

Buzan and Coleman (1998) have produced a highly recommended series of GCSE study books for a range of set literature texts that illustrate this process effectively. For example, they will take the main characters from a text and allocate them symbols that epitomise their role in the text. So, Lennie in John Steinbeck's novel *Of Mice and Men* could be represented by a rabbit, which suggests both his love of soft things, the secret dream he shares with his companion George, the way George controls him and so on. The discussion itself of the choice of an appropriate image for a character sums up a range of issues associated with that character and the future use of an agreed image will remind the student of these issues as an almost subconscious revision strategy. This technique is not only confined to characters within a text but is also used for themes. Friendship and misuse of power are among the major themes in this novel. Friendship could be symbolised by clasped hands, two smiling heads together – misuse of power by a whip or a boot. Again the discussion of suitable images helps to establish the nature of friendship or power. It is sometimes difficult to decide whether to allow individual students to keep their own images or to insist on uniformity within the group. The advantage gained from a student personalising images has to be weighed up against the advantage of having common images for group revision work. Important literary devices, such as plot structure, setting, language style, can have symbols attached either as cues to remind students to mention them in exam situations or as reference points in the text to enable students to locate examples. With these it is probably more useful to have agreed common images set by the teacher.

All these images can be used within either a wholistic concept map or the analytic sequential structure of a time-line, list, family tree (see chapter 10) or storyboard. Students can often help themselves to remember complex sequences like the events in one of Shakespeare's plays with the minimum of writing. The advantage also of this is that an imager will be able to use a snapshot of the whole board or map in the mind's eye to capture the content in memory later.

When it comes to revision, these symbols are invaluable for a number of purposes:

- when devising and revising concept maps as plans for exam type answers
- for memory aids in the examination itself. Students can swiftly draw the symbols on a piece of rough paper at the start of the exam to focus their attention upon the core of the book and its themes

Buzan and Coleman's books are not the only literature study-support books that use visual techniques. The ILEA series (1990) also offers a range of more visually based activities that are particularly helpful to imagers. Buzan and Coleman, however, focus upon organising information into manageable chunks for examination purposes and then apply mind-mapping and visualising techniques to this in a way that can then be applied to other texts and subjects.

This process is applied here to English literature, but it is obviously equally effective with other subject areas especially where concepts may be wordy and can be summed up visually in a way that cues in to information stored in the student's memory.

Figure 9.8 is an example of using visual symbols in the form of a mind map to collect information for an exam answer.

Question: who would you consider most to blame for the tragedy of Eva Smith? Use the events from the play to back your answer.

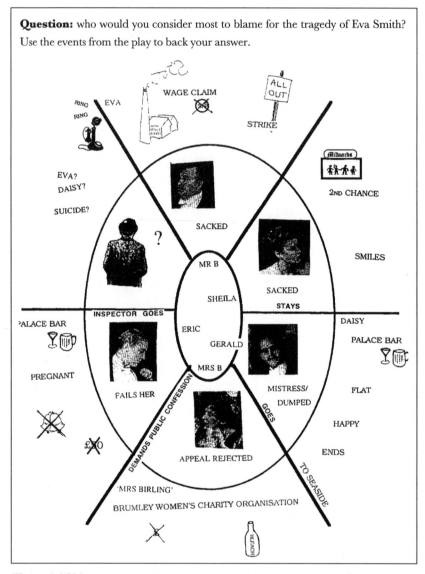

Figure 9.8 Using a concept map to prepare an answer to an exam question.

Earlier in this chapter Buzan's work books are introduced. These encourage students to select keywords from topic areas and associate them with images. They can then be incorporated into mind maps. These keyword images are obviously equally useful in an examination situation where a quick plan has to be compiled either for writing or for supporting answers dictated to an amanuensis. Students can jot images down onto rough paper or onto the question paper next to key concepts in the questions. Chapter 7 looks in more detail at the use of concept maps with amanuenses.

Here is an illustration of the strengths of a dyslexic imager:

Lucy, aged 12, has just been bought a self-assembly cabin bed. Her mother was about to assemble it from the written instructions when she was called away. On her return the bed was up, and Lucy was on it. She had simply looked at the illustration on the box, automatically disregarded the written instructions and built her self-assembly cabin bed perfectly from the picture she had in her mind's eye. Lucy, however, had enormous difficulties when it came to writing up practical tasks for science or design and technology in school or when it came to explaining how she did things.

Spelling techniques for imagers

Introduction

How difficult is English spelling?

> My spelling is wobbly ... It's good spelling, but it wobbles.
> (Winnie the Pooh, Milne 1926)

A simple but clear way of looking at English spelling is that it is a mixture of:

* words that follow phonologic rules, such as 'brave', 'dentist' and 'point'
* words that follow orthographic rules to do with word building from affixes or word origins
* words that do not, at first glance, follow these rules and need to be learnt almost as icons or pictures

This is very simplistic and may well cause problems to some spelling experts. However, the purpose of this book is not to get embroiled in debates about spelling. It is aimed at students of secondary-school age and above and so attempts to suggest ways of compensating for spelling difficulties rather than systematic ways of building spelling skills. By the time a student enters a GCSE course, the pressure is on to absorb and use information. Time for building spelling for spelling's sake is strictly limited and many dyslexic students have had enough. It is essential that they should be happy with a range of spelling supports, such as dictionaries, spell checkers, computer programs and helpful friends and relatives. Any time remaining for focusing upon spelling needs to be directed towards the most essential words. These will be a range of essential sight words, agreed with the student:

- Those on the common sight word list (see Appendix 4). These words look so deceptively simple – a child of 7 should surely be able to spell these! Look again at words like 'have', 'are', 'one'; a cursory glance will reveal that the majority of them are phonically irregular words which cannot be sounded out. This therefore makes them very hard for anyone with a weak visual memory for words. It can, however, be desperately embarrassing to be caught out making mistakes with these.
- Words connected with the individual, for example addresses.
- Words that must be spelt correctly for specific subjects either for accuracy of information in a scientific or practical subject or, arguably, to prevent the writer from looking stupid in subjects such as English literature, for example *Shakespeare, character* and *scene.*

These words will, of course, consist of a mixture of phonically regular and irregular words. They will be single-syllable and multi-syllable. It is likely to help any student to analyse the make up of a word they are trying to spell, and there is a range of excellent books available to do this. Many of these books also help the student to extrapolate from one word they are studying to a family of similar words. A few books that have been particularly useful will be found in the further reading section at the end of this book. The more students engage with words they are attempting to learn to spell, the more thorough the processing will be and the more likely they are to be retained. But what is the most successful way for any student, dyslexic or non-dyslexic, to process spelling target words?

Some research suggests (Mortimore 1995, Brooks and Weeks 1998, 1999) that students with literacy difficulties tend to be more successful when using their strongest channel to learn spelling. There are a range of ways that seem at first glance to draw more either upon verbal/auditory modes or upon visual processing, but it is, in fact, hard to be certain exactly what type of processing is really going on when students attempt to learn to spell. A seemingly visual mode of presentation may in fact be being processed in a multi-sensory way involving simultaneous letter naming or sounding. The students themselves may not be totally aware of how they are doing it. The most successful approach seems to be, yet again, to offer practice in a range of techniques and see what works best. The useful DFEE research report on individual styles in learning to spell (Brooks and Weeks 1998) provides a wide range of style-based methods and suggests weekly trials with each one to discover each child's most successful approach.

Image-based techniques

Here are some techniques that seem to be more image based. All techniques suggested have been successful for someone! The most widely successful are presented first. An important general point for dyslexic students is that it is useful to establish at the start how many words each student will attempt. Many individuals with severe dyslexia will struggle with more than three or four words in a set. Totals can sometimes be increased by ensuring that the words are part of a closely related family, for example: *war, warm, ward, warn, warning*, etc.

With all these techniques, it seems that, for dyslexic individuals, much of the success lies in regular daily practice between tests. Topping (1992), the pioneer of the concept of paired reading and other peer tutoring practices, suggests that the idea of children supporting each other is well-suited to spelling. It also has extra social advantages, such as boosting self-esteem.

Here is Topping's nine-step process a version of simultaneous oral spelling.

1. read word – together and alone
2. choose cues (visual or verbal) for the word
3. say cues together
4. speller says cues, helper writes the word
5. helper says cues, speller writes the word.
6. speller says cues and writes word
7. speller writes word fast
8. speller reads word
9. at end of each session, speller writes all words fast and goes through the steps again for each error

These following points seem to be very important.

- helper must cover each try
- speller checks own try
- if try is wrong, do previous step again
- helper must praise!

The following methods are all individual rather than paired:

Look – Cover – Write – Check

1. look at each word carefully – (about ten seconds)
2. cover the word
3. write word out
4. check back with the original spelling and underline any mistakes for extra care

This can also be done on a computer – typing the word out without looking at the screen.

Words within words

Some students have real difficulty working from sound and find it easier to examine a word visually to chunk it into smaller words, for example *im-port-ant*. They may then use visual links, such as a bottle of port or an ant to fix it in their minds. It sometimes helps them to pronounce words exactly as they are written, for example Fe *bruary* with the accompanying image of the pint of beer! All students should be encouraged to look at words really carefully to examine how they are put together and pick up on both areas that they get wrong, which can be highlighted in different colours, or for cues to help with memory, for example h*ear* with your *ear* – w*hat* a *hat*!

Neuro-linguistic programming/visualisation

The first time this technique is used it will need some visualisation work.

1. Ask the student to imagine his/her house and see it in the mind's eye. How many windows are there? What colour are they painted? What shape are they? What colour is the front door?
2. Observe where the student looks while visualising. This will

indicate his/her spontaneous way of visualising images in the mind's eye:
These two steps are only used to establish the visualising direction the first time that the technique is tried.

3. The student now picks a word to learn, for example *because.*
4. Divide it into syllables *be-cause.*
5. Look in the same direction as when visualising the house.
6. Hold the first syllable in the mind's eye until it is really clear. Colour it – *be.*
7. Say the letters forwards.
8. Say the letters backwards.
9. Write the letters with your eyes closed.
10. Do the same for the second syllable – *cause.*
11. Put the syllables together to make the whole word – *because.*
12. See it.
13. Say the letters forwards.
14. Say them backwards.
15. Say them forwards and write the word with your eyes closed.

There are variations on this that omit the forwards/backwards letter naming or substitute writing the word on a large piece of card and holding it in the student's visualisation direction for seeing it in the mind's eye. They all may seem rather cumbersome but do seem to work well for some students.

Visual delay

This process can be recorded onto a tape so that the student can use it independently or it can be used by a class with the teacher leading them. It can be used with up to 15 words, but many dyslexic students prefer to work with much smaller numbers. The students choose their words and either the students or the teacher writes them on a pile of cards. The students make sure they can read all their words fluently. They turn them face down on the table. They then follow this process for each word.

The teacher says:

1. 'Over': the student turns the card over and looks carefully at the word – five seconds

2. 'Cover': turn the card over and 'see' the word clearly
3. **After 15 seconds** – 'Write': the student writes the word
4. 'Check': the student checks the word with the original and focuses on any errors

At the end of the session students should try to write as many words from memory as they can. It seems to be important that the students should do each word twice. As each one takes about half a minute, it is up to the teacher to work out how many words to work on. Daily practice, weekly testing and provision of a new list have been very effective for some dyslexic students. These are particularly good ways of working with common irregular words. Some practitioners advocate using short phrases rather than single words.

Visual mnemonics

Some students find these helpful for a few really important words. There are lots of old favourites using acronyms of the letters that cause problems.
*suc*cessful dressing involves two *c*ollars and two *s*ocks!
The door's blocked *because* *b*ig *e*lephants *c*an't *a*lways *u*se small *e*ntrances.
Again this is a technique that only appeals to some who usually like to devise their own mnemonics. Other see it as merely adding more detail to remember.
As with all the suggestions, try it and see.

Chapter summary

Not all dyslexic people are naturally imagers. Some use this pathway by default.

Anyone can be helped to visualise and can benefit from exploring this method of making learning more real. This section introduces a range of strategies all aimed at utilising and developing visualising skills.

The key to this section has to be: picture this. Train your mind's eye and value its skills.

To help imagers and many dyslexic students take information in, educators should:

- Use visual presentations – film, diagram, symbols.
- Reinforce verbal presentations with visual cues whenever practical.
- Keep visual presentations uncluttered. Break them into chunks visually with colours, lines or boxes.
- Be alert for signs of physical eye strain.
- Help students to try out resources, such as coloured overlays.

To help imagers and many dyslexic students process and store information, educators should:

- Encourage students to create documentaries in their minds for any subject.
- Turn concept maps into pictures.
- Generate keywords and link these words with images.
- Develop 'umbrella' concepts in a range of subjects and express these as images.
- Help students to interact with text and to provide visual markers for verbally presented information.

To support imagers with both oral and written tasks, educators should:

- Reduce stress levels in oral situations by providing much opportunity for visual reinforcement and practice.
- For written tasks, they can help students to use more visual frames and to build in detail and description by using the senses.

The chapter also introduces the structure of English spelling and describes some more visual ways of learning to spell.

Chapter 10 provides strategies to support verbalisers and to help them develop their ability to use words.

CHAPTER 10

Verbal strategies

Introduction: The power of the word

This chapter introduces a range of strategies that can be used either to complement the style of the verbal or auditory learner or to help develop these skills. Why might it be important to develop auditory skills? Two reasons stand out:

It has already been suggested that a high proportion of secondary-school material, particularly in language-orientated subjects, tends to be presented to the auditory-verbal mode. Wood's (1988) research into how children learn also suggests that skilled silent readers translate visual material into subvocal language when memorising and that, by the age of 16, skilled readers recall more from written information than visual modes, such as video.

Verbal learners are likely to be comfortable with presentation through the auditory-verbal mode, but imagers and many dyslexic learners may find themselves at a disadvantage. It must not, however, be taken for granted that dyslexic people will automatically fall into this group.

> I love playing with the words and juggling with the meanings – it fires me up. (Max, 18, dyslexic poet)
>
> I've never been able to read very well because of my dyslexia. But I heard a lot of poetry when I was growing up, particularly at the church my parents went to. I would learn from Jamaican records and street poets. I used to love rhyme and music. (Benjamin Zephaniah, writer, *Dyslexia Contact* May 2000)

A significant group of dyslexic learners will be verbalisers. Many dyslexic students are marked out by the discrepancy between their verbal dexterity and their literacy skills. Some of these may also not suffer from the more usual memory problems. For example, Nicholas Parsons, the radio and TV presenter, stated in *Dyslexia Contact*:

> Dyslexic people are usually blessed with good memories and excellent recall. It has certainly been my survival kit in coping with the disadvantages and handicap that come with the inability to read at normal speed. My ability in this respect is way below average, but what is committed to memory is way above. (*Dyslexia Contact* May 2000)

Teaching and learning strategies to help verbal learners

This three-part section corresponds with the three stages of learning:

Getting the information in   –   modes of presentation
Processing the information   –   storing and revising
Getting the information out   –   modes of expression

Strategies for getting information in – modes of presentation

> My tutors on the Dip HE noticed that I was very audile. They advised me to do my essay plans on a Dictaphone. It helps me structure my work, whereas before there was no structure to my work because of the difficulty I had getting it onto paper. I also tape my lectures because of the difficulty in taking notes. It enables me to go back and listen to the tape so I can improve my notes. (Alex Hawthorne, dyslexic research student)

Verbalisers use **sound**; they respond strongly to words. They will therefore want written or spoken information along with action, demonstration or images. It seems that they recall abstract, acoustically complex, unfamiliar text better than concrete, highly visual, descriptive text (Riding and Calvey 1981). They will prefer the teacher to talk through what they are demonstrating and will like to put their experience or learning into words as soon as possible after it has taken place. Asking a verbaliser to help explain a process to a neighbour will be helping both students in different ways.

Studies have shown that verbalisers tend to read better than imagers (Riding 1998). Many verbalisers may well prefer to be given references and written information and asked to research or study independently. Dyslexic verbalisers, however, often find that their laborious reading prevents access to the printed medium that they find most useful. There are a number of ways around this, all of which involve using the voice:

- working from taped material provided by others
- taking a Dictaphone into a lesson or lecture and listening to it later rather than trying to make notes at the time
- recording any television or radio programmes and listening again
- reading text aloud to themselves
- working with partners to talk their way through new information or prepare brief presentations to other groups
- forming discussion groups for revision and projects
- creating their own revision material or notes on a high quality recorder such as the ARROW machine[1]
- using a text-to-voice software programme. Text-to-voice software offers an enormous advantage to non-dyslexic verbalisers and all dyslexic students. There are some very good systems around. Keystone or textHelp both read text aloud from the computer screen and can be used in a range of ways. Here are some suggestions:
    a) enable dyslexic students to hear what they have written and decide if it makes sense
    b) enable students to listen to and alter spelling attempts before spell-checking
    c) enable students to read text that has been downloaded from sources such as CD Roms or the internet
    d) reading e-books, for example any classics that are out of print can be downloaded into a text-to-voice program from: http://promo. net/pg/index.html; Listening Books is an easy to operate talking books library

---

[1]ARROW, an acronym for Aural-Read-Respond-Oral-Written, is a multi-sensory approach to teaching information and skills central to speaking, spelling and listening. It is based upon research results showing that children learnt spelling more successfully from their own voices than those of others (Lane 1992). Thus students listen or read information, record it onto a high-quality tape machine, listen to the fact, stop the tape, repeat the fact and then write it. The most useful machines also have an echo facility whereby the student can easily echo information several times to reinforce it. Auditory spellers are likely to find this a successful strategy for learning common sight words. Many students find that this is also a highly successful way of learning to read new vocabulary or information as they can use their tape on a regular daily basis to learn lists of words or facts until they are secure.

e) reading material that has been scanned onto the computer from any text using a scanner. (This can be anything from complete books to pieces of the student's own notes. Kurzweil 3000 is a useful scanning system. It also provides spell-checking and work-prediction facilities with text spoken and tracked by colour. The further reading section at the end of this book contains further information about other software and sources of advice or help.)

All these methods help students to compensate for laborious reading. There are, however, other ways in which verbalisers can capitalise on their facility with words. These include the following:

- Students can be encouraged to talk through what they are actually doing *as they do it.*
- Students can be encouraged to explain what they have learned to each other.
- Use role play and drama; with younger children, use actions as well as language while making connections and telling stories.
- Students can be encouraged to articulate what they are about to write. Some students like to tape their ideas before writing anything. This can then be used to generate a mind map choosing the most comfortable structure.
- Use pairs and partners to generate suggestions, discuss texts or problems before writing and compare ideas.

Recap

Verbalisers are likely to prefer listening and talking as a means of gathering information. However, this may disadvantage dyslexic readers; so a range of ways of presenting information verbally needs to be available. This can include:

- oral work of all kinds
- use of hardware and IT

Strategies for processing, storing and revising

Like imagers, verbalisers will tend to prefer either wholistic or sequential ways of storing information. Any of the processing techniques suggested for wholists or analytics may be useful to verbal learners, depending on their position on the wholistic-analytic scale. Unlike imagers, their preferred medium will be words. They are quite likely to be happy with a mind map but will tend to label mind maps and use keywords to trigger concepts and sequences. Much of this section will focus upon ways of developing vocabulary and using words to structure and process.

It is useful if teachers are aware of their own tendencies, as these are likely to be reflected in the ways they present information and the language that they use. Verbalisers need to be given the opportunity to put information into their own choice of words. They tend to recall semantically complex material better than highly visual, descriptive and imaginable material. As discussed frequently, encouraging students to transform information across modes will be useful, particularly to encourage the non-complementary analytic-verbalisers whose ability to visualise the whole picture may be seriously limited. A study by Riding and Dyer (1980) suggests that, while imagers (unlike verbalisers) generate images spontaneously without conscious effort, verbalisers can generate images if consciously encouraged to do so. It adds to the flexibility of their learning if they are reminded of this approach.

This should be remembered when utilising concept maps with verbalisers. They will get as much benefit as imagers from the use of concept maps as advance organisers and note-taking strategies. However, for verbalisers, the identification and use of keywords when taking notes helps to unearth the underlying skeleton structure that the writer has used to get the ideas across. When reading text to collect notes, they can highlight keywords or, if listening, they can write them down either randomly or in whatever shape suits them. They can then organise them into a structure.

Students can start off by being given keywords and then, after reading or listening to the relevant information, asked to develop them into a family-tree structure, which gives the main points of the topic. Figure 10.1 is an example of this family-tree structure. They can be helped by using questions such as: What do they do? Where do they come from?

To enable verbalisers to get the most out of their preferred mode, it is essential to help to build the necessary vocabulary.

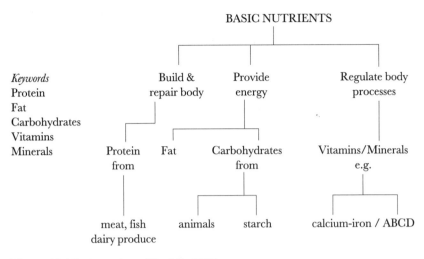

Figure 10.1 Basic nutrients (Hamblin 1981).

Subject teachers who do not consistently work with students with learning difficulties sometimes underestimate both the language difficulties their mainstream students may have and the wide-ranging effect this can have on their attitudes and actions. Some of the trying behaviour teachers have to deal with may well be masking underlying problems with language. The 'Speech and language difficulties' section in the further reading section at the end of this book provides insights into this area. There is also a growing body of evidence that many dyslexic students also suffer from language deficits. Any teacher working as a SENCO or to support dyslexic students should, as a priority, ensure that other members of staff are aware of any students with this hidden difficulty, how it can affect classroom interactions and where to go for support for these students and themselves. Staff are generally very aware of students with major learning difficulties, but this is a subtle area that can go unrecognised.

By the time students begin GCSE exam courses, it is arguably too late to spend time working individually on general language development. Most of the work must of necessity go on within the general classroom; so it is important that all teachers are made aware of the need to introduce and define subject-specific vocabulary. They should ideally also be aware of any students for whom language may be a problem so that they can carry out simple support measures for them such as:

- asking them to repeat important instructions back to the teacher or a study partner
- providing written instructions for any tasks that have to be performed independently
- providing access to lists of vital subject vocabulary both prior to and during the topic so that they have the words to place within whatever structures they use to help organise their learning
- working through any test or instruction vocabulary, for example 'compare', 'define', 'distinguish'. (A list is provided later in the chapter.)

Many teachers do actually report that these measures have helped improve performance, not just for less academically able groups but also in some of their most able classes!

Most English teachers will have a range of successful strategies for building vocabulary. Some of the most useful are those employed when building word association for creative writing and poetry. Games such as starting with one word and each student in turn providing the first word they can think of, brainstorming words on a large sheet of paper from a central word or object, comparing unlikely word associations or giving a group an object like a brick and getting them to find as many associations as they can. These are all common within English class-rooms and are an invaluable way of using the stronger members of a group to enrich those whose vocabulary is impoverished.

Some teachers have the luxury of working individually to develop language and vocabulary with students at this late stage, even if it is only for a short, weekly session. It is really important to kill as many birds with one stone as possible. For example:

- When working through more advanced structured reading schemes, such as Units of Sound Levels 2 and 3 (Bramley 1975), be sure to work to check knowledge of word meanings as well as decoding. Any oral activities, such as 'find the word in the list that means … is the opposite of …' both helps the student to use semantic knowledge to put down traces of the word in memory, practises skimming skills and also extends vocabulary. You can also deal with word categories and relationships in a similarly informal way. 'This word is "lorry". What other types of transport can you think of?'

- If a dyslexic student is working to improve decoding skills, it is crucial to liaise with a subject teacher to obtain a list of relevant vocabulary both to practise with and to define. Alternatively, look at general examination vocabulary or even specific subject test papers.
- When working to improve reading fluency, sections from relevant course texts can be used.

It is not sufficient to introduce new vocabulary; the student must retain it and be able to use it. The most recent research suggests that a three-pronged attack is the most successful:

1. A student should define the new word.
2. A student should count and say the syllables.
3. A students should identify and say the first sound.

This means that the student has established traces for this new word in the three-most-common types of word identification stored in the lexicon – *meaning, phonological pattern* or *initial sound.*

It is really useful for any secondary-support teacher to build up a store of subject-specific vocabulary, ideally in conjunction with subject teachers. Copies of standard textbooks in use or the revision guides provided by the examination boards are a helpful source. Finding out which topics are being taught at what stage in the school year is ideal, but not always realistic. There is, however, no substitute for liaison with subject teachers. Mainstream school life is so pressured that some subject teachers, with the best intentions, can see the special needs of students in their groups as an implicit criticism of their repertoire of teaching strategies. These teachers need to see support staff as useful allies who will lighten their load rather than increase it.

For some dyslexic students, simply having the opportunity to go over the topics that they have been taught that week makes an enormous difference to retention and confidence. It doesn't matter if the support teacher's knowledge of chemistry stopped at the end of primary school! Students are frequently delighted to find that someone who seems so competent in some areas has, like them, great gaps in others. It also focuses their attention on the gaps in their own knowledge that need to be plugged. Their task for the week can be to ask their subject teacher to answer these questions so that they can tell you. By the time they have done this, they should remember it!

Semantic and content mapping are both excellent techniques that combine vocabulary building with using words to predict and organise. They are, therefore, a particularly useful approach for verbalisers. They do, however, provide support for both verbal and visual learners and are useful exercises, which work on several levels:

- For a student with a limited vocabulary, they provide the chance to extend vocabulary and check understanding of concepts.
- For the articulate verbaliser, they are types of advanced organisers or ways of preparing a student for a topic.
- For the analytic verbaliser who may have problems seeing links and transferring knowledge from one content area to another they can be used to bridge areas within a topic. For example, if students are studying Victorian England, looking at scientific inventions, art projects and social conditions, a semantic map can be drawn up to show how each section relates to the central idea of the whole topic – Figure 10.2 shows a semantic map drawn up for the topic 'Victorian England'.

Heimlich and Pittelman (1986) provide an excellent introduction to this approach, which was originally suggested by the schema theorists Johnson and Pearson (1984) as part of their work aimed at improving reading comprehension.

A semantic map is very similar to the kind of concept map described in chapter 7 and is prepared in the same way. It is, however, nearly always used as a classwork tool, either as preparation for a topic or as a study technique to design a map of content information from a text. When used as preparation for studying a topic, the following steps can be followed:

1. The classwork topic is written on the board.
2. The students collect individual rough lists of all the words they can think of related to the topic.

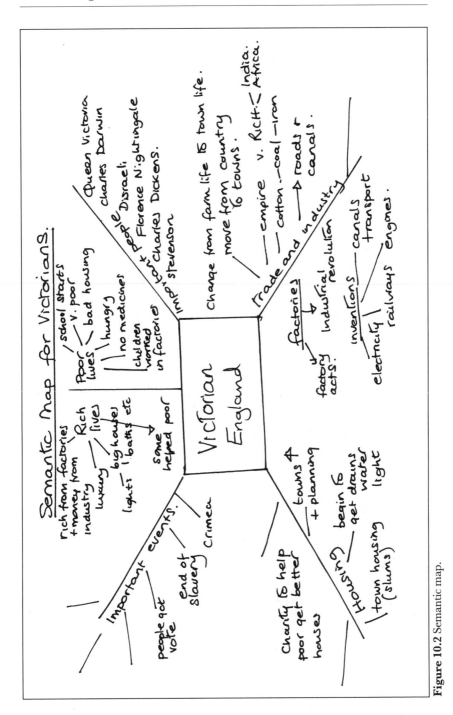

Figure 10.2 Semantic map.

3. Word lists are shared orally, and all words are written on the class concept map as <u>categories</u>. This gives students practice in classification. It is up to the teacher whether categories are provided prior to writing the words on the board or if students are asked to work out categories as they go.
4. Discussion of the map is probably the most valuable part of the exercise. It provides new words plus meanings, shows further meanings for old words, allows students to see relationships and gives much opportunity for expressive language use. It also gives the teacher some idea of the level of prior knowledge within the class.

This technique can obviously be integrated into the SQ section of the SQ3R technique described in chapter 7.

A <u>content map</u> is similar to Levy's concept mapping from chapter 7. The difference from a semantic map is that it is used for processing material already gained either from text or other modes of study rather than generating material. It is a three-staged strategy that divides information into three categories: main idea, secondary categories and supporting details. It is a three-stage process:

1. Identify main idea, write it in the centre of the paper. Draw up to six lines radiating out.
2. Skim read or listen to/watch text to find the second category headings. Write them on the lines.
3. Try to remember as many details or facts as possible for each of the categories. Add them to the maps.

After this stage a range of activities can take place depending upon the purpose of the map. It is always useful, however, for a group to share their individual maps and create a group map that can then either be reproduced for everyone or else individuals can augment their own. These maps will tend to be verbal in that they will utilise language rather than visual symbols. They also give much opportunity for language building.

Figure 10.3 shows an example of a content map.

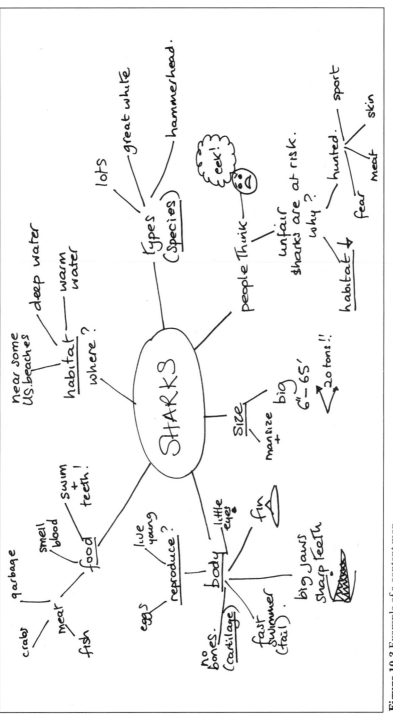

Figure 10.3 Example of a content map.

Recap

Verbalisers will find word-based information easier to deal with than descriptive, visual material. They will need practice converting material into this mode. Their concept maps will use words rather than images. Do not take it for granted that all verbalisers will be articulate and good with language! Some students become verbalisers due to a combination of the response to the predominant teaching style in secondary schools and their difficulties with visualising. Many verbalisers may need help with vocabulary building to enable them to take advantage of their preferred mode.

Semantic or content mapping is an effective way of simultaneously providing structure and new vocabulary. All students can benefit from being helped to develop and use vocabulary – particularly vocabulary that is relevant to specific subjects. Forging a supportive relationship with mainstream-subject teachers will be of enormous value to everyone.

Strategies for getting information out – creating text, writing frames for verbalisers

Verbalisers may need as much help as visualisers in organising their written work. They will prefer to work from mind maps or more sequential frames according to where they fall upon the Wholistic-Analytic continuum. They will, however, tend to prefer working with words to working with images. Some students, dyslexic and non-dyslexic alike, seem to have been dealt the proverbial double whammy. They may have problems with auditory processing, yet their visual difficulties are far worse! (A checklist for visual processing difficulties is provided in appendix 3.) They frequently end up as verbalisers by default. These verbalising students may well need unexpected help. They may be depending upon words as their learning mode, yet suffering from an impoverished vocabulary, both for receptive and expressive language. They will frequently have difficulties not just with understanding and generating subject vocabulary but also with the kind of vocabulary that can move them on from one stage in a piece of writing to the next. This is also a way of helping students who tend to get stuck in the middle of a piece.

There is more detail about providing writing frames in chapter 7, based on the Lewis and Wray model. They provide not only frames for the different types of writing but also selections of phrases that can move students through the creation of a piece of text. Students whose knowledge of word meanings is quite extensive find the more abstract, structure-creating words – such as prepositions – very hard. Providing a range of these in addition to a frame gives students a model for future use, which will stand them in good stead throughout their academic career and beyond. In fact, one of the current GCSE grade criteria includes use of such words and phrases.

Here is a non-exhaustive list of suggestions for text structuring phrases:

STARTERS

- To begin with...
- Although not everyone would agree, I want to argue that...
- I have several reasons for this point of view. My first reason is...
- I think that...
- You will need...
- First you...
- I want to explain why...
- There are different reasons why...
- There are differing explanation as to why/what/how...
- I would like to suggest that...
- There are several reasons why...
- Before I ..., I thought that...
- To begin with...
- It starts by...

CONNECTIVES

- moreover
- although
- on the other hand
- as a result
- a further point they make is
- a further reason is

- in addition to these points
- because
- furthermore
- first
- next
- therefore

ENDINGS

- My conclusion is...
- Finally...
- Consequently...
- I think I have shown that...
- These facts/arguments show that...
- So now you can see why...
- Despite any arguments to the contrary, I believe...
- Bearing all this in mind, I have decided/come to the conclusion that...
- Despite all the evidence I would argue that...
- As a result...

Figure 10.4 is an example of a comparison grid using a range of phrases.

Here is another list of conjunctions and prepositions and time words that sometimes cause problems both for writing and for listening.

CONJUNCTIONS

if	for	since	unless	yet	while	because	
and	that	until	whether	but	when	though	although

PREPOSITIONS

aboard	behind	from	through	about	below	in	above	
beneath	into	to	across	beside	near	towards	between	
of	under	against	beyond	off	along	by	on	up
among	down	opposite	upon	around	over	with	at	
except	past	within	for					

Time words

before	after	at	during	between	past
since	until	till	to	about	beyond

GCSE COURSEWORK
WIDE READING

**What do different writer think the future will be like?
Compare different versions.**

(Using a comparison Grid)

	Ray Bradbury	H.G. Wells The Time Machine
Opening	Both____and _____ write about the future. In some ways their visions are similar but there are some major differences...	
People	In____, Bradbury gives us a picture of ...	H.G. Wells's people also... but they are different in that they...and...
Houses and Food	Both the... and the ... live comfortable lives. But everything else about them is different. For example (1.) ... Also (2)	while ...
Is it a good society?	Neither society is particularly good. Bradbury thinks ...	Wells feels that...
Your opinion?	This society is good. In some ways	There are also good points about
Good		
Bad	However.	Wells also...
Sum up		

Figure 10.4 Example of a comparison grid.

Marks (1998) provides more. This is a highly practical handbook of suggestions for helping mainstream students cope with a range of speech and language disorders. It also includes lists of test-vocabulary terms and textbook language.

Verbalisers are as likely as imagers to use writing frames successfully. They are simply more likely to use words than pictures while planning them.

Recap

Both verbalisers and imagers will benefit from the use of frames.

Some verbalisers and dyslexic learners will need help generating the words or phrases that connect parts of a text. Providing these or sentence starters for transition points will help the writing to flow.

Voice-recognition software or voice-activated systems (VAS) – talking to computers

Voice-recognition software is arguably as useful to imagers as verbalisers. However, it has been placed within the verbalising chapter as it is dependent upon a student's ability to generate verbal information, which is then processed by the computer.

What are voice-activated systems or VAS?

A voice-activated system uses voice-recognition (VR) technology. Through the installation of a sound card into the computer, people can speak to their computers, and the speech will be converted into text on the screen. It was not originally designed for dyslexic people, more for business use. However, many people with dyslexia have found it liberating. There are two forms of software:

- continuous speech; this is where the speaker can speak at a natural pace
- discrete or spaced speech; for this the speaker needs to pronounce each word separately with a short but deliberate pause after each

word, rather like dictating to a secretary. Experience has found that this version is more successful with dyslexic students as it helps them to focus upon the writing. The more modern computer programs use continuous speech but can be adapted to operate in the discrete mode.

For dyslexic users it has been found to be essential that the computer program is run in conjunction with a screen reader which reads the words as they appear on the screen so that the user can be sure that the text corresponds with their spoken words.

Use of a VAS can provide a real breakthrough for dyslexic students, particularly for older students at secondary or further education level, but they are not a panacea, and there are some drawbacks:

- All speech-recognition computer programs have to be trained to respond correctly to the user's voice.
- Experience has proved that the further a user's voice deviates from an adult-male standard English voice, the longer the training will take. Thus girls, younger boys or people with strong regional accents will have more difficulty in making the machine produce the words they want.
- Ideally, students should be trained and supported by somebody who is an expert user and who is available to offer support over a period of time, as the computer program starts by introducing a limited amount of vocabulary and builds up over time.
- Impulsive students will frequently become impatient that they are not getting perfect results immediately. VAS can then easily become yet another tool that has failed, confirming the student's impression that he or she is hopeless!
- In a school environment, background noise can be a problem as can be ensuring that children's personal voice files do not get overwritten by other users. These are, however, management problems that should be solvable.

Overall, those students who have mastered the use of VAS find that it is well worth the effort and is particularly useful for producing coursework and essays at GCSE and higher-education levels.

VAS is a particularly useful tool for strong verbalisers, who are happy working orally with words since, when working properly, it is like having your own mechanical amanuensis. For others, who are less spontaneously fluent, it is a good way to proofread uncorrected drafts, providing they can read their own work easily. There is no danger that they will forget ideas if they are already captured in rough. Students who find it hard to generate ideas using VAS often find it very helpful at the proofreading stage.

What programs are the most user-friendly?

Cotgrove (2000) supplies a helpful rundown on the available systems and the hardware required to run them successfully.

The Dragon Systems, including Dragon Dictate, classic discrete speech and Dragon Naturally Speaking, have all been used widely and successfully with dyslexic students. The iANSYST web pages at www.dyslexic.com provide a regularly updated review of developments as well as useful resources, such as the Earlswood School training routines.

For checking the accuracy of text as it appears on the screen, the most effective echo-back system is Keystone supplied with Dragon Dictate by Aptech (World Wide Sounds) of Newcastle.

BECTa is also evaluating ways of using VAS. Results and a range of helpful suggestions can be found on their website at www.becta.org.us/inclusion/speechrecog/userforum/index.cfm/.

Developing phonological awareness

This section applies to both verbalisers and imagers with dyslexia, but it is included in this chapter as the strategies suggested involve sound and verbalising. A common weakness for a large proportion of dyslexic people, both verbalisers and imagers, lies in the area of phonological processing. (This is a well-researched area and much is available in terms of phonological assessment instruments and programs to develop phonologic skills. For further information see work by Snowling and Stackhouse (1996) and suggestions in the further reading section at the end of this book.)

Although many individuals with dyslexia are often extremely adept with the semantics or vocabulary of language, even dyslexic verbalisers may well have problems with processing and remembering sound patterns for reading, spelling or memorising. These students can often be identified by their extreme low scores on non-word reading tests. These are tests where students are asked to decode non-words, for example:

- dut
- threep
- gonplat

To do this successfully, they have to rely upon phonologic knowledge, both of letter-sound links and syllable patterning, rather than visual memory. Phonologically disordered individuals with dyslexia will score many years below their chronological age. The Graded Non-word Reading Test (Snowling et al., 1996) provides an age-related baseline assessment. Another rough way of assessing whether students are relying upon visual or phonological cues for reading is to ask them to read a series of sentences, including homophones, and to state if they are correct. For example:

- To ride on a train, you must pay a fair.
- He put his hand through the pain of glass.
- The child loved his teddy bare.

Students who make errors with these are likely to have poor phonological-analysis skills.

Verbalisers with dyslexia will be likely to respond well to the verbal strategies described in this section. They may, however, suffer from a range of phonological weaknesses including:

- weak auditory memory for words
- poor discrimination between similar words and sounds
- poor linkage between sound and symbol both when reading and spelling (this obviously exacerbates spelling problems when the dyslexic also suffers from a weak visual memory and therefore has to rely upon phonological spelling skills)
- inability to develop the phonological decoding skills that allow unknown words to be identified through their letter patterns
- problems with accessing the right word from similar-sounding words when generating talk or writing.

There is also the possibility that some dyslexic students may be verbalisers by default due to the lack either of stronger visual pathways or the encouragement to use the visual mode. The following questions are often asked:

- If a dyslexic student suffers from poor phonological processing skills, should time be spent attempting to develop these skills?
- Would it not be more realistic to attempt to build compensatory visual or kinesthetic approaches?

The answer is that this must depend upon the age and goals of the student. If it does seem a priority to develop phonological awareness, there are a range of well-researched and tested phonological assessment and development programs available. Several chapters in Hulme and Snowling's (1997) collection of papers from the BDA International Conference discuss a range of approaches. One example of an assessment battery is the PhAB or Phonological Assessment Battery (Frederikson 1995); Sound Linkage: An Integrated Programme for Overcoming Reading Difficulties (Hatcher 1994) is a reliable system for developing phonological awareness. The Lindamood (1997) approach with its emphasis on sensory feedback is also interesting. These programmes do demand, however, considerable hours of study and practice. The present book is aimed mainly at students at secondary school and above, whose education time is running out. Is it worth spending precious time on the possibly unsuccessful task of developing phonological awareness in dyslexic people who have so many other demands upon their time?

I am dyslexic and therefore a creative speller. (Thelma Good, theatre critic)

Using phonological awareness to improve proofreading skills

Dyslexic spelling is one of the most difficult skills to improve. Later in the chapter some suggestions for helping verbalisers to improve sight-word spelling appear. In general, however, by the time a student embarks upon GCSE courses there is insufficient time and frequently zero motivation to follow spelling courses. It is really a case of providing compensatory strategies and encouraging students to hone their proofreading skills. As described earlier, dyslexic students should always be encouraged to produce written work in three stages:

brainstorm ━━━▶ writing frame ━━━▶ text

Because it is hard for them to focus both on ideas and accuracy, it is suggested that they do not worry about accuracy of punctuation or spelling until they have produced a rough draft of the text. Some students feel very uncomfortable relying upon their own spelling efforts, even at this early stage. For these, it is best simply to give them the spellings they ask for as quickly as possible so that they are not distracted from the flow of ideas. Once they have produced what is, in effect, an ideas' draft, a decision has to be made. Do they always need to go through the stage of producing a neat copy? For many non-dyslexic and virtually all dyslexic students, the production of an error-free neat copy is really onerous. It is a secretarial task, and it is boring. For the dyslexic individual, however, it can represent hours of tedious work, at the end of which there will still be errors glaringly obvious to anyone but the writer.

There has to be a really good reason for putting a severely dyslexic writer through this activity regularly. Although giving practice in proofreading techniques, it is highly unlikely to improve general spelling skills in any measurable way. It is far more constructive for the student to choose to proofread a piece of work thoroughly for a special purpose. It could be a piece of work for a coursework folder or a display. In this case there is a really good incentive to get the work as error-free as possible.

How should the student go about it? There are a range of possibilities. These include:

- using a computer spell checker
- using a dictionary
- using voice-recognition software

Why is phonological training relevant here? If a writer does not have a strong mental image or picture of the spelling of a word, it will cause difficulties. Research suggests that naturally good spellers store visual images of words in their mental lexicon, which they then gain access to instantly. They know if words 'look' right and often use the strategy of writing alternative spellings to select the correct one. The majority of dyslexic learners, even those who seem to have visual strengths, are unable to do this with more than the most basic sight vocabulary. They are thrown back onto using the sounds within words – or *phonemes* and attempt to represent words from appropriate letter strings – or *graphemes*. Dyslexic writers with reasonable auditory and phonological skills may thus end up with spelling that is logical and readable but wrong. For example:

> Thay sor the flars in the gardn.

This is unlikely to cause a reader major difficulties and likewise will probably not defeat any of the more phonically based computer or hand-held spell checkers available. However, write it like this:

> The sa the frs in the grdun

and things won't be so easy! Whether the writer is using a dictionary or electronic support, it is important to be able to isolate sounds within words and produce logical, recognisable spelling. Some dyslexic students with that level of spelling difficulty would be able to read their work; others wouldn't. For them, arguably, the world of predictive software (details of which are given in the further reading section at the end of this book) is probably one solution. For everyone attempting independently to proofread text, the development of the ability to isolate and represent sounds must be a priority.

A practical approach to developing phonological awareness

There is a range of multi-sensory programmes for developing spelling. Reid's handbook *Specific Learning Difficulties* (1994) provides a useful overview. The focus in this chapter, however, is on a less-familiar approach, that of the THRASS (Teaching Handwriting, Reading and Spelling Skills) system devised by Davies (1992). This programme arguably has some drawbacks for teaching dyslexic students with poor visual memory for letter patterns in words, in that they will find choosing the 'correct' spelling from a range of phonic alternatives virtually impossible. However, it can be effectively adapted to help build the phonological skills to support proofreading skills. It is particularly useful for the following reasons:

- It turns the concept that one letter represents one sound on its head.
- It suggests that the English language consists of 44 phonemes or sounds, and that spelling consists of finding the most likely grapheme, or letter string, to represent each sound. There are 120 common graphemes.
- It provides the 44 sounds in the form of a box chart. Each box represents one phoneme and shows the most common graphemes for that phoneme.
- This chart can be reduced to easily carried pocket size and used as a resource to build words from their phonemes. Alternatively, it can be taped to the wall beside each computer terminal.

The program provides a range of ways of listening to, segmenting, learning and practising the phonemes correctly, which builds phonological discrimination. It also provides a CD Rom for practising the phonemes independently and in a multi-sensory way. This is a useful tool for helping to build a range of phonological skills. Phono-Graphix (McGuinness 1998) is another system which follows the same principle that written words are made up of sound pictures that represent individual sounds.

It can be used to develop proofreading skills in the following way. Many dyslexic students have real difficulty hearing sound in words and therefore representing these words in text. This is one way to help. There are three lines of attack:

1. Help students to separate out or segment the different sounds within words, for example *hedge* has three sounds or phonemes: *h – e –* and *j*. It is <u>essential</u> that the intrusive voiced schwa *ur* is not included in unvoiced phonemes such as *h*. *Hedge* is not pronounced *hurejur*!
2. Teach students the 44 voiced and unvoiced phonemes in a multi-sensory way. Davies and Lane provide a rap tape that some students enjoy. For many dyslexic learners, the most effective method is to feel the sensations and analyse the parts of the mouth

used to make each phoneme. For some students only the difference between movements they feel within their mouths between different sounds can help them distinguish them. For example *f* is made by grabbing your *bottom lip* between your front teeth and blowing. To make *th* grip your *tongue* between your teeth and blow. To feel the difference between unvoiced *p* and voiced *b* stick your finger on your voice box and feel the buzz come and go. Lindamood and Lindamood (1997) suggest systematic ways of doing this.

3. Students need to be very familiar with the location of the phonemes on the THRASS chart if they are to locate them quickly enough to prevent frustration. It is, therefore, vital to work physically and kinesthetically with the chart. (This also has the effect of focusing attention and reinforcing the multi-sensory element of the activity.) The THRASS CD Rom also provides reinforcement.

These three strands must run concurrently. Ideally, students should have had the opportunity to try out this approach and become familiar with the support at the earliest possible time in secondary education if they are not to feel patronised. They should also be shown how it can be helpful in practice as soon as practicably possible. One suggested way is to:

1. Practise counting the phonemes in words right from the beginning, ensuring that the schwa is eliminated. Some individuals with dyslexia will find this very hard to start with but should improve with practice and encouragement.

2. As soon as the students are able to start to navigate the THRASS chart, provide them with regular practice with phonemic segmentation charts (Figure 10.5). For this practice the students listen to a word and count the phonemes (a). They then use their THRASS chart to attempt the spelling, ensuring that they have the right number of phonemes (b). They then feed their attempt into some sort of spell checker and write the corrected response (c).

3. It is often really useful to provide a group with some carefully selected words to try out with spell checkers so that they can find out for themselves how much more likely a spell checker is to

Word	Number of phonemes	Attempt	Checked
brick	4	b r i c	brick
catch	3	k a c h	catch

Figure 10.5 Phonemic segmentation chart.

come up with the word they want once they have got their spelling attempt as close as possible to a phonic alternative.

4. Encourage students to develop the habit of counting the phonemes in any words they need to spell. It can be useful to have a written task that needs proofreading on the go so that they can get used to the idea that, when they ask for help with a spelling, the teacher will not provide the spelling but support them through the process of phonemic segmentation and their building the word with the THRASS chart. Those who find this approach helpful will start to internalise the process for independent use. They may even encourage others who are slower to pick it up! Those who try valiantly and hate it are going to need a different strategy.

Developing phonological awareness is helpful for proofreading in three of the main approaches: either using a dictionary, computer or hand-held electronic spell checker.

Electronic spell checkers

Students are often really tempted to put their work through a computer spell checker before attempting to improve the accuracy of the spelling. They see this as a short cut to accuracy, despite advice to the contrary! A nasty but often effective way of proving the point is to allow some poor soul to put a piece of work through an automatic computer spell checker without improving the spelling attempts and then to read the perfectly spelled gibberish that the computer will offer (having kept a copy of the original, of course!).

Here is the computer spell checker's version of a section of a piece of GCSE media coursework discussing the direction of a scene from a film version of *Romeo and Juliet*:

> I wooed not have woolsack in the back grown. I wood still keep the heavy berthing. Romeo and Mercutio wood have a mainly huge and Tybalt's fruition that hey is gown to get bet so he grabs peas of glass and runs at him.

Any coursework marker unfamiliar with dyslexic-style spelling would be likely to struggle to locate the ideas in this. It is often less confusing to deal with non-words than to be sent off down the wrong track by the meaning of substituted words. The text should have read:

> I would not have music in the background. I would still keep the heavy breathing. Romeo and Mercutio would have a manly hug, and Tybalt's frightened that he is going to get beaten; so he grabs [a] piece of glass and runs at him.

These points would gain marks; arguably the earlier version might not!

When using electronic spell checkers of any sort, being able to produce a readable, reasonably logical/phonic misspelling will reduce failure and frustration. It will not, of course, improve the spelling-age-related score in any official spelling test! There is, in fact, no test-related way of presenting evidence of improvement in readability of spelling, which is a shame, as it is a major achievement for many dyslexic students.

Dictionaries

Using a standard dictionary is often hard for dyslexic students, even if they are fairly competent readers. A student with a poor visual memory for words will have trouble trying to find any word with ambiguous initial sounds. For example, *about* sounds as if it starts with *u* or *ur* and *prepare* sounds like *pri*-pare.

The standard alphabetic English dictionary is not organised upon phonic lines, but there are alternative sound-based dictionaries, such as the Aurally Coded English or ACE dictionary or the less-common consonant sound-based dictionary (Morrison 1987). In the ACE dictionary, words are grouped under sound categories into one-, two-, three- or more syllable-length columns. To be able to use this very helpful support, a writer must be able to isolate sounds.

Examination and revision techniques for verbalisers

> My spelling and reading were so poor, my short-term memory appalling. So I listened in lessons and developed my memory instead of writing notes. I didn't write during my A levels. I dictated essays to a secretary. (Billy Broadbent, dyslexic student at Leeds Metropolitan University, cited in Williams 1999)

Using an amanuensis

The verbaliser is arguably better adapted to the exam situation than the imager who may well dry up in the face of an examination question. Dyslexic candidates can apply for an amanuensis, and this should be particularly helpful to verbalisers. They must be given the opportunity to practise, and they must be in the habit of using a plan to structure their answers. Chapter 8 explores working with amanuenses.

Examination language

Chapter 7 introduces the use of keywords for structuring examination answers.

Don't forget that many students, including some verbalisers, have difficulty with interpreting examination terminology. Working through definitions and practising a range of anticipated test terms for any subject area can be really helpful to both dyslexic and non-dyslexic students. Obviously, it helps dyslexic learners if these words are practised until they are part of their sight-reading vocabulary. Even dyslexic students with exam concessions can end up simply with 25% extra time so any way of speeding up their processing of exam tasks must be worthwhile. Here is a list of general test and examination vocabulary. It is obviously useful for individual subject areas to compile their own and to pass their lists on to the SENCO (Special Educational Needs Co-ordinator) in the school.

List of keywords for examination questions

compare	contrast	criticise
define	describe	discuss
distinguish	differentiate	evaluate
explain	illustrate	interpret
justify	outline	relate
state	summarise	trace

Spelling techniques for verbalisers

A range of basic general points are made in chapter 9, which briefly discusses:

- the nature of English spelling
- how much spelling is essential
- research support for matching learning style with spelling technique

The main conclusion is that the most successful approach is to offer practice in a range of techniques and see what works best. Brooks and Weeks's (1999) DFEE research report provides a wide range of style-based methods and suggests weekly trials with each one to discover each child's most successful approach. Chapter 9 provides a range of proven techniques that seem to be more image based, with the most widely successful presented first. This chapter focuses on the use of sound. Small whiteboards are highly recommended for use in working on spelling words.

Using THRASS to refine phonemic awareness

General practice with THRASS has already been described. It can, of course, be applied to learning lists of words. The students should follow the process described in this chapter:

1. count phonemes
2. use the THRASS chart to build the word
3. check the correct spelling and try to visualise the shape
4. use the phonemic knowledge to build the word each time they practise it

Onset-rime technique

Spell out the word using plastic or wooden letters or letters written on cards. Break up the words into onset-rime, for example *plate* has the sounds *pl – ate*. *Dentist* has the sounds *d – en/ t - ist*.

Move the letters as you spilt the word. Move them back together as you say the whole word. Students can also write the whole word as they say it.

Own-voice technique

The student writes the spelling list. Then using his or her own voice and, ideally, a high-quality tape recorder that has an echo-replay facility the child records the whole word on tape, spells the individual letter names and then repeats the whole word:

$$plate - \underline{p} \; \underline{l} \; \underline{a} \; \underline{t} \; \underline{e} \; plate$$

The important aspect of this technique seems to be regular practice of the words so that the child can echo and re-echo the words, ideally writing the word after each repetition. Dyslexic students should be given a copy of the word list and their own tape so that they can go through the words daily before the next test.

Simultaneous oral spelling (Bradley 1994)

The student writes the spelling list. The teacher then writes each word correctly, saying the letter name as it is written. The student then writes the word saying each letter's name as it is written. The student then says the whole word and checks it is correct against the teacher's. This can obviously be practised at home with a family member or at school with a friend.

Using rhythm and music to help with spelling

Some students find that spelling words to song tunes is really useful. Commercially produced tapes for common sight words are available, but it is usually more effective for students to make their own in the privacy of their own homes!

Using the computer

Computer systems using voice can be used in a range of ways too.

The Units of Sound System is now on a program for PCs and Imax. Students can read, highlight, listen and write. They can highlight, listen and then write. Students can use any read-back program to type words in and listen to the outcome, repeating until the words are all accurate. Programs such as 'My Words' and 'Write Out Loud' are useful for this. There are some commercially produced programs that are useful, but few of these offer the leeway for students to compile their own lists.

The advantage of using tape recorders or computers is that students can work independently to reinforce their spellings after initial support from a teacher or classroom assistant. With all these techniques, it seems that, for dyslexic spellers, much of the success lies in regular daily practice between tests. Topping (1992), the pioneer of the concept of paired-reading and other peer-tutoring practices, suggests that the idea of children supporting each other is well-suited to spelling. It also has extra social advantages, such as boosting self-esteem.

Here is Topping's nine-step process, a version of simultaneous oral spelling:

1. read word – together and alone
2. choose cues (visual or verbal) for the word
3. say cues together
4. speller says cues, helper writes the word
5. helper says cues, speller writes the word
6. speller says cues and writes word
7. speller writes word fast
8. speller reads word
9. at end of each session, speller writes all words fast and goes through the steps again for each error

The following points seem to be very important.

• helper must cover each try
• speller checks own try
• if try is wrong, do previous step again
• helper must praise!

Recap

Choose number and nature of words to be learnt carefully.

Students should try out different techniques and choose their own.

Verbal learners are likely to have more success with verbal or sound-based techniques, but this should not be taken for granted!

Any techniques must be reinforced daily.

Use friends, relatives, classmates, IT and tape recorders or a Walkman to reinforce.

I don't know why that Johnson bloke bothered to put his dictionary together. Making spelling wrong or right just caused trouble for people like Shakespeere or Shaspeyr or Shakespeare or me. No one got at Shakespeare's manuscripts and stuck red ink all over his spelling. We're just more creative spellers, him and me! (Jake, dyslexic university student)

Chapter summary

There are a number of reasons why it is important to develop the verbal mode. A high proportion of teaching in secondary-school education tends to be verbal, and all students will benefit from verbal skill. Some students with dyslexia are articulate, natural verbalisers; others are forced to use this pathway by default, despite experiencing difficulty with word finding or phonology.

Verbalisers respond more strongly to words. Students with dyslexia need to be given ways to compensate for difficulties with reading, vocabulary or phonological processing.

To help verbalisers take information in, educators should:

- use text or verbal presentations, but provide ways to get around reading difficulties such as use of tape, IT and a range of oral work with other students
- encourage students to articulate as they work

To help verbalisers process and store information, educators should:

- help students to use verbal concept maps
- use a range of methods to introduce and retain both general and subject-specific vocabulary
- use techniques such as semantic or content mapping to generate vocabulary and help students to structure verbal work

To support verbalisers with written tasks, educators should:

- help students to use verbal writing frames and grids
- provide a range of connective vocabulary plus sentence starters to take dyslexic writers from one stage of a text to another

This chapter also examines the use and scope of voice-activated software and ways of helping students to develop phonological awareness to enhance their spelling and proofreading skills.

It provides a range of more sound-based techniques for learning spelling.

Chapter 11 examines some ways to help students remember what they have learnt.

PART SIX
What Were Those Last Ten Chapters About?

CHAPTER 11

Helping students to remember

Introduction: Dyslexic students and memory

It could be claimed that this whole book is about memory, as it aims to help all students to use their strongest channels to interact with and experience or internalise information at a deeper, often more emotional level. There are, of course, many different types of memory. The most vivid and long-lasting tend to be sensory:

- visual – pictures in the mind
- auditory – sounds: how about 'our' tune?
- kinesthetic – linked with movement or feeling: the ability to ride a bicycle
- tactile – physical sensations
- taste – flavours: the tastes of our childhood
- smell – a particular scent can transport us back to another moment in time

Using these forms of memory should help any student, whatever the learning style.

The introduction to chapter 6 of this book provides a brief outline of current memory theory plus suggestions for further reading. It discusses the major difficulties dyslexic students can experience and suggests the most useful type of support. To reiterate:

Dyslexic students may well have difficulties in two areas of memory function: phonological processing and automatisation. There is some further suggestion that there may be difficulties in the 'organising' department – the central executive – and some evidence of a lack of confidence in their ability to retain facts.

257

They are likely, therefore, to need support in three fundamental areas:

- compensation for poor auditory or phonological skills
- the kind of support which will reduce the possibility of overload
- encouragement in the use of thinking strategies, such as:
    monitoring
    testing
    revising
    prediction
    planning
    evaluating

The strategies suggested throughout this book aim to:

- set the preconditions for learning – low stress, high motivation
- reduce the load on memory through structuring, condensing and chunking
- encourage students to interact in a range of ways with the material that they are learning
- make information memorable – **see** it, **hear** it or **be** it
- move from the concrete to the abstract
- use the power of the sensory memory

There is a range of books and computer programs available with the specific purpose of developing memory skills. Those included in the further reading section at the end of this book are highly recommended in that the activities outlined are both practical and fun.

Learning style and memory

The various strategies presented here and in the recommended sources are useful for all students, dyslexic and non-dyslexic alike. However, some are more visually based; some are more verbal. Some seem to add more information to be memorised along with the target facts, which may simply overload a vulnerable dyslexic. It is important to be aware of the style and strengths of the individual learners and to enable them to select the most comfortable methods.

As with other aspects of study, specific aims need to be clear. All methods can be tried out for different purposes, for example encouraging visualisers to use verbal strategies to enrich their skills allowing wholists to develop sequential abilities through the use of structured questioning techniques or giving analytics practice in developing big-picture frameworks.

Memorising or learning does not take place at a steady rate. Research into learning physical skills, such as typewriting, seems to indicate a four-stage process:

1. the introductory stage: little progress seems to be made because the student is unfamiliar with the activity
2. the student starts to make rapid progress
3. despite effort, no progress seems to be made

However, providing the student perseveres, this usually turns out to be a consolidating phase where, eventually:

4. progress again becomes rapid until a peak of expertise is reached

The message that this sends is that very little can be memorised instantly. Initial acquaintance with any information places it purely into the short-term memory where it is likely to decay within less than half a minute, unless reinforced. For example, pick a random number from a phone book, read it once trying consciously to remember it. Then write it down from memory. This may well be easy. However, now pick another number from the book; don't write it down, just leave it for five minutes and do something else. Will you then be able to remember either number? The answer is probably no. The first number had been processed sufficiently to stay in the short-term memory long enough to write it down. The second number then interfered with the traces of the first, eliminating it and, because nothing had been done to reinforce the second number, it had faded completely from the short-term memory by the time the number was needed. This example emphasises the two important features of memorising:

• process information
• to shift it into the long-term store, reinforce at regular intervals to prevent it from decaying or being displaced

It is also important to be aware of how the memory works so that reinforcement can be timed for maximum effect. Within 24 hours, 80% of the information learnt can be lost (Mitchell 1994). To transfer information from short-term memory to automatic long-term memory it must be reviewed regularly starting, ideally, before students forget what they have learnt. Mitchell suggests six reviews at intervals of:

- 5 minutes
- one day
- one week
- one month
- three months
- six months, by which time it should be in long-term memory

For students with memory difficulties, she suggests:

- 5 minutes
- one hour
- one day
- two days
- one week
- one month
- six months

Figure 11.1. shows a memory-strategy preference graph

Possible preferred modes of expression			
Text (1) Speech (2) Diagrams (2) Picture (3)	ANALYTIC VERBALISER	ANALYTIC IMAGER	Diagrams (1) Picture (2) Text (2) Speech (3)
Speech (1) Text (2) Picture (2) Diagrams (3)	WHOLIST VERBALISER	WHOLIST IMAGER	Picture (1) Diagrams (2) Speech (2) Text (3)

Figure 11.1 A memory-strategy preference graph adapted from Riding and Rayner (1998).

The keys to successful memorising seem to be **awareness** of style, **timing** and **variation of strategy**.

Making things easier to remember – key memory aids

Key memory aids

> I am a theatre reviewer these days so often have to order what I have seen and heard. Years of being dyslexic have developed a good memory for what I see and hear. I take some notes during the performance. Interestingly, I have bad short-term memory problems – i.e. I can't remember what I have just done, but I have good medium- and long-term memory. I have developed a skill as a minute writer over the years using my memory. (Thelma Good, theatre critic)

Many dyslexic students feel that they have lousy memories and fear that they will be unable to remember important information. They often do not realise that knowledgeable people do not necessarily need to have good memories. These people use sources when they need to find information and often keep references and notes. Only essential key points really need memorising. It is, however, true that some things seem much harder to remember than others. There are two important questions to answer here. What is it that makes some things easier to remember? How can we use this to make the hard things easier?

What is it that makes some things easier to remember? Think of something that you find easy to assimilate and recall. You will usually find that it scores high on the following factors:

- **understanding** – you are really on top of it or it is closely linked with real experience
- **relaxation** – you don't feel threatened by it – you are relaxed about it
- **motivation** – you want to remember it because you will use it
- **fun** – you enjoy learning about it

Whether it's learning to rock and roll or finding out about Formula One racing, these types of things seem to go in quickly and stay in place.

How can this be used to make the hard things easier? The obvious answer is to take a more difficult area and find ways of increasing the score on these factors. The first one, **understanding**, is arguably the most crucial. If you understand something, you immediately become more **relaxed** about it and can look around for ways of making it more **fun** or, at least, more distinctive – even if only through pairing up with a friend to keep each other awake. **Motivation** is a trickier one. It can be hard to get keen on a minor member of the nine or more examination subjects a 16-year-old student feels compelled to take. It is perhaps important at this point either to see it as part of a long-term goal to get on to a particular course or to attempt to imagine some situation where it might become crucial – impressing your new, glamorous French neighbour with your fluency in the language, perhaps!

Establishing understanding

Students must **reconstruct** information in order to understand it better. This is emphasised constantly throughout this book, and a range of cross-modal strategies is provided. Ways of linking information, either to a student's experience or to past knowledge, are also suggested:

- Link to experience by finding an example from experience of each point studied: in geology, where have you seen that rock formation? In English Literature, who does that character remind you of? Link to past knowledge by making a map of everything you can remember about the topic then add in the new information.

Topics should be linked and mapped and all inessential material should be cut out. For people with dyslexia in particular, it is vital to avoid overload and to provide them with clear, uncluttered material from which they can revise.

What makes material memorable?

Many study-skills books have used this activity, but it is well worth revisiting.

A list of twenty words follows. Time yourself; you have one minute to memorise as many as you can.

father
banana
Marilyn Monroe

tree
aluminium
and
ball
sex
because
violin
terrapin
ball
dangerous
fan
pencil
west
pillow
ball
blue
jellyfish

Now write down as many as you can. The order doesn't matter.
Compare your list with the original. It is likely that it will contain the
words 'sex' and 'Marilyn Monroe'.

Why? Because they stick out from the others as being different.
For the same reason you may have 'jellyfish' or 'aluminium'. You
may also have 'ball'. Why? Because it occurred three times. Your
other words are likely to be from the first or last five words in the
group. Bland little words from the middle like 'and' or 'because' are
likely to have been overlooked. This gives a good idea as to what
makes things memorable. Things need to:

- **stand out** – either because they are different or attention grabbing
- be **repeated**
- come from the **beginning** or the **end**

There are some simple ways of helping this process.

- To make things **stand out**, we can use association to create
  memorable cues. There are two ways of doing this: one is a very
  verbal strategy and will be dealt with in the section; the other is

more simple, multi-sensory and direct. Take a word like 'fan'. What do you think of? Do you think of a Japanese geisha with a beautiful fan? Do you think of a Liverpool supporter with a scarf? Do you think of a pop fan? Make a link with the strongest association and make it as visual or experiential as you can.

The images should be as dramatic, funny or disturbing as possible. We all remember the emotional and the unexpected. Literature students presented with an onion each while trying to understand why the onion should be a metaphor for love, discovered, among other things, that, like love, it will make you cry and that the memory (in this case the smell) lingers long after it has been taken away or lost. They also remember the shock on the faces of the unexpected visitors who found the classroom covered in onion skins and stinking of onion! These students now only have to conjure up the smell of an onion and they know exactly what to write in an exam question about the use of unexpected metaphors.

- It is easy to make a habit of **repeating** things.
- It is also easy to create more **beginnings** and **endings**. If the original twenty words had been chunked into groups of four, it is likely that more would have been remembered. This reminds us that not only does information need to be divided into bite-sized chunks but also study time benefits from being divided into manageable units with set targets for each section. Thirty minutes is probably long enough for most adults to be able to concentrate on revision. After that they need a break, probably to move about. Then they will be able to come back, **review what they learnt over the past half-hour session** and get started again; this creates more beginnings and endings.
- Another advantage of chunking items into groups is that it encourages a learner to make **associations** between things. Take 'father', 'banana', 'Marilyn Monroe' and 'tree'. Imagers can create all sorts of interesting pictures linking these items together! Verbalisers may find a quick anecdote springs to mind. Notice that one of the words is a **stand out** word. It often helps to have one of these as the focus for the others. There will be more suggestions as to the practical use of associations in the 'useful techniques' section.

Lists are, of course, not the only type of information that need to be memorised. Topics need to be internalised by interaction in the ways that are suggested in previous chapters. The memory rules described above obviously apply to learning lists but also have some use in topics. For example, topics can be divided up into subsections to provide more beginnings and endings. The student should focus on each subsection as though it is all that has to be learnt. Then, when confident, he or she should look back for links to previous sections and forward to the next. The final sections of both chapters 7 and 8 offer suggestions as to how students can personalise topic sections and strategies for learning them.

Obviously, at some point in exam preparation, dyslexic students will come up against the kind of learning they find hardest – a list of some sort that has to be memorised. It could be the four factors that speed up an electric motor, the seven main parties in the Weimar Republic or the order in which Shakespeare wrote his plays. This is where these memorable features and the techniques described next can be really helpful.

Recap

For dyslexic students, the aim is to reduce the load that will need processing and to allow individuals to select from a range of approaches the one that suits them best.

Remember:

- **understanding**
- **relaxation**
- **motivation**
- **fun**

Use: repetition, beginnings and endings, associations and the unexpected.

Useful techniques

None of these strategies is new. Many of the most creative were invented thousands of years ago by the Greeks and have passed the test of time. The fact that many of the suggestions are now validated by contemporary psychology is a testament to the insight of these thinkers.

The main thrust of the following techniques is to attempt to impose some type of linking structure upon the target items, or facts to be remembered, through the use of a range of types of association. Thus the student can learn a smaller number of more densely packed units. It is rather like providing a shopping basket for the brain's retrieval department. For dyslexic students, a principal aim must be to reduce the load on the memory, therefore any technique that seems to be suggesting they learn even more in the way of memory cues will be regarded with deep suspicion. Consequently, any such techniques have not been included unless proved valuable by experience.

Two main types of techniques are described: rules and structures. The first type of association involves developing an unchanging rule system that can then be linked imaginatively with the target information. The other type involves creating structures around the items to be remembered.

It is hard to know which system wholists or analytics might prefer. Arguably, a system involving logical sequences should appeal more to analytics, while a rule system building structures around a central point maybe more wholistic. As always, the only answer is to try both.

Similarly, while inferring that imagers are more likely to relate to visual techniques and that verbalisers are more likely to respond to words, it is not always easy to spot which technique appeals predominantly to one mode or the other, for two reasons. First of all, it is hard to pinpoint exactly what form of processing is involved in a complex task, such as memorising. Even if a student is creating verbal associations, there is no proof that the visualising process is not equally strongly involved. Secondly, the aim of any memorising technique is usually to process the information as thoroughly as possible, therefore students will be encouraged to engage all forms of sensory memory. However, certain students will be drawn more to one type of technique than another, and, arguably, this will be connected to their preferred learning style. It seems oversimplistic, therefore, to attempt to group the types of technique under umbrella terms such as 'verbal' or 'visual', although some attempt to distinguish between them has been made.

Rule systems

These types of systems attempt to set up an unchanging framework into which new target items can be slotted. The target items are linked with the unchanging frame through visual or verbal association in as

striking a way as possible. It is essential that students should be practised in creating associations. Some verbalising and visualising techniques are outlined in chapters 9 and 10. Two methods are described
here. The first seems more verbal:

1. The number/rhyme system
This system uses the numbers one to ten as the unchanging frame
but replaces the numbers with concrete objects, chosen by the
student, that rhyme with the number. For example:

one	gun
two	blue
three	tree
four	door
five	hive
six	bricks
seven	heaven
eight	plate
nine	wine
ten	men

So, if students have to remember three crops: rice, corn and apples,
they start with the word *gun* and the word *rice* and combine it in as
pictorial, absurd or rude way possible to create a vivid image. Maybe
they think of a gun firing rice puddings and then move on to 'blue'
corn and apple 'tree'. Imagers are likely to find creating a picture
and freezing it in the memory more successful. Verbalisers may find
a more anecdotal or verbal approach more helpful. Try this out with
a group with any list of words. Ask them to try to remember the
words without cues as a first timed trial then provide cues and see if
this improves memory. It usually does, which will give the students
an incentive to try it out for themselves.

2. The *loci* or *place* method
This was invented by the Greeks. It is a more visual, experiential
method. To use it the students need to think of a preferably unchanging place or route that they know inside out. It could be their room or
the walk to school. They need first of all to take themselves around this
route seeing everything very clearly. They then need to choose ten
clear objects from the route and write them down, numbering them

from one to ten. These objects/places need to be very clear in the mind's eye. The target items need to be associated with these things in a similar way as with the number /rhyme method. This needs to be done in the mind's eye, either through purely visualising these items in the places or on the objects or else through using absurd combinations. The key to success is, firstly, that the chosen objects are really firmly in the memory and, secondly, that the associated image is really vivid. This is an inventive method that often really appeals to dyslexic students whose imaginations are frequently wonderfully offbeat! It also uses long-term memory of a familiar environment rather than a list of cue words.

Creating structures **around the target items**

This approach takes the target items as the starting point and then builds them into an associative structure. Here are two methods: chains of association and using acronyms.

1. Creating a chain of association.
This is a sequential method that can be adapted to suit both visualisers and verbalisers. The aim is to create links between each item starting with the first in the list. It works best if the links are as absurd or visual as possible. So, if students have to remember a list of 15 vital survival items to take on an expedition starting with a knife, a compass and a pair of walking boots, they could imagine the knife cutting into a cake-sized compass with one slice marching off on little legs in a pair of walking boots. The rest can be built up in as surreal a way as possible and run through the mind several times.

Often it helps if the images can be built up into an actual story. Many science teachers have used this method to help students remember the order of the planets.

It is also possible to 'translate' more abstract ideas into physical events. For example, if a student was trying to remember the abstract themes contained within a novel – for example loneliness, power struggles, jealousy – these could be built into a short scenario.

Bartlett and Moody (2000) give a lovely example of the way to remember memory techniques such as **highlighting** keywords, using **spider diagrams** or making **associations**. They imagine an artist looking out on the neon-signs (**highlights**) of the city. He sees a **spider** drop on to his painting and remembers (**associations**) a film he had seen about tarantulas.

Verbalisers and imagers will obviously find the most comfortable way to do this. Wholists may prefer the neatness of a story to a chain of association.

2. Using *acronyms.*
These methods take the first letter of each target item and use it to make silly sentences. For example, to remember the colours of the spectrum – red, orange, yellow, green, blue, indigo and violet – one student made up the following sentence after going to watch a football match:

really 'orrible **y**obs **g**et **b**undled **i**nto **v**ans

complete with a mind's eye cartoon of a van with a rainbow on the side!

Using a word. This is great if the items make a useful word, particularly if the students can then use association to link it with the topic. Nonsense words aren't quite so helpful, particularly for dyslexic students with phonological processing problems. It is probably better to go for the silly sentence.

Any of these techniques should be used selectively for really crucial items. In some ways a student is being asked to memorise more. It is only going to be helpful for those who find the time taken to create imaginative and visual structures for memorising is repaid by the success of the method.

Chapter summary

For dyslexic students, it is crucial to:

- reduce overload
- interact with the material
- use the creative power of the imagination
- create structures or rules to organise the information to be memorised

Last words:
A caution

Nothing is as simple as it seems. The jury is still out over a number of issues discussed in this book and research is ongoing. Two of the most central are:

- Is learning style subject specific or universal? Diagnosing a learning style does not necessarily mean that a particular student will automatically operate in this way across all areas of learning.
- Are dyslexic students likely to favour a visual style of learning? Research evidence is still inconclusive.

The existence of these uncertainties means that it is probably unwise to attempt purely to cherry-pick the sections of this book that relate to the learning style which interests you. Learning is a fiercely complex process. Experience dictates that the most successful approach for dyslexic students is the multi-sensory route. Evidence for the existence of learning style preferences must suggest that multi-sensory approaches may also work for mainstream learners and that an over-concentration on talking and listening may be hampering their learning too. The techniques described should not be exclusively for dyslexic students. Two main priorities are emphasised throughout:

1. Learners need to be given the chance to develop awareness of their own learning strengths and the encouragement to take responsibility for using them.

2. Educators need to be aware of their priorities when presenting
   information. Are they aiming to teach subject material or to
   develop learning strategies? If the first, students should be
   encouraged to use the most comfortable mode. If the second,
   verbalisers should be encouraged to use the visual mode to activate the areas of the brain that generate images; wholists should
   be guided through more analytical procedures and so on.
   However, it is worth remembering that some dyslexic learners,
   contrary to expectation, feel overloaded by multi-sensory presentation. Being sensitive to the individual student's needs has to be
   the key.

Researchers suggest that the more we expand our repertoire of
learning skills, the more able we become to absorb and retain information. They warn us to 'use it or lose it'. Students of all types can
only benefit from being shown how.

Assessing the reading level of texts

The Fogg Index of Readability

Devised for journalists by Robert Gunning of the Robert Gunning Clear Writing Institute of Santa Barbara, California.

Take a sample piece of writing of about 150 words long.
Calculate the average number of words per sentence   (e.g. 12)
Count the number of words of three or more syllables   (e.g. 15)
Express this as a percentage of the whole   10%
Add average word number and percentage together   12 + 10 = 22
Divide by 2.5   8.8
So reading age = roughly 9 years.

This is obviously quite laborious, but familiarity will give you a 'sense' of how difficult a passage is. The *Guardian* and *The Times* are aimed at around 11 to 12

The *Daily Mail* is around 10. Research shows that 50% of readers get lost if a sentence exceeds 14 words (Rose 1993), and 80% lose it after 20 words.

Strategies for kinesthetic learners

These students are most successful when learning through experience or touch. Arguably, any younger child whose understanding of abstract concepts is still underdeveloped is going to appreciate the chance to learn in this way along with the other strategies that have been introduced. Some older dyslexic students also benefit from this:

> I gave the presentation on dyslexia as I wanted to give people an understanding of what dyslexia is and how it affects the child and their family. After the presentation, I was given feedback. I was asked why I use my hands when speaking and if I had been taught any sign language to aid my difficulty. The hand movement that is used seems to be a way of expressing my point of view and also helps me with my thought process. It seems that dyslexics could be using their hands as a compensatory adaptive strategy. A difficulty that some dyslexics have is with homophones. When looking at the signs for some of the homophones, we found that there was a difference between the signs and homophones. This meant that there was more of a distinction between the signs for 'there' and 'their'. I found that the signs have helped me focus on the individual words and helped me understand the meaning of the words. (Alexander Hawthorne, dyslexic research student who is hoping to carry out a research project into this area)

Kinesthetic learners prefer:

- To learn through hands and touch. The feel of wooden letters in a velvet bag may help them learn sounds/symbol links more effectively.
- Concrete action – let's build it first and **then** explain how. Do the experiment in science.

- Drama – use role play and improvisation to understand characters and situations in humanities.

Some may find using their hands to sign helps them retain information.

APPENDIX 1

Visual processing deficit checklist

Some types of dyslexia are more related to visual processing problems than phonological processing. Others combine the two. These are not the type of visual difficulties that are always picked up by routine eye tests. It is always worth discussing the possibility of visual processing difficulties with students. This checklist was devised by Melanie Jameson, quoted by Bartlett and Moody (2000), and has much in common with checklists provided by Holland for use by classroom teachers to establish if there might be a need for more in-depth screening.

See the website: www.essex.ac.uk/psychology/overlays

Have you been prescribed glasses?
Does reading make you tired?
Do you often lose your place when reading?
Do you reread or skip lines when reading?
Do you ever read words/numbers back to front?
Do you miss out words when reading?
Do you tend to misread words?
Do you use a marker or your finger to keep the place?
Are you easily distracted when reading?
Do you read for pleasure?
Do you get headaches when you read?
Do your eyes become sore or water?
Do you screw your eyes up when reading?
Do you read close to the page?
Do you push the page away?

Do you prefer dim light to bright light for reading?
Does white paper (or a whiteboard) seem to glare?
Does it all become harder the longer you read?
Does print become distorted as you read?

A common sight word list

a	could	had	may		under
about	cut	has	me	said	up
after		have	men	saw	upon
again	did	he	much	say	us
all	do	help	must	see	use
always	does	her	my	seven	very
am	done	here	myself	shall	
an	don't	him		she	
and	down	his	never	show	walk
any	draw	hold	new	sing	want
are	drink	hot	no	sit	warm
around		how	not	six	was
as	eat	hurt	now	sleep	wash
ask	eight			small	we
at	every	i	of	so	well
ate	exit	if	off	some	went
away		in	old	soon	were
	fall	into	on	start	what
be	far	is	once	stop	when
because	fast	it	one		where
been	find	its	only	take	which
before	first	it's	open	tell	white
best	five		or	ten	who
better	fly		our	thank	why
big	for	jump	over	that	will
black	found	just	own	the	wish
blue	four			their	with
both	from	keep	pick	them	work
boy	full	kind	play	then	would
bring	funny	know	please	there	write
brown			pretty	these	
but	gave	let	pull	they	yellow
by	get	light	put	think	yes
	give	like		this	you
call	go	little	ran	those	your
came	goes	live	read	three	
can	going	long	red	to	
carry	good	look	ride	today	
clean	got	made	right	too	
cold	green	make	round	try	
come	grow	many	run	two	

Case Studies

Jack and David

(Names have been changed)

1. JACK

Jack is introduced at the start of chapter one. Observing his behaviour and his pattern of strengths and weaknesses, it seemed clear that he was far more of an imager than a verbaliser, despite having no language problems. He also seemed to be more of a wholist than an analytic. Subsequently, his scores on the CSA revealed that he was indeed a wholistic imager. How does this tie in with his relative strengths and weaknesses?

- His strengths are his active practical mind; his inventiveness, his ability to visualise and to create visual representations, his ability to remember detail when really engaged and his willingness to experiment with ways of working in order to take responsibility for himself.
- His weaknesses are his unwillingness to verbalise or experiment with words, his inability to remember detail when reading or otherwise disengaged, his lack of confidence in his ability to write at any length and, obviously, his struggles with literacy and the effort he has to expend in this area.

What approaches have helped Jack?

It was clear that he needed ways to store information, particularly once he started being able to cope with longer texts.

He also needed support with planning his writing to encourage him to keep going. He found the following approaches effective.

1. He was taken through the Levy techniques (described in chapter 7) of selecting the main facts in any text or watched programme and mapping them. He then watched videos and used a whiteboard to create a brain-image. Spontaneously, he used the standard Buzan-style mind-map format and created icons and drawings to represent key points. Others in the group were very impressed with his maps. Next, he practised the same techniques while listening to information, following progressively more difficult and longer texts. He was consistently encouraged to visualise all information, preferably experiencing it. Success with this began to make him realise that his memory wasn't that bad after all when given the right props. This reduction in anxiety in its turn improved his recall. He was happy to apply this same technique to reading texts, taking a whiteboard or rough paper and stopping at frequent intervals to create a mind map. He then used his own 'notes' to confirm answers to comprehension questions, which meant that he seldom had to reread. If he did have to do so, his mind map gave him an idea of whereabouts in the text he might search.

2. He had no confidence in his ability to write. The first time he completed a 200-word story he was thrilled and disbelieving. He was shown the brainstorming techniques, which are summarised in chapter 7, but did not particularly warm to them. He also found the story chains unhelpful. He did, however, really take to Wray's writing frames and found that, once he had a basic set of paragraph headings, he was able to keep going and flesh out the paragraphs. Understandably, he didn't like working from a page with a lot of words on it. He preferred to have simple headings and generate his own information. Sometimes he prepared his writing frames on paper, sometime on the computer, leaving spaces to fill in with information. He always worked on computer, finding the word-prediction software 'Co-Writer' particularly helpful and using 'My Words' or 'Write Out Loud' to read his written text to him.

He continues to work to develop his use of vocabulary and is now prepared to attempt more complex words, particularly to describe activities or processes. He is reluctantly discovering that he can play with words.

The next step is likely to be the use of voice-recognition software to enable him to use some of the more complex vocabulary that he knows. He may also very well find, in time, that he begins to feel more comfortable with some of the approaches that he initially rejected.

Jack has been rewarded with real success. He spontaneously makes use of these techniques throughout his schoolwork and expects to continue to do so beyond school. Reading is still difficult for him; so he tends to use the talking books and click readers on the computer when he wants to enjoy a book and has read a wide range this way. He is looking forward to trying out the voice-recognition software and anticipates combining it with writing frames to produce more sophisticated work.

The techniques that have worked for him do seem to match his learning style in that he uses frames to provide structure both for writing and for recalling the content of texts. He also gravitates towards the visual mode. He is, however, a good oral presenter and will, no doubt, be a successful salesman of anything, such as the lazy mixer shown below, that he invents!

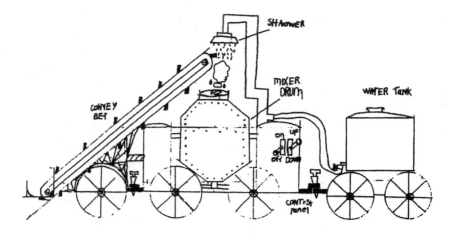

Figure A 5.1 The lazy mixer.

2. David

David's difficulties were rather different from Jack's. The highly articulate and intelligent son of a family of barristers, he had muddled through a couple of preparatory schools with literacy skills well below his potential, until at 12, the family realised that there really was something wrong with his ability to learn in the conventional way and that, if he were not to spend a good proportion of his school career outside the classroom for cheeking the teachers and setting himself up as student union rep., something radical had to be attempted. He was thus enrolled in a specialist college for dyslexic students. At the age of 12, his reading age was around 9, which meant that the stories he enjoyed were too difficult for him to read independently. His previous teachers had also been consistently disappointed by the thinness of his written work. Few of his original ideas and none of the sophisticated vocabulary he had used to express them seemed to survive the writing process.

What was David's cognitive style?

Again, initially there were no formal diagnostic tools available; so an estimation of David's learning style was arrived at by observing his strengths and weaknesses. He was obviously highly verbal, scoring off the top of the scale on the British Picture Vocabulary Test and using complex structures and vocabulary in his spoken language. He played with words both with wit and also in writing poetry, which gave him real pleasure.

His listening skills were excellent, and he not only picked up the outline of topics but also remembered detail. However, this was not the case when reading, where he frequently would misread longer words, guess them and end up well away from the intended meaning. This was obviously beginning to cause him real frustration.

When storing information, he would always try to use words and was a great 'list' man. Unfortunately, his struggles with spelling meant that he would forget a lot of information while trying to spell. He was extremely scathing abut mind-map techniques when they were first introduced to him and obviously far preferred to arrange things in hierarchies or chains.

The overall picture was of a strong verbaliser with analytic rather than wholistic strengths. However, his intelligence meant that he was quite capable of seeing those links and connections that some analytics find hard to identify. When he was eventually assessed on the CSA, he did score as an analytic verbaliser but was not particularly far down the analytic scale.

What are David's relative strengths and weaknesses?

David's strengths are clear. He is a very bright boy with a real gift for and love of language. He is a talented drama student with a fund of ideas. He is also determined and motivated with a real understanding of the nature of his difficulties. His weaknesses stem from the discrepancy between his verbal abilities and his literacy – both reading and spelling. He was also attempting to use verbal and analytic structures to organise and store information and was coming up against problems caused by this discrepancy between speaking and writing. It has also been suggested that using this verbal sequential mode places a greater strain upon memory. Add to this the fact that his reading skills were yet to become automatic and it is not surprising that the resulting overloads caused him to lose many of his ideas between his head and the paper.

He needed to find ways to:

- improve his ability to store information
- plan work more effectively
- use more ambitious vocabulary in written work

How was his learning managed?

Like Jack, David's school offered a mixture of individualised multi-sensory and group strategies to develop reading – both decoding and comprehension skills. He spent some time focusing upon the use of syllable division to help him decode the complex keywords that might send him off down the wrong track in a factual text. By 16, he was reading fluently, although still needing time to focus and absorb complex factual or technical material. He also chose to use computers and became a fast typist. He tried a range of computer programs but tended simply to stick to Microsoft Word, although using text-to-speech software for proofreading.

Initially, David was resistant to the use of any form of mind map, clearly stating his preference for lists. However, he was aware that his strategy was not producing the results he wanted. He agreed to experiment but, presumably influenced by his style profile, kept returning to his earlier strategy claiming loudly that nothing else worked. By this stage the rest of his teaching group were, automatically and happily, using concept maps; so the teacher was also tending to use them for presenting material and storing ideas while acknowledging to David that it was up to him to use the strategies that suited him best.

The breakthrough came when David started to practise using an amanuensis for exams and was encouraged to create a plan before starting to dictate. At this stage, with the pressure of exams upon him, he finally began to find that a mind map allowed him to use association techniques and juggle information more effectively. He did, however, always stick to verbal labels. During the pre-GCSE revision phase, he was caught using this so-called wholistic technique consistently and, as in the manner of the soap commercials, was not prepared to exchange them for his old soap powder! This really does show that learners really do need to experiment with techniques.

Enabling David to use the full scope of his vocabulary does remain problematic. A couple of strategies have been helpful. He is a good poet; so one approach has been for him to plan descriptive pieces by condensing the language as though he were drafting a poem. He then expands it into continuous prose when writing his piece. He has also found the senses frame (which is described in chapter 9) helpful for capturing images. With more factual work, he has started to use voice-recognition software so that he can dictate his ideas. He does, however, find the slow pace of this frustrating. Another approach he has tried is taping his ideas and then using the tape to make a transcript. This is not particularly easy but, for pieces of untimed coursework where he is highly motivated to get a mark that reflects his ability, it has been successful. The focus has consistently been on using words rather than images, and, for someone as articulate as David, this has been the obvious route.

His reading has improved considerably, but it is still not easy enough for him to be able to lose himself in a demanding book. He has made much use of taped books and also used books that have been scanned onto the computer. For exam revision, again he has used tapes and CDs and made use of revision sites on the internet. He learns well by ear but has made considerable use of concept maps to process the information and commit it to memory.

Outcomes

David is now on course for higher education, with a stronger aware-ness of how to also manage his study and written expression and avoid the areas where he is weak. He makes very good use of any form of amanuensis and will have no problems using the right kind of dyslexia support in higher education! He will, no doubt, continue to make the best use of his superior verbal skills and has managed to move away from the rigid analytical approach that he was attempt-ing to use towards a far more flexible approach to planning texts and storing information. It has, in fact, paid David to experiment with approaches that were not his first, instinctive choice.

References

Andersen-Wood, L. and Smith, B. R. (1997) Working with Pragmatics. Bicester Oxford: Winslow

Ausubel, D. P. (1981) Educational psychology: A cognitive view. New York

Backhouse, G. (2000) Assessment and Report Writing for Special Arrangements at GCSE, GCE, VCE, GNVQ available from Patoss PO Box 10, Evesham, Worcs WR11 6ZW or patoss@evesham.ac.uk

Baddeley, A. D. (1986) Working memory, Oxford: Oxford University Press

Baddeley, A. D. and Hitch, G. (1974) 'Working memory'. In Bower, G. A. (ed.) Recent advances in learning and motivation, 8, 47-90, New York: Academic Press

Banner, G. and Rayner, S. (1997) Teaching in style: Are you making the difference in the classroom? Support for Learning, Vol.12 No.1 pp.15-18

Barkley, R. A. (1990) Attention-deficit hyperactivity disorder: A handbook for diagnosis and treatment. New York: Guilford

Bartlett, D. and Moody, S. (2000) Dyslexia in the Workplace. London: Whurr

Bath, J. B., Chinn, S. J. and Knox, D. E. (1986) The Test of Cognitive Style in Mathematics. East Aurora, New York: Slosson (out of print, see Chinn, 1998)

Biggs, J. B. (1987) Student Approaches to Learning and Studying. Hawthorn Victoria: Australian Council for Educational Research

Blagg, N., Ballinger, M., Gardiner, R., Petty, M. and Williams, G. (1988) Somerset Thinking Skills Course. Blackwell/Somerset County Council

Bradley, L. (1984) Assessing Reading Difficulties: A Diagnostic and Remedial Approach (second edition). London: Macmillan Education.

Bradley, L. and Bryant, P. E. (1978) Difficulties in auditory organisation as a possible cause of reading backwardness. Nature, 271, 746-747

Bradley, L. and Bryant, P. E. (1983) Categorising sounds and learning to read: A causal connection. Nature, 310, 419-421

Bramley, W. (1975) Units of Sound – from Units of Sound Productions. Pool Green: Neston, Wiltshire.

Brenneker, E. M. (2001) Dyslexia Contact

Brooks, P. and Weeks, S. (1999) Individual Styles in Learning to Spell: Improving Spelling in Children with Literacy Difficulties and All Children in Mainstream Schools Crown Copyright: DFEE Her Majety's Stationery Office, St. Clements House, 2-16, Colegate, Norwich, NR3 1BQ

Buzan, T. (1982) Use Your Head, BBC Books

Buzan, T. and Coleman, R. (1998) A Guide to Of Mice and Men. London: Hodder and Stoughton.

Cane and Cane (1979) in The Gifted Child Quarterly, Spring 1979, Vol XXIII No. 1, pp. 160-166

Carbo M., Dunn R. and Dunn K. (1986) Teaching Students to Read Through Their Individual Learning Styles. Englewood Cliffs, New Jersey: Prentice Hall.

Case, R., Hayward, S., Lewis, M. and Hurst, P. (1988) Toward a neo-Piagetian theory of cognitive and emotional development. Developmental Review, 8 1-51

Chasty, H. (1985) What is dyslexia? In Snowling, M. J. (ed.) Children's Written Language Difficulties. Windsor: NFER Nelson

Chinn, S. J. (1998) Diagnostic Inventory of Basic Skills and Learning Style in Mathematics. London: The Psychological Corporation

Chinn, S. J. (2000) Informal Assessment of Numerical Skills. Mark: Mark College

Chinn, S. J. and Ashcroft, R. (1998) Mathematics for Dyslexics: A Teaching Handbook (second edition). London: Whurr

Chinn, S. J., McDonagh, Van Elswijk, R., Harmsen, H., Kay, J., McPhillips, T., Power, A. and Skidmore, L. (2001) Classroom studies into cognitive style in mathematics for pupils with dyslexia in special education in the Netherlands, Ireland and the UK. British Journal of Special Education, 28, 80-85.

Coleman, J. and Hendry, L. (1989) The Nature of Adolescence (second edition) London: Routledge

Cooper, P. and O'Regan, F. (2000) A Teacher's Guide to the Management of AD/HD. London: Routledge

Coopersmith, S. J. (1967) The Antecedents of Self-Esteem: California: Consulting Psychologists Press

Coren, S. (1993) Left-Hander: Everything you need to know about Left-Handedness. London: John Murray

Cotgrove, A. (2000) Voice-activated Systems in The Dyslexia Handbook 2000 (ed. I. Smythe). Reading: BDA

Cramond, B. (1994) 'The relationship between Attention-deficit Hyperactivity Disorder and creativity'. Paper presented at the Annual Meeting of the American Educational Research Association (New Orleans, LA. 4-8 April 1994)

Csóti M (2001) Social Awareness Skills for Children: London: Jessica Kingsley.

Culshaw, C. and Waters, D. (1984) Headwork Series. Oxford: Oxford University Press

Cummins, J. (1978) Bilingualism and Minority Language Children. Ontario: Ontario Institute for Studies in Education

Daines, B., Fleming, P. and Miller, C. (1996) Speech and Language Difficulties. NASEN

Davies, A. (1992) Handwriting, Reading and Spelling System. London: Heinemann

De Fries J. C., Alarcon, M., Olson, R. K., Dennison, P. E. and Dennison, G. E. (1997) Genetic Aetiologies of Reading and Spelling Deficits: Developmental Differences. In Hulme, C. and Snowling, M. (eds.) Dyslexia: Biology, Cognition and Intervention. London: Whurr

Dennison, P. E. and Dennison, G. E. (1989) Brain Gym: Teacher's edition revised. Ventura, CA: Edu-Kinesthetics, Inc.

Dimond, S. (1972) The Double Brain. Edinburgh: Churchill Livingstone

Donaldson, M. (1978) Children's Minds. Glasgow: Fontana

Dunn, R. (ed.) (1995) Learning Style Network Review of Articles and Books. School of Education and Human Services, St. John's University, New York

Dunn, R. and Dunn, K. (1991) Teaching Students Through their Individual Learning Styles. A Practical Approach. National Association of Secondary School Principles. Reston, VA: Prentice-Hall

Edwards, J. (1994) The Scars of Dyslexia: Studies in Emotional Reactions, London: NY Caswell

Entwistle, N. (1981) Styles of Learning and Teaching. London: David Fulton

Entwistle, N. (1988) Motivational factors in students' approach to learning. In Schmeck, R. R. (ed.) Learning Strategies and Learning Styles. New York and London: Plenum

Eysenck, H. J. (1967) Biological Basis of Personality. Charles C. Thomas: Springfield, Illinois

Eysenck, H. (1976) The Measurement of Personality. Medical and Technical Pub Co: Lancaster

Fawcett, A. J. and Nicolson, R. (1994) The Dyslexia Screening Test. The Adult Dyslexia Index: University of Sheffield

Feuerstein, R. (1979) The Dynamic Assessment of Retarded Performers: The Learning Potential Assessment Device, Theory, Instruments and Techniques. Baltimore: University Park Press

Fey, M. E. (1999) Speech-language pathology and the early identification and prevention of reading disabilities: Perspectives. Winter 13-17

Flavell, J. H. (1987) Speculations about the nature and development of metacognition. In Weinert, F. and Kluwe R. (eds.) Metacognition, Motivation and Understanding. London: Lawrence Erlbaum

Frederikson, N. (ed.) (1995) Phonological Assessment Battery (PhAB) Windsor: NFER Nelson

Freeley, M. E. (1987) Teaching to both hemispheres. Teaching, K8 Aug-Sept, 65-75

Freeman, R. (1991) Mastering Study Skills. Macmillan Master Series. London: Macmillan

Frith, U. (1995) Dyslexia: can we have a shared theorietical framework? In Frederickson, N. and Reason, R. (eds.) Phonological assessment of specific learning difficulties. Educational And Child Psychology 12: 6-17

Frith, U. (1997) Brain, Mind and Behaviours in Dyslexia. In Hulme, C. and Snowling, M. Dyslexia: Biology, Cognition and Intervention. London: Whurr

Fisher, R. (1995) Teaching Children to Think. Stanley: Thornes

Galaburda, A. M. (ed.) (1993) Dyslexia and Development: Neurobiological Aspects of Extraordinary Brains. Cambridge, MA: Harvard University Press

Galton, M. and Willcocks, J. (eds.) (1983) Moving from the Primary Classroom. London: Routledge and Kegan Paul

Garner, S. and Rippon, G. (1997) 'Relationship between functional organisation of the brain and reading and spelling skills in learner readers'. Paper presented at BDA 4th International Conference, York

Gathercole, S. E. and Baddeley A. D. (1993) Working Memory and Language. Hove: Lawrence Erlbaum Associates

Gazzaniga, M. S. and Ledoux, J. E. (1978) The Integrated Mind. New York: Plenum Press

Geisler-Brenstein, E. and Schmeck, R. R. (1995) The Revised ILP: A Multifaceted Perspective on Individual Differences in Learning. Carbondale: Southern Illinois University

Gelb, M. (1997) Mind Mapping. Available from: Nightingale Conant, Long Road, Paignton, Devon

Geschwind, N. and Galaburda, A. M. (1987) Cerebral Lateralisation, Biological Mechanisms, Associations and Pathology. Cambridge, MA: MIT Press

Given, B. (1997) 'Why learning style instruction is effective: a neuroscientific Explanation'. Paper presented at BDA 4th International Conference, York

Given, B. and Reid, G. (1999) Learning Styles: A guide for teachers and parents. Red Rose Publications

Goedkoop, G. (2001) Double diagnosis or developmental diversity in Smythe, I. (ed.) The Dyslexia Handbook 2001 London: BDA

Gordon, M. (1991) AD/HD: A Consumer's Guide GSI

Graham, K. G. and Robinson, H. A. (1989) Study Skills Handbook. International Reading Association: Delaware

Gregorc, A. R. (1982) Style Delineator. Maynard, MA: Gabriel Systems

Grigorenko, E. L. (2001) Developmental Dyslexia: An Update on Genes, Brain and Environments in Journal of Child Psychiatry, 42, 1, 91-125

Gross, R. and McIlveen, R. (1998) Psychology: A New Introduction. London: Hodder and Stoughton

Hamblin, D. (1981) Teaching Study Skills. Oxford: Basil Blackwell

Harman, C. A. and Freeman, R. (1984) How to Study Effectively: Self-Help Series available from National Extension College 18, Brooklands Avenue, Cambridge CB2 2HN

Hatcher, P. J. (1994) Sound Linkage: An Integrated Programme for Overcoming Reading Difficulties. London: Whurr

Heimlich, J. E. and Pittelman, S. D. (1986) Semantic Mapping: Classroom Applications; International Reading Association. Newark: Delaware

Holloway, J. (1995) Specials, Study Skills. London: Folens

Holloway, J. (1999) The Learning Kit: an Inclusive Approach to Studying (Photocopiable resource book for study skills): Connect Publications

Holloway, J. (2000) Dyslexia in Focus at Sixteen Plus; An Inclusive Teaching Approach NASEN

Honey, P. and Mumford, A. (1986) Using Your Learning Styles: Maidenhead, Berkshire: Peter Honey

Hughes, M. (1999) Closing the Learning Gap. London: Network Educational Press Ltd

Hulme, C. and Snowling, M. (eds.) (1997) Dyslexia: Biology, Cognition and Intervention. London: Whurr

Hynd, G. W. and Hiemenz J. R. (1997) Dyslexia and Gyral Morphology Variation. In Hulme, C. and Snowling, M. (eds.) (1997) Dyslexia: Biology, Cognition and Intervention. London: Whurr

Irlen, H. (1991) Reading by the Colors. New York: Avery Publishing Group Inc.

Jensen, E. (1994) Super Teaching: The Learning Brain. Stafford: Turning Point

Johnson, D. and Johnson, F. (1982) Joining together: Group theory and group skills. Englewood Cliffs, NJ.: Prentice Hall, Inc.

Johnson, D. D. and Pearson, P. D. (1984) Teaching Reading Vocabulary (second edition). New York: Holt, Rinehart and Winston

Keefe, J. W. (1982) Assessing Students' Learning Styles: an Overview. In Keefe, J. W. (ed.) Student Learning Styles and Brain Behaviour. Reston, VA: National Association of Secondary School Principals

Keefe, J. W. (1987) Learning Style Theory and Practice. Reston, VA: National Association of Secondary School Principals

Keefe, J. W. (1995) Annotated Bibliography. St. John's, Jamaica: Learning Styles Network

Kilpatrick, G. McCall, D. and Palmer, S. (1982) I See What You Mean; 1 and 2. London: Oliver and Boyd

Kirby, J. R. (1988) Style, Strategy and Skill in Reading. In Schmeck, R. R. (ed.) Learning Strategies and Learning Styles. New York and London: Plenum

Klein, C. (1995) Diagnosing Dyslexia. London: Basic Skills Agency

Klin, A., Volkmar, F. R. and Sparrow, S. S. (eds.) Asperger Syndrome. New York: Academic Guildford Press

Lane, C. (1992) Now, Listen, Hear. Special Children (54) pp. 12-24

Levine, M. D. (1992) Keeping a Head in School. Educ. Publisher. Available from the Helen Arkell Dyslexia Centre

Levine, M. D. (1993) All Kinds of Minds. Educ. Publisher. Available from the Helen Arkell Dyslexia Centre

Levine, M. D. (1993) PEEX and PEERAMID assessment batteries for ages 6-9 and 9-16. Educ. Publisher. Available from the Helen Arkell Dyslexia Centre

Levy, E. (1993) A New Image: Brain Imagery to improve memory and reading comprehension speed: Emily B. Levy

Lewis, M. and Wray, D. (1995) Developing children's non-fiction writing. Leamington Spa: Scholastic

Lindamood, C. and Lindamood, P. (1997) Auditory Discrimination in Depth. Austin, Texas: Pro-Ed.

Locke, A. and Beech, M. (1991) Teaching Talking: A Screening and Intervention Programme. Windsor: NFER Nelson

Lunzer, E. and Gardner, K. (1979) The Effective Use of Reading. London: Heinemann Educational Books for The Schools Council

Marks, A. (1998) Supporting Young People with Language impairments in secondary mainstream schools – a practical guide. Worthing: Priority Care, NHS Trust

Martin, D. and Miller, C. (1996) Speech and Language Difficulties in the Classroom London: David Fulton

Martin, N. (1999) 'Specific Learning difficulty. It is more than a literacy problem.' article: High Peak College, University of Derby

Mason, M. (1990) Illuminating English, Book 3, Writing for Learning. Wigan: Training Research Agency Consultancy Enterprises Ltd.

Mayo, P. and Waldo, P. (1994) Scripting: Social communication for adolescents (second edition) Eau Claire, WI: Thinking Publications

McGuinness, C. (1998) Reading Reflex. London: Penguin

McLean, B. Study Skills. Available from the Helen Arkell Dyslexia Centre

Miles, T. R. (1983) The Bangor Dyslexia Test. Cambridge: LDA

Miles, T. R. (1993) Dyslexia: The Pattern of Difficulties (second edition). London: Whurr

Miles, T. R. and Gilroy, S. (1986) Dyslexia at College. London: Methuen

Milgram, R., Dunn, R. and Price, G. E. (1993) Teaching and counseling gifted and talented adolescents. Westport, CT: Praeger

Miller, A. (1991) Personality types: learning styles and educational goals Educational Psychology 11, 217-238

Milne, A. A. (1926) Winnie the Pooh. London: Methuen

Mitchell, J. (1994) An Introduction to Study Skills and memory: a workbook available from the Communication and Learning Skills Centre, 131 Homefield Park, Sutton, Surrey SM1 2DY

Moran, A. (1991) What can learning styles research learn from cognitive psychology? Educational Psychology, 11, 239-245

Morrison, M. L. (1987) Word Finder, The Phonic Key to the Dictionary. Available from Pilot Light, Stone Mountain, Georgia. GA300960905 PO Box 305

Mortimore, M. (1995) Dyslexic students learning to spell: unpublished classroom study. University of Cardiff

Mortimore, M. (1998) A comparison of learning style in dyslexic and non-dyslexic undergraduates. MEd Dissertation, University of Cardiff

Moseley, D. (1996) The ACE Spelling dictionary. Wisbech: LDA

Nelson, T.O. (ed.) (1992) Metacognition: Core readings. Boston: Allyn and Bacon

Newton, M. and Thompson, I. (1982) The Aston Index. Cambridge: LDA

Nicolson, D. and Ayres, H. (1997) Adolescent Problems: A Practical Guide for Parents and Teachers, London: David Fulton

Nicolson, R. and Fawcett, A.J. (1990) Automaticity: A new framework for dyslexia research? Cognition 30, 159-182

Nicolson, R. and Fawcett, A.J. (1994) Comparison of deficits in cognitive and motor skills in children with dyslexia. Annals of Dyslexia, 44, 147-164

Nicolson, R. and Fawcett, A.J. (1995) 'Dyslexia is more than a phonological disability'. Dyslexia: An International Journal of Research and Practice, 1, 19-37

Nippold, M. A. (2000) Language Development during the Adolescent Years: Aspects of Pragmatics, Syntax and Semantics: Topics in Language Disorders: February; 20 (2): 15-28

Nisbet, J. and Shucksmith, J. (1986) Learning Strategies. London: Routledge and Kegan Paul

Nist, S. L. and Mealey, D. (1991) Teacher directed comprehension strategies. In Flippo, R. F. and Caverly, D.C. (eds.) Teaching reading and study strategies at the college level. Newark: IRA

O'Connor, J. and Seymour, J. (1990) Introducing Neuro-Linguistic Programming. London: Thorsons

Ornstein, R. E. (1972) The Psychology of Consciousness. San Francisco: W. H. Freeman

Osmond, J. (1994) The reality of dyslexia. London: Channel Four Books

Ostler, C. (1999) Study Skills A Pupil's Survival Guide: Ammonite

Ostler, C. and Ward (2001) Advanced Study Skills, A Student's Survival Guide for AS, A Level and Advanced. VCE Wakefield: SEN Marketing

Paris, S. G. and Lindauer B. K. (1976) The role of inference in children's comprehension and memory for sentences. Cognitive Psychology, 8, 217-227

Pask, G. (1988) Learning Styles, Teaching Strategies and Conceptual or Learning Style. In Schmeck, R. R. (ed.) Learning Strategies and Learning Styles. New York and London: Plenum

Peer, L. (1997) A Young Person's Guide to Dyslexia. London: BDA

Peer, L. (1997) Your Personal Survival Kit, Preventing Parental Burn-Out. London: BDA

Peer, L. (2001) The Survival Kit, initiated by young dyslexics for other young Dyslexics. London: BDA

Pickering, S. (2000) 'Working memory and Dyslexia': Lecture notes produced for MRC Working Memory and Learning Disability Programme. University of Bristol

Pollock, J. and Waller, E. (1994) Day-to-day dyslexia in the classroom. London: Routledge

Portwood, M. (2000) Understanding Developmental Dyspraxia – a textbook for students and professionals. Roehampton: David Fulton Publishers

Pumfrey P. D. and Elliott, C. D. (1990) Children's Difficulties in Reading, Spelling and Writing. London: Falmer Press

Pumfrey, P. D. and Reason, R. (1991) Specific Learning Difficulties (Dyslexia) Challenges and Responses. Windsor: NFER Nelson

Quicke, J. (1992). Thinking Skills: An analysis of intellectual processes and their relation to education. In Support for Learning vol. 7 no. 4 1992

Race, P. (1992) '500 Tips for students'. Polytechnic of Wales, Pontypridd, CF37 1DL

Rapin, I. (1996) Developmental Language Disorders: A Clinical Update. New York: Guildford Press

Rawlins, W. K. (1992) Friendship Matters: communication, dialectics and the life course. New York: DeGruyter

Raymond, S. (2001) Supporting Dyslexic Pupils across the Curriculum: SEN Marketing. London: Fulton

Rayner, S. and Riding, R. Towards a categorisation of cognitive styles and learning styles. Educational Psychology, 17, 5-27

Reid, G. (1994) Specific Learning Diffficulties (Dyslexia) A Handbook for Study and Practice. Edinburgh: Moray House Publications

Richardson. A. and Stein, J. (1993) Personality Characteristics of Adult Dyslexics. In Wright, S. F. and Groner, R. (eds.) Facets of Dyslexia and its Remediation Amsterdam: Elsevier Science Publishers B. V.

Riddick, B. Farmer, M. and Sterling, C. (1997) Students and Dyslexia, Growing up with a Specific Learning Difficulty. London: Whurr

Riding, R. J. (1991a) Cognitive Styles Analysis: Birmingham, Learning and Training Technology

Riding, R. J. (1991b) Cognitive Styles Analysis User Manual Birmingham. Birmingham: Learning and Training Technology

Riding, R. J. (1994) Personal Styles Awareness Package. Birmingham: Learning and Training Technology

Riding, R. J. (1997) On the nature of cognitive style. Educational Pychology, 17, 29-45.

Riding, R. J. (1998) 'The validity and reliability of the CSA'. Information sent by R. J. Riding

Riding, R. J. and Calvey (1981) The Assessment of verbal-imagery learning styles and their effect on the recall of concrete and abstract prose passages by eleven-year-old children. British Journal of Psychology 72, 59-64

Riding, R. J. and Cheema, I. (1991) Cognitive styles: an overview and integration Educational Psychology, 3 and 4, 193-215

Riding, R. J. and Douglas, G. (1993) The effect of cognitive style and mode of presentation on learnning performance, British Journal of Educational Psychology, 63, 297-307

Riding, R. J. and Dyer, V. A. (1980) The relationship between extraversion and verbal-imagery learning style in twelve-year-old children. Personality and Individual Differences 1, 273-9

Riding, R. J. and Mathias, D. (1991) Cognitive Styles and preferred learning mode, reading attainment and cognitive ability in eleven-year-old children. Educational Psychology, 11, 383-393

Riding, R. and Rayner, S. J. (1995) Personal Style and Effective Teaching. Birmingham: Learning and Training Technology [what is this place?]

Riding, R. J. and Rayner, S. (1998) Cognitive Styles and Learning Strategies. London: David Fulton

Riding, R. J. and Staley, A. (1998) Self-perception as learner, cognitive style and business studies course students' course performance. Assessment and Evaluation in Higher Education, 23.

Riding, R. J. and Watts, M. (1997) The effect of cognitive style upon the preferred format of instructional material. Educational Psychology 17, 179-83

Riding, R. J. and Wright, M. (1995) Cognitive Style, personal characteristics and harmony in student flats. Educational Psychology, 17, 179–183

Riding, R. J., Glass A. and Douglas, G. (1993) Differences in thinking: cognitive and physiological perspectives Educational Psychology,13, 267-277

Rinaldi, W. (1992) The Social Use of Language Programme. Windsor: NFER Nelson

Rippon, G. and Brunswick, N. (1997) 'Patterns of Lateralisation and Cognitive Differences in Dyslexic and Normal Readers', paper presented at the 4th BDA International Conference, York

Rippon,G. Brunswick, N. and Garner, S. (1997) 'Early Cognitive Neuropsychological Profiles and Development of Reading Skills', paper presented at the 4th BDA International Conference, York

Rose, S. P. R. (1993) The Making of Memory. London: Bantam

Rose, C. and Goll, L. (1992) Accelerate Your Learning, A World Of Opportunity in Your Hands: Six Super Skills. USA: Accelerated Learning Systems Ltd.

Schmeck, R. R. (ed.) (1988) Learning Strategies and Learning Styles. New York and London: Plenum

Sharma, M. C. (1989) Mathematics Learning Personality Math Notebook vol. 7 nos.1 and 2

Shaw, S. and Hawes, T. (1997) Effective Teaching and Learning in the Primary Classroom: A practical guide to brain compatible learning: Network Educational Press

Silva, K. Lunt, I. (1982) Child Development, a first course. London: Penguin

Singleton, C. and HEFC (2001) Dyslexia. In Higher Education, policy, provision and practice, The report of the National Working Party on Dyslexia in Higher Education from SEN Marketing available via email sen.marketing@ukonline.co.uk

Singleton, C. and Thomas, K. (1994) Computerised Screening for Dyslexia. In Singleton, C. (ed.) Computers and Dyslexia: educational applications of new technology. Hull: Dyslexia Computer Resource Centre

Smith, A. (1996) Accelerated Learning in the Classroom. Stafford: Network Educational Press

Smith, A. (1997) Accelerated Learning in Practice. Network Educational Press. Stafford: Accelerated Learning UK

Smythe, I. (2001) Checklist for dyslexic adults. In Smythe, I. (ed.) The Dyslexia Handbook 2001. London: BDA

Smythe I (ed.) The Dyslexia Handbook 2001. London: BDA

Snowling, M. J. (ed.) (1985) Children's Written Language Difficulties. Windsor: NFER Nelson

Snowling, M. J. (2000) Dyslexia: A Cognitive Developmental Perspective. Oxford: Blackwell

Snowling M. J. and Stackhouse, J. (eds.) (1996) Dyslexia, Speech and Language: A Practitioner's Handbook. London: Whurr

Snowling, M., Stothard, S. E. and McLean, J. (1996) The Graded Non-Word Reading Test, Bury St. Edmunds: Thames Valley Test Company

Stackhouse, J. and Wells, B. (1997) Children's Speech and Literacy Difficulties, A Psycholinguistic Framework. London: Whurr

Stanovich, K. E. (1988) Explaining the difference between the dyslexic and the garden-variety poor readers: the phonological core model. Journal of Learning Disabilities, 21, 590-604

Stein, J. F. and Walsh, V. (1997) To see but not to read: the magnocellular theory of dyslexia. Trends in Neuroscience 20 (4) 508-14

Steffert, B. (1996) 'Sign Minds and Design Minds; the trade off between visual spatial skills and linguistic skills', paper given at the 2nd international conference on dyslexia in higher education. Learning across the Continuum. University of Plymouth

Svantesson, I. (1998) Learning Maps and Memory Skills (second edition). London: Kogan Page

Tallal, P. (1988) Developmental language disorders. In Kavanagh, J. F. and Truss (Jr), T. J. (eds.) Learning Disabilities: Proceedings from the National Conference. Parkton, MD: York Press

Tallal, P., Allard, L., Miller, S. and Curtiss, S. (1997) Academic Outcomes of Language Impaired Children. In Hulme, C. and Snowling, M. (eds.) Dyslexia, Biology, Cognition and Intervention. London: Whurr

Tennant, M. (1988) Psychology and Adult Learning. London: Routledge

Thompson, L. J. (1969) 'Language disabilities in men of eminence'. Bulletin of the Orton Society, XIX, 113-121

Thomson, M. E. (1984) Developmental Dyslexia. London: Edward Arnold

Topping, K. J. (1992) Cued Spelling Training Tape: Kirklees Metropolitan Council

Torgesen, J. K. (ed.) (1990) Cognitive and behavioural characteristics of children with learning disabilities. Austin, TX: Pro-ed Inc.

Torrance, E. P. and Rockenstein, Z. L. (1988) Styles of Thinking and Creativity. In Schmeck, R. R. (ed.) Learning Strategies and Learning Styles. New York and London: Plenum

Turner, M. (1997) The Assessment of Dyslexia. London: Whurr

Vail, P. (1997) 'Theory's fine; but what do I do Monday?' Paper presented at the 4th BDA International Dyslexia Conference, York

Vasta, R., Haith, M. M. and Miller, S. A. (1992) Child Psychology, the Modern Science. New York: John Wiley

Vinegrad, M. (1994) A revised Dyslexia Checklist. Educare No. 48, March 1994

Vivian, V. (1998) Specific Learning Difficulties, Dyslexia: Literacy Strategies for the Classroom: available from Croydon Special Educational Needs Support Service, Davidson Professional Centre, Davidson Road, Croydon, CRO 6DD

Volkow, N. (2001) Interview in the Newsletter Journal of the American Medical Association, September 2001

Vygotsky, L. (1978) Mind in society: the development of higher psychological processes. Cambridge, MA: Harvard University Press

Webster, A. and McConnell, C. (1987) Special Needs in OrdinarySchools: Children with developmental dysphasia. In Wyke, M. (ed.) Developmental Dysphasia. London: Academic Press

Wechsler, D. (1981) Wechsler Adult Intelligence Scale Revised. San Antonio: Psychological Corporation

Wechsler, D. (1981) Wechsler Intelligence Scale for Children (third edition). San Antonio: Psychological Corporation

Weinert, F. and Kluwe, R. (eds.) (1987) Metacognition, Motivation and Understanding. London: Lawrence Erlbaum

Weinstein, F. E. and Van Mater Stone, G. (1996) Learning Strategies and learning to learn. In De Corte, E. and Weinert, F. E. (eds.) International Encyclopaedia of Developmental Psychology, 419-23. London: Pergamon

West, T. (1991) In the Mind's Eye. Buffalo, New York: Prometheus Books

Whyte, J. (ed.) (1989) Dyslexia: Current research issues Irish Journal of Psychology, 10,121-135

Wilkins, A. J. (1995) Visual Stress. Oxford: Oxford University Press

Wilkins, A. J., Lewis, E., Smith, F., Rowland, E. and Tweedie, W. (2001) Coloured overlays and their benefits for reading. Journal of Research into Reading 2001-24 (1)

Williams, E. (1999) Dyslexia: no longer a closed book. Times Educational Supplement 29 October 1999

Winner, E., Von Karolyi, C. and Malinsky, D. (2000) Dyslexia and Visual-Spatial Talents: No Clear Link Perspectives, Spring 2000 26-30

Witkin, H. A. (1969) Some Implications of Research on Cognitive Style for Problems of Education. In Whitehead, J. M. (ed.) Personality and Learning 1. Milton Keynes: Open University Press

Wood, D. (1988) How Children Think and Learn. Oxford: Blackwell

Wray, D. and Lewis, M. (1997) Extending literacy: children reading and writing non-fiction. London: Routledge

Yuill, N. and Oakhill, J. (1991) Children's problems in text comprehension. Cambridge: Cambridge University Press

Zenhausern, I. (1982) Education and the Left Hemisphere. In Keefe, J. W. (ed.) Student Learning Styles and Brain Behaviour. Learning Styles Network Conference

National Association of Secondary School Principals, St. John's, Jamaica: National Association of Secondary School Principals

Further Reading
A non-exhaustive list of useful references

Areas of interest

1. Dyslexia: background and research
2. Dyslexia: practical support and strategies (this does not include specific literacy programmes, which are well documented in Reid 1994)
3. Dyslexia and stress
4. Other syndromes sometimes co-existing with dyslexia:
    a. ADHD
    b. Dyspraxia
    c. Speech and language difficulties
5. IT
    a. Dyslexia – websites and software
    b. Learning styles
6. Learning Style
    a. Research background
    b. Using style
    c. Practical strategies
7. Accelerated learning and related approaches
8. Memory
9. Study skills
10. Dictionaries
11. Schema theory and memory
12. Miscellaneous

1. Dyslexia: background and research

There is now a very wide range of books available. The following can provide an introduction, which combines research background with teaching suggestions.

Miles, T. R. (1993) The Pattern of Difficulties (second edition). London: Whurr
Reid, G. (1994) Specific Learning Difficulties (Dyslexia). Moray House Publications
An excellent and wide-ranging introduction to the area including detailed reference lists of practical teaching programmes.
Snowling, M. (2000) Dyslexia. A Cognitive Developmental Perspective (second edition). Oxford: Blackwell
Snowling, M. and Stackhouse, J. (eds.) (1996) Dyslexia, Speech and Language: A Practitioner's Handbook. London: Whurr

2. Dyslexia: practical support and strategies

Membership of the British Dyslexia Association brings many benefits both to teachers, parents and dyslexics, among which is the excellent and upbeat official magazine *Dyslexia Contact*.

Bartlett, D. and Moody, S. (2000) Dyslexia in the Workplace. London: Whurr. A really practical guide to help dyslexic adults compensate for dyslexic difficulties in a range of workplaces.
Holloway, J. (1995) Specials! Study Skills. Folens. Excellent: photocopiable and practical.
Holloway, J. (2000) Dyslexia in Focus at Sixteen Plus: an Inclusive Teaching Approach. NASEN. Informal learning style checklists for use with students, plus a range of excellent strategies, including study skills, to help older students.
McLean, B. Study Skills. Helen Arkell Dyslexia Centre
Ostler, C. and Ward, F. (2001) Advanced Study Skills from SEN Marketing at 618, Leeds Road, Outwood, Wakefield, telephone: (01924) 871697 or email: sen.marketing@ukonline.co.uk
Vivian, V. (1998) Specific Learning Difficulties, Dyslexia: Literacy Strategies for the Classroom: available from Croydon Special Educational Needs Support Service, Davidson Professional Centre, Davidson Road, Croydon, CRO 6DD, telephone: (020) 8656 66551.
A highly practical resource prepared for the purpose of supporting classroom teachers through inset sessions. It covers everything from early identification to special exam arrangements in a highly accessible way and provides useful lists of resources to support all aspects of teaching dyslexic students.

3. Dyslexia and stress

Miles, T. R. and Varma, V. (1995) Dyslexia and Stress. London: Whurr
Peer, L. (1997) A Young Person's Guide to Dyslexia. London: BDA
Peer, L. (1997) Your Personal Survival Kit, Preventing Parental Burn-Out. London: BDA
Peer, L (2000) The Survival Kit, initiated by young dyslexics for other young dyslexics. London: BDA

4. Other syndromes sometimes co-existing with dyslexia

a. ADHD

Cooper, P. and O'Regan, F. (2000) A Teacher's Guide to the Management of AD/HD. London: Routledge

Gordon, M. (1991) AD/HD: A Consumer's Guide. GSI

b. Dyspraxia

Portwood, M. (2000) Understanding Developmental Dyspraxia – a textbook for students and professionals. London: David Fulton Publishers.
An authoritative review of dyspraxia.

c. Speech and language difficulties.

For a readable and accessible introduction to this area see:

Daines, B., Fleming, P. and Miller, C. (1996) Speech and Language Difficulties. NASEN

Martin, D. and Miller, C. (1996) Speech and Language Difficulties in the Classroom. London: David Fulton Publishers

For a general introduction with very practical suggestions for helping students in secondary mainstream settings:

Marks, A. (1998) Supporting Young People with Language Impairments in Secondary Mainstream Schools – a practical guide. Worthing: Priority Care NHS Trust, available from Trust Headquarters, Arundel Road, Worthing, West Sussex BN13 3EP

For a more in-depth analysis linking in with dyslexic difficulties:

Stackhouse, J. and Wells, B. (1997) Children's Speech and Literacy Difficulties: A Psycholinguistic Framework. London: Whurr

For information about the social use of language or pragmatics see:

Andersen-Wood, L. and Smith, B. R. (1997) Working with Pragmatics. Bicester: Winslow

Watson, J. (ed.) Working with Communication Difficulties. Edinburgh: Moray House Publications

There are a number of programmes for developing the social use of language, including:

Locke, A. and Beech, M. (1991) Teaching Talking: A Screening and Intervention Programme. Windsor: NFER Nelson

Rinaldi, W. (1992) The Social Use of Language Programme. Windsor: NFER Nelson, but these tend to be targeted at primary school children

For adolescents see:

Csóti M. (2001) Social Awareness Skills for Children. London Jessica Kingsley. Although aimed at younger children, this is very adaptable.

Johnson, D. and Johnson, F. (1982) Joining together: Group theory and group skills. Englewood Cliffs, N. J.: Prentice Hall, Inc.

Mayo, P. and Waldo, P. (1994) Scripting: Social communication for adolescents (second edition) Eau Claire, WI: Thinking Publications

Rawlins, W. K. (1992) Friendship Matters: communication, dialectics and the life course. New York: DeG

5. IT

a. Dyslexia – websites and software

<u>Website</u>

Source of experts and expertise on dyslexia: www.DyslexiaA2Z.com

<u>Software</u>

Advice on downloading from a whiteboard or flip chart to laptop or electronic copy board:

Sahara Presentation Systems PLC (0208 319 7700) or http://www.sahara-products.com

<u>Hardware to aid with note taking</u>

Digital Palmcorder Camcorder NV-DS33 (Panasonic 08701 578 577) will record an entire lecture and download it onto a computer.

<u>Interactive software to change a whiteboard into a computer screen</u>

www.hp.com/uk

http://www.openebook.org/ebooks.htm

<u>Listening to scanned text away from the computer</u>

The Road Runner from Ostrich Software can store 2000 pages of text in a 120 gms box running on two small AA batteries (Omnysys Ltd. 01522 685050)

<u>Mini-recorder that will play though a coupler</u>

Norcom 2500 audio mini recorder http://www.image-management.com

Penfriend:from Penfriend Ltd. 30, South Oswald Road, Edinburgh EH9 2HG, or admin@penfriend.ltd.uk. Free Demo from www.penfriend.ltd.uk

<u>Predictive software typer with speech</u>

Co-writer

<u>Text-to-speech software</u>

textHELP – scan, speak, spell, predict, pronounce, perceive: from textHELP Systems Ltds, Enkalon Business Centre, 25 Randalstown Road, Antrim, N. Ireland or telephone 0800 328 7910 or www.texthelp.com

Readingpen II

A fully portable electronic dictionary that scans words and pronounces them aloud ianSYST Ltd 01223 426644 sales@dyslexic.com or The White House, 72 Fen Road, Cambridge, CB4 1UN www.dyslexic.com

<u>Voice-recognition software</u>

Dictation Software www.dyslexic.com/dictcomp.htm

Iansyst (01223 420101) http://www.dyslexic.com/dicnload.htm

Wordswork

> Programme designed for dyslexic undergraduates to develop a variety of skills available from Alphabetics Ltd, 43 Northolme Road, London N5 2UX telephone: (020) 7359 1565, website: www.wordswork.co.uk or email: wordswork99@yahoo.com

<u>IT Consultants</u>

See also Bartlett, D. and Moody, S. (2000) Dyslexia in the workplace: London: Whurr (p. 203) for list of consultants.

b. Learning styles

Mind mapping on the computer www.inspiration.com or iANSYST's site at www.dyslexic.com/inspir.htm.

6. Learning Style

a. Research background

Riding, R. and Rayner, S. (1998) Cognitive Styles and Learning Strategies. London: David Fulton

b. Using style

Given, B. and Reid G. (1999) Learning Styles, a guide for teachers and parents. Red Rose Publications. Lots of good ideas, including detailed descriptions of Circle of Knowledge and team learning. Also contains a wide list of other books on learning style plus brief critiques.

Honey, P. and Mumford, A. (1986) Using Your Learning Styles: Maidenhead, Berkshire: Peter Honey

Milgram, R., Dunn, R. and Price, G. E. (1993) Teaching and counselling gifted and talented adolescents. Westport, CT: Praeger

Riding, R. (1994) Personal Styles Awareness Package. Birmingham Learning and Training Technology

Riding, R. and Rayner, S. J. (1995) Personal Style and Effective Teaching. Birmingham Learning and Training Technology

c. Practical strategies

Culshaw, C. and Waters, D. (1984) Headwork Series. Oxford: Oxford University Press. An excellent classroom and individual resource providing experience in a range of different modes and styles.

Fisher, R. (1995) Teaching Children to Think. Stanley Thornes
A useful introduction to creative thinking, critical thinking and problem-solving.

Heimlich, J. E. and Pittelman, S. D. (1986) Semantic Mapping: Classroom Applications International Reading Association. Newark: Delaware
Ways of developing curriculum-based concept maps and developing vocabulary

Dennison, P. E. and Dennison, G. E. (1989) Brain Gym: Teacher's edition revised. Ventura, CA: Edu-Kinesthetics, Inc.
Activities to help develop skills associated with both hemispheres of the brain.

Mind mapping: Resources available from Buzan Centres Ltd., 54 Parkstone Road, Poole, Dorset BH15 2PG or email: Buzan@Mind-Map.com

Get Ahead (video) £13.99 Brain Power for Kids (book) £4.99 + £3.00 p&p

Mind Mapping – Michael Gelb. Nightingale Conant, Long Road, Paignton, Devon
Multi-mode maps and frames

Kilpatrick, A., McCall, P. and Palmer, S. (1982) I See What You Mean Books 1 and 2. Oliver and Boyd.
Lots of different activities for practising moving from one mode to another

Lewis, M. and Wray, D. (1995) Developing children's non-fiction writing. Leamington Spa: Scholastic.
Essential for introducing and practising the use of writing frames.

Mason, M. (1990) Illuminating English – Book 3 Writing for Learning. TRACE (Training Research Agency Consultancy Enterprises Ltd.) Bridgeman Terrace, Wigan WN1 1TX.
Practice in spotting and using the structure of different types of writing.

7. Accelerated learning and related approaches

Accelerated learning

The following two books are available from The Accelerated Learning Centre

Crown Buildings, Bancyfelin, Carmarthen SA33 5ND or telephone: (01267) 211880/211886 or visit their website at: www.accelerated-learning.co.uk or email learn@accelerated-learning.co.uk

Smith, A. (1996) Accelerated Learning in the Classroom: Network Educational Press.
The first book in the UK to apply new knowledge about the brain to classroom practice.

Smith, A. (1997) Accelerated Learning in Practice.
Contains over 100 tools to help students accelerate their own learning.

Related approaches

Chris Gamble's work for Mind Kind Educational Ltd. is interesting.

Dickinson, C. (1988) Effective Learning Activities. Network Educational Press
Practical activities to improve learning in the secondary school.

Hughes, M. (1999) Closing the Learning Gap. Network Educational Press Ltd.
Introduces information about how the brain learns best based on recent research. Applies this to teaching practice, gives many practical suggestions and requires teacher-readers to examine and evaluate the effectiveness of their own styles of teaching.

Rose, C. and Goll, L. (1992) Accelerate Your Learning: The Super Skills Supplement.
Contains six 'super skills' including lots of ideas for learning through imagery and co-operative group learning. Available from Accelerated Learning Systems Ltd. at 50 Aylesbury Road, Aston Clinton, Aylesbury, Buckinghamshire, England.

Shaw, S. and Hawes, T. (1997) Effective Teaching and Learning in the Primary Classroom
A practical guide to brain compatible learning: Network Educational Press.

8. Memory

(See also accelerated learning and study skills sources)

Blagg, N., Ballinger, M. and Gardner, R. (1988) Somerset Thinking Skills Course: Module 7 Organising and Memorising: Simon and Schuster Education in association with Somerset County Council.

Materials from the Communication and Learning Skills Centre (CALSC), 131, Homefield Park, Sutton, Surrey SM1 2DY or telephone: (020) 8642 4663 or at info@calsc.co.uk or www.caslc.co.uk.
Includes Mastering Memory, to improve visual and auditory short-term memory.
Time to Revise, KS1-3; Timely Reminders, KS4 and adults; to improve revision and recall.

9. Study skills

See also the section on mind mapping and the Ostler books described under the dyslexia section (2).

Freeman, R. (1991) Mastering Study Skills; Macmillan Master Series. London: Macmillan.
A very helpful chapter on memory. Varied presentation with lots of activities for the reader. Quite a lot of text.

Graham, K. G. and Robinson, H. A. (1989) Study Skills Handbook. Delaware: International Reading Association
Clearly presents theory behind range of study skills plus practical suggestions; targets teachers of older secondary-school students.

Harman, C. A. and Freeman, R. (1984) How to Study Effectively: Self-help Series. National Extension College 18, Brooklands Avenue, Cambridge CB2 2HN.
This is aimed at further and higher-education students and can also be followed through a correspondence course guided by an experienced tutor. It has some excellent ideas, particularly for preparing for exams, but has a lot of text and could be rather daunting for an unsupported dyslexic student. Useful as a source for ideas for someone supporting a dyslexic student.

Holloway, J. (1999) The Learning Kit: an Inclusive Approach to Studying (Photocopiable resource book for study skills) Connect Publications, telephone (01273) 400118. Very useful.

Svantesson, I. (1998) Learning Maps and Memory Skills (second edition). London: Kogan Page
Very clearly explained and demonstrated with some interesting background. Targets secondary-aged and older students.

The website for the Counselling and Psychological Services (CAPS) describes the Ten Study Traps and offers advice on how to avoid them. www.unc.edu/depts/unc_caps/TenTraps.html

10. Dictionaries

Phonetically based dictionary

Moseley, D. (1996) The ACE Spelling Dictionary. Cambridge: LDA.
Dictionary using only consonant sounds, e.g. 'n d p n d n t' = 'independent'.

Word Finder, Morrison, M. L: Pilot Light, PO Box 305, Stone Mountain, Georgia, US.
Commercially produced tapes for learning the spelling of common sight words.

11. Schema theory and memory

Gathercole, S. and Baddeley A. (1993) Working Memory and Language. Hove: Lawrwnce Erlbaum Associates

Lewis, M. and Wray, D. (1995) Developing children's non-fiction writing. Leamington Spa: Scholastic

Nist, S. L. and Mealey, D. (1991) Teacher directed comprehension strategies. In Flippo, R. F. and Caverley, D. C. (eds) Teaching reading and study strategies at the college level. Newark: IRA

Rose S.P.R., (1993) The Making of Memory. London: Bantum.

Vasta, R., Haith, M. M. and Miller, S. A. (1992) Child psychology, the modern science. New York: John Wiley

Yuill, N. and Oakhill, J. (1991) Children's problems in text comprehension. Cambridge: Cambridge University Press

12 Miscellaneous

Listening Books – 12, Lant Street, London SE1 1QH or telephone 0171 407 9417

Index

mathematics
  diagnostic inventory of basic skills
    and learning style in maths 37
  IANS37
  learning style in 37, 160
  profile 37
memory 53, 63, 99–106, 132, 174,
    257–269, 300, 301
  aids 261–5
  and dyslexia 62, 63, 257–58
  auditory memory 53, 56, 63, 100
  long term memory (ltm) 63, 100,
    260
  procedural memory 63, 101
  review intervals 260
  rule systems 266–7
  semantic memory 63, 100–101
  short term memory (stm) 49, 63,
    100, 259
  techniques for association 265,
    267–9
  visual memory 53, 56, 63, 100, 195
  working memory 63
mental models *see* frames
metacognition 12, 13, 27, 96, 104,
    107–8
Miles 56, 75, 77
mind maps 22, 23, 42, 131–6, 149,
    198–9, 299, 301 *see also* brain-
    imaging, imaging, concept maps
mnemonics 220
models 13–14, 16
models of learning style 13, 14–21
modes of expression *see* written work
motivation 15, 118–9, 258
multi-sensory approaches 43, 95, 140,
    189, 245, 270

narrative writing 147, 169–174, 176–8
    see also story chains and story
    boards
nature / nurture debate 8
neurodevelopmental diversity 30
Neuro-linguistic Programming 35, 218
Nicolson and Fawcett 50, 56, 63, 75,
    106
non-word reading tests 241

observing learning style 34–37
oral presentations 205
organisation 130–9 *see also* dyslexia

Pentonville Prison Project 74
personality 8, 15
Personal Styles Awareness 113
Phonographix 245
phonological awareness 240–247
phonological processing 49, 53, 54, 56,
    59, 105–6, 240–242 *see also* audi-
    tory processing
phonological working memory 103
physiological styles 18, 29
Piaget 9, 25
pragmatics 70, 159–60, 198, 297
presentation modes 26
  analytics 161–4
  verbalisers 223–5
  visualisers 194–7
  wholists 122–9
processing 8, 39, 95, 96 *see also* under
    analytic, verbal, visual, wholistic
    learners
  approaches to 7
  types 15, 16
  differences 4
  gender 28
proof reading 240, 242–9
  dictionaries 248–9
  mechanical supports 240, 247–8

quantitative and qualitative learners
    37–8
question word bank 150
question word frames 128, 142, 161–5,
    179
questionnaires 31–4, 52, 56–7

reading
  for information 123, 202–3
  for research 126–129, 161
recap 13, 38, 93, 97, 129, 140, 148,
    167, 176, 181, 204, 211, 225,
    234, 238, 254, 265
reflective experience 29, 31